J. PETER BRUZZESE

Exchange Server 2007

HOW-TO

SAMS 800 East 96th Street, Indianapolis, Indiana 46240 USA

Exchange Server 2007 How-To

ISBN-13: 978-0-672-33048-3
ISBN-10: 0-672-33048-2

Library of Congress Cataloging-in-Publication Data

Bruzzese, J. Peter.
Exchange server 2007 how-to / J. Peter Bruzzese. — 1st ed.
p. cm.
ISBN 978-0-672-33048-3
1. Microsoft Exchange server. 2. Client/server computing. 3. Electronic mail systems. I. Title.
QA76.9.C55B799 2009
005.4'476—dc22
2008043870

Printed in the United States of America

First Printing December 2008

Trademarks

Warning and Disclaimer

Bulk Sales

Sams Publishing offers excellent discounts on this book when ordered in quantity for bulk purchases or special sales. For more information, please contact

U.S. Corporate and Government Sales
1-800-382-3419
corpsales@pearsontechgroup.com

For sales outside of the U.S., please contact

International Sales
international@pearson.com

Editor-in-Chief
Karen Gettman

Executive Editor
Neil Rowe

Development Editor
Mark Renfrow

Managing Editor
Kristy Hart

Project Editor
Andy Beaster

Copy Editor
Deadline Driven Publishing

Indexer
Lisa Stumpf

Proofreader
Seth Kerney

Technical Editor
Ronald Barrett

Publishing Coordinator
Cindy Teeters

Book Designer
Gary Adair

Compositor
Gloria Schurick

Contents at a Glance

Table of Contents

5 Manage Recipients

6 Manage Organization Permissions and Mailbox Settings

About the Author

J. Peter Bruzzese is an independent consultant and trainer for a variety of clients including CBT Nuggets (the Exchange 2007 Video Series) and New Horizons. During the past ten years, Peter has worked with Goldman Sachs, CommVault Systems, and Microsoft, to name a few companies. His focus has been and continues to be corporate support and training. He has specialized in Active Directory, Exchange support, education, and certification training. He holds the following certifications: Microsoft's MCSA 2000/2003; MCSE NT/2000/2003; MCITP: Messaging with Exchange 2007; and MCT; Novell's can; Cisco's CCNA; CIW's CIW Master and CIW Certified Instructor; and CompTIA's A+, Network+, and iNET+.

Peter enjoys taking complex technical topics such as Exchange and breaking them down into something easy to understand and enjoyable to learn. He has a love for the way messaging works and appreciates the improvements Microsoft has made to Exchange with each release.

Peter has a monthly column with Realtime Publishers called Exclusively Exchange, which formed his free site www.exclusivelyexchange.com. At this site, you can watch screencasts about Exchange 2007 SP1, read Peter's blog postings about Exchange and PowerShell, and locate assistance from others in the Exchange community. He also created a variety of miniature training clips to assist others in learning more about networking, Office 2007 (including Outlook 2003 and 2007 clips), and Vista (www.cliptraining.com). Peter believes that short training sessions in a familiar environment yield greater results.

Peter is also a contributor to *Redmond* magazine, *WindowsITPro* magazine, and several tech sites. He is a speaker for the TechMentor conferences, Microsoft TechEd conferences, the IT360 Tech conferences in Canada, and more recently, the TEC conference. His conference sessions focus mainly on Exchange. Finally, he writes the Enterprise Windows blog for InfoWorld.

You can catch up with Peter at mailto:jpb@cliptraining.com.

Dedication

For my wife, Jennette, who continues to race me to the corner... or now, more appropriately, to the crib. And to our son, Lucas Grey, whose smile is, well... everything.

Acknowledgments

Franklin D. Roosevelt said, quite modestly, "I'm not the smartest fellow in the world, but I can sure pick smart colleagues." I use the term modestly because Roosevelt was a Harvard graduate and a Columbia Law major (although he never completed the law degree, as he passed the New York State Bar exam prior to his graduation). Roosevelt was wise to keep smart colleagues. Personally, I often feel that having done that myself, I owe them more than the words here. The people I acknowledge here have assisted me professionally (some without even knowing it), increased my knowledge regarding Exchange, or encouraged me to pursue more in my life.

First and foremost, I'd like to thank Loretta Yates and Neil Rowe. They have shown a tremendous amount of confidence in me as a technical author. This has led to the creation of many different educational products, including the book you are holding, and I appreciate very much the trust they placed in my hands each time they give me a green light to go forth and create.

My Exchange colleagues are some of the finest, most intelligent people on the planet. Really, it's true. Take Brien Posey, for example. He has written more than 3,000 technical articles, written or contributed to 27 books, and was in charge of IT security for Fort Knox. It's a privilege for me to work with him and collaborate with him on projects and public-speaking assignments. Another impressive Exchange guru that I'm privileged to know is Bharat Suneja, who is the author of the Exchangepedia.com blog and the author of *The Complete Reference: Exchange 2007*.

In addition, I appreciate the articles and books written by folks like Jim McBee, Scott Schnoll, Henrik Walther, and Brian Tirch (the Exchange Genie). And, I certainly would know much less regarding Exchange if it weren't for the Exchange Team (msexchangeteam.com) and the many articles the team posts.

Others I work with in the technical field and conference circuit who have been good friends and coworkers include David Solomon, Alan Wright, Toby Malina, Greg Shields, Don Jones, Mark Minasi, Rhonda Layfield, Derek Melber, Ed Scannell, Lafe Low, Doug Barney, Elaine Home, Sheila Molnar, Brian Winstead, Nick Cavalancia, Stonna Edelman, Laurie Wells, Tim Duggan, Ronald Barrett (the technical editor on this book and co-author in times past), and others.

On a personal note, I'd like to thank my wife and best friend, my family, and all my friends who are always supportive in these endeavors. They watch as I work continuously on one project or another, never fully understanding what it is I do (not that I am able to explain it well in layman's terms), but always hoping somehow that my ability to establish a global messaging environment for a 100,000 people is going to translate into an answer to the ultimate question of, "So, what kind of computer should I buy?" or "Hey, is that Vista stuff any good?" to which I happily reply "I don't really know" and "I've heard good things."

Finally, I'd like to thank all the folks at Sams who deserve a tremendous amount of praise for the ability they have to take the manuscript I hand in and morph it into the book you are holding. I could never accomplish this level of undertaking without the help of project editor Andy Beaster, development editor Mark Renfrow, the technical editor Ronald Barrett, copy editor Ginny Munroe, proofreader Seth Kerney, indexer Lisa Stumpf, and cover designer Gary Adair.

We Want to Hear from You!

As the reader of this book, *you* are our most important critic and commentator. We value your opinion and want to know what we're doing right, what we could do better, what areas you'd like to see us publish in, and any other words of wisdom you're willing to pass our way.

You can email or write me directly to let me know what you did or didn't like about this book—as well as what we can do to make our books stronger.

Please note that I cannot help you with technical problems related to the topic of this book, and that due to the high volume of mail I receive, I might not be able to reply to every message.

When you write, please be sure to include this book's title and author as well as your name and phone or email address. I will carefully review your comments and share them with the author and editors who worked on the book.

Email: `consumer@samspublishing.com`

Mail: Neil Rowe
Executive Editor
Sams Publishing
800 East 96th Street
Indianapolis, IN 46240 USA

Reader Services

Visit our website and register this book at informit.com/title/9780672330483 for convenient access to any updates, downloads, or errata that might be available for this book.

INTRODUCTION

Using This Book

- How To Educate Yourself About Exchange 2007 SP1
- How To Benefit from This Book
- How To Continue Expanding Your Knowledge

How To Educate Yourself About Exchange 2007 SP1

In truth, whenever you pick up a book that catches your eye, flip to an article that draws your interest, or research and locate a site or blog that interests you, you are attempting to educate yourself in some way. Perhaps it is a subject you already know or one for which, you can extract the information you need much faster and easier than a novice because of your preexisting knowledge.

The motivation behind education varies from person to person. Some simply love to learn to enhance their own knowledge of a subject, even if they never intend to use that knowledge in the working world. Some, on the other hand, are required to learn to perform a job. A messaging engineer, much like a physician, must keep up with the latest practices and techniques to stay on top of the profession he has chosen.

Most Exchange books are 800, 900, or even 1,500 pages in length! And for some, that is just the kind of book they need to accomplish their messaging goals. However, this book is a "how-to" book. It's designed to give an administrator what she needs to understand the concepts involved in managing an Exchange 2007 SP1 environment and to perform the necessary tasks.

There are many ways to educate yourself about Exchange 2007 SP1. You can review books, articles, and websites, but for on-the-job, in-the-trenches, step-by-step information, look no further than this book!

How To Benefit from This Book

We've designed this book to be easy to read from cover to cover. The goal is to gain a full understanding of Exchange. We divided the subject matter into 12 easy-to-navigate and easy-to-use chapters:

- Chapter 1, "Introduction to Exchange 2007 SP1"
- Chapter 2, "Consider Deployment Scenarios"
- Chapter 3, "Install Exchange 2007"
- Chapter 4, "Manage Storage and Databases"
- Chapter 5, "Manage Recipients"
- Chapter 6, "Manage Organization Permissions and Mailbox Settings"
- Chapter 7, "Configure the Client Access Server"
- Chapter 8, "Administrate Transport Settings"
- Chapter 9, "Design and Deploy Disaster Recovery Settings"
- Chapter 10, "Design and Deploy High Availability for Exchange 2007"
- Chapter 11, "Configure a Unified Messaging Server"
- Chapter 12, "Monitor and Troubleshoot Your Exchange Environment"

In each of these chapters are subheadings that focus on the primary elements of design and deployment of that portion of Exchange.

Under the subheadings are scenario-problem introductions. These serve as starting points for the administrator to consider. At times, the information provided helps you deal with a specific problem that you might face. Typically, a scenario is described that enables the administrator to determine whether this direction is needed for his particular organization.

The solution that follows each scenario-problem includes additional information about a particular technology or design element to consider before providing step-by-step instructions. This additional information is provided so that you have more than just commands, but also the underlying reasons for the instructions.

When additional information is needed that doesn't fit neatly into the subject matter or it is essential that the message stand out to attract your attention, we use a note.

NOTE This is an example of a note.

At other times, when a task that is performed through the Exchange Management Console (EMC) is shown to you in PowerShell through the Exchange Management Shell, we use a special note that looks like this:

PS NOTE The cmdlet through the Exchange Management Shell to move a storage group path is Move-StorageGroupPath-Identity "Name of Storage Group" -LogFolderPath:"New Location Path" -SystemFolderPath:"New Location Path."

Perhaps the most important aspect of the how-to premise is the provision of step-by-step instruction that walks you through each and every step of the wizards and dialog boxes that Exchange provides in the GUI console. Along with clear instructions on managing and configuring your Exchange organization, we provide clear figures and screenshots of only the most important elements you face visually while working with your Exchange servers.

How To Continue Expanding Your Knowledge

Certainly there are more books, articles, and websites you can and should consider to expand your knowledge of Exchange 2007, especially because Exchange 2007 will continue to evolve and change as Microsoft adds more features, fixes, and enhancements. How does one stay on top of this flood of information about Exchange?

Several websites are invaluable and should be added to your Favorites at work. They include the following:

- The Microsoft Exchange Team Blog (http://msexchangeteam.com)—Truly, this is the finest resource on the Internet for Exchange information because it comes directly from the creators of Exchange and the finest instructors and MVPs Exchange has to offer.
- TechNet for Exchange 2007 (http://technet.microsoft.com/en-us/library/bb124558.aspx)—In addition to the Exchange team itself, this is the best location for organized, clear, up-to-date information about Exchange 2007.

In addition, several blog sites from Exchange gurus are worth investigating, including the following:

- http://exchangepedia.com/blog (by Bharat Suneja)
- http://exchange-genie.blogspot.com (by Brian Tirch)
- http://mostlyexchange.blogspot.com (by Jim McBee)
- http://robichaux.net/blog/ (by Paul Robichaux)
- http://blogs.technet.com/scottschnoll/ (by Scott Schnoll)

These are just a handful of the ones I personally enjoy; you can easily find more. Choose the ones you feel are most helpful to you.

Last, but certainly not least, you are welcome to visit my website (http://www.exclusivelyexchange.com) for free Exchange education. It includes links to articles I wrote, a variety of interviews, and so on. You might be most interested in the collection of free screencasts for Exchange and PowerShell.

CHAPTER 1

Introduction to Exchange 2007 SP1

IN THIS CHAPTER

- An Overview of Exchange 2007 SP1
- Choose Your Exchange Server Roles
- Determine Your Server Type: Server 2003 or 2008
- Choose Your Exchange 2007 Version
- Choose the Right Hardware for the Role
- Ensure the Needed Software Is Installed First
- Ensure Components Are Installed Per Server Role
- Plan Your Exchange Storage Architecture

An Overview of Exchange 2007 SP1

You may be new to Exchange and perhaps you are new to messaging servers in general, but one thing is certain: You are not new to email. Email has become the underlying foundation for a new civilization based upon global communication. According to estimates, more than one billion people utilize email in one form or another with that number growing to two billion by 2012. With the increase in email use comes the need for advances to the underlying messaging infrastructure—the servers behind it all—to provide additional features, as well as the necessary disaster recovery, high availability, and storage architecture solutions that people might not know they need.

What is the end result? The answer is new server applications every couple of years. This brings us to the subject of our book: Exchange 2007 SP1. Exchange 2007 SP1 is the latest in messaging servers from Microsoft. It's new, it's impressive, and it's different. With those differences, messaging administrators have much to concern themselves with because the new features come with an entirely new set of interfaces. Yes, there is more than one interface. Exchange 2007 has the Exchange Management Console (EMC), shown in Figure 1.1, which is the GUI console. It also has the Exchange Management Shell (EMS), shown in Figure 1.2, which is the command-line interface (CLI). Before you say, "I'll stick with the GUI," it's important to mention that there are some things that can be done only in the CLI. Not to worry, we will get you through it.

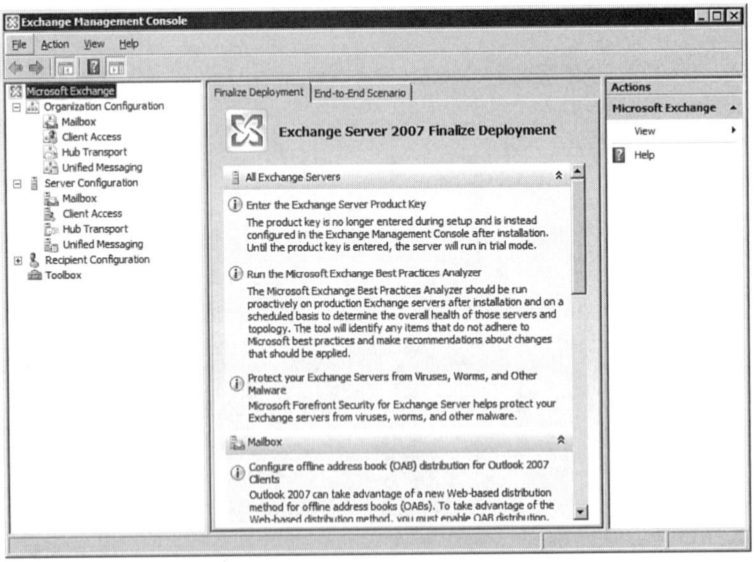

FIGURE 1.1
The Exchange Management Console (EMC) for Exchange 2007 SP1.

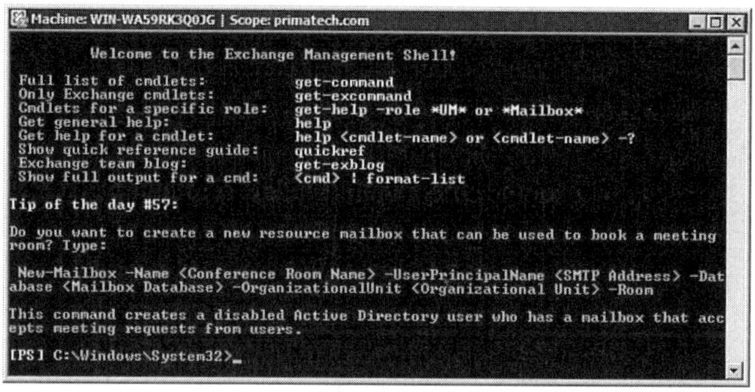

FIGURE 1.2
The Exchange Management Shell (EMS).

If you are new to Exchange or if you are moving from a previous version to Exchange 2007, you might be curious about what new features it has to offer.

New Features for Exchange 2007

Here is a quick list of features that Exchange 2007 offers:

- Active Directory integration—Beginning with Exchange 2000, there has been a connection between Active Directory (AD) and Exchange in the underlying catalog of users and their details. However, with Exchange 2007, trust is put into the capability of AD to route information. So, routing groups (an important aspect in Exchange 2000/2003) are eliminated completely with the AD site topology handling the routing needs of Exchange.
- Autodiscover—Connected to the Client Access Server role (to be discussed shortly), this new feature in Exchange assists in connecting a remote user to his mailbox server. In addition to optimizing bandwidth in assisting remote users, this feature benefits the internal client connections in that it helps to automatically configure Outlook profiles. Note: The Autodiscover service is only available for Outlook 2007 clients. Earlier versions, including Outlook 2003, do not have the ability to use the service.
- Availability—This service helps determine the availability of your Hub Transport (HT) servers in an effort to load balance inbound and outbound connections from mailbox servers. This not only enhances the flow of mail but also prevents the failure of a single Hub Transport server from stopping your flow of mail. The best part is that this is handled automatically and requires no configuration on the part of the administrator.
- EMC and EMS—As mentioned earlier, there are new administrative interfaces to work with in Exchange 2007. The EMC is somewhat familiar to us and mimics the feel of the System Manager, although with a more intuitive structure, and the new Actions pane helps present the options available. The EMS is based on the new scripting language PowerShell 1.0, which is a CLI that enables you to perform powerful administrative tasks with a simple set of commands called cmdlets (pronounced command-lets).

- High availability—Exchange RTM offered three flavors of high availability, with SP1 providing an additional one. Three of these use a technique called continuous replication, which plays off Exchange storage architecture to provide secondary copies of your Exchange mailbox database. With Local Continuous Replication (LCR) and Standby Continuous Replication (SCR), you do not need clustering services, whereas Cluster Continuous Replication (CCR) does use active/passive clustering technology. Single Copy Clusters (SCC) are similar to the high availability services from Exchange 2003.
- Performance enhancements—The required platform for Exchange 2007 is 64-bit hardware and software, which improves performance and capacity. Combined with the improved architectural features, by making the step toward 64-bit, an increase in the memory cache size, an increased number of storage groups, and an increased number of information stores per server are possible.
- Unified Messaging—One of the server roles we discuss in this chapter is Unified Messaging, which is a feature-rich solution for many organizations that want to unify their email, voice mail, and incoming faxes. It might require the purchase of some new hardware or an effort to use older hardware. However, it might be worth the cost and effort because it doesn't simply provide one location access for those items mentioned; it also provides multiple access solutions (such as phone, Outlook Web Access, mobile devices, and so on).

The list continues with items that relate to the new server roles (for example, antispam agents in the transport server roles), disaster recovery solutions, and with tools that adhere to best practices or troubleshoot your server. As you look through this how-to guide, note items such as transport rules and managed content settings, journaling, and so on. Exchange 2007 is a substantial and impressive release.

Additional Features with SP1

The release of SP1 includes some changes from the RTM version. None of these changes are major in the overall structure and design, but they do provide features and fixes that might make your experience with Exchange more enjoyable.

These features include the following:

- Deployment options—Enhancements that enable Exchange 2007 SP1 to install and run better on a server that is running Server 2008.
- ActiveSync improvements—Additional policy settings have been added to the mobile policies you can create. A remote wipe confirmation and Direct Push improvements have been added in an effort to compete more fully with BlackBerry.
- Outlook Web access improvements—These enhancements are more for the benefit of your users in that they now have the ability to access their deleted items. A monthly calendar view has also been added. Users can create and edit server-side rules. Public folders are supported through the /owa virtual directory. S/MIME support has also been included. Additionally, several customization features have been provided.

- POP3/IMAP4 Interface—If you worked with the RTM of Exchange 2007 and had to make adjustments to the POP or IMAP settings, you quickly learned that there was no GUI interaction available, and you had to go through the EMS. Microsoft heard its customers' concerns about this, and now an administrative interface exists in the EMC.
- Public folder management—As mentioned, the RTM was missing some key elements in the GUI to administer Public folders and that led you to the EMS. SP1 adds those management features into the EMC.

These are just a few of the enhancements (many are behind the scenes, such as the improvements made to transport algorithms), but there are others like the new SCR high availability option we mentioned earlier. There is also now the capability to import and export with .pst files, and there are other new enhancements to the Unified Messaging role.

Your Next Step

It might be hard to determine what you need to do next. Before you begin installation, you need to first make a few decisions, including the following:

- What server role (or roles) should I install?
- What hardware and software should I concern myself with, including which version of server should I use—2003 or 2008?
- Depending on the server role and my view of Exchange architecture, how should I plan my disk configuration? Let's begin with an understanding of roles. However, we are going to switch to the how-to format of the book so that you begin getting used to the structure.

Choose Your Exchange Server Roles

Scenario/Problem: Exchange 2007 has five different server roles you can install. How do you know which one to install?

Solution: The choice might be easy if you are dealing with a small environment where you plan to use one Exchange Server. In that case, you need to install the Typical server roles, which include the Mailbox role, the Client Access Server role, and the Hub Transport role. We discuss the step-by-step installation of roles in Chapter 3, "Install Exchange 2007."

If you need to install roles one at a time, which role is designed to handle which responsibilities? Consider the following five server roles:

- Mailbox (MB)—Hosts mailbox databases and public folder databases. Ordinarily, you can install the MB role with other roles on a single server (with the exception of the Edge Transport) unless you plan to use cluster services to provide CCR or SCC high availability options within Exchange.

- Client Access Server (CAS)—This role is similar to the front-end server for the Exchange 2000/2003 infrastructure and provides connections to a mailbox through Outlook Web Access (OWA), ActiveSync for Mobile devices, Outlook Anywhere, POP, and IMAP support. It also provides free/busy data through the availability service and supports the autodiscover services.
- Hub Transport (HT)—This role is similar to the Bridgehead server of Exchange 2000/2003. All mail coming in and out of your organization goes through the HT role. This means transport rules established on the HT role enable you to control mail while in transit. It relies completely on Active Directory to have a logical infrastructure in place to support the flow of mail.
- Unified Messaging (UM)—Provides Voice over IP (VoIP) with your mailbox. Email, voicemail, and incoming faxes can all come in to your Inbox. You can check the messages and calendar through multiple access interfaces (phone, email, or web browser). For this to work, you need a telephony expert for the installation and configuration of the telephony infrastructure (or the reconfiguration of your existing infrastructure). You might have a legacy Private Branch Exchange (PBX) that will work with a VoIP Gateway, or you can purchase a new IP-PBX.
- Edge Transport (ET)—This role is not a part of the Active Directory (and cannot be installed with any other role) but resides on the perimeter of the network using Active Directory Application Mode (ADAM) and synchronizes with the HT servers on the internal network. Its purpose is to provide additional security, antivirus, and antispam to your messaging organization. It's a recommended but not required role.

Determine Your Server Type: Server 2003 or 2008

Scenario/Problem: You have your new 64-bit server. Which flavor of Windows Server operating system should you install?

Solution: The choice might be in your hands, unless you've already made the decision to use the RTM version of Exchange, in which case you must go with Server 2003. The RTM of Exchange 2007 cannot be installed on a server running 2008. However, you can use SP1 on a server running both 2003 and 2008.

Keep in mind, however, that a network that includes Server 2008 domain controllers can still have a Server 2003 running Exchange 2007 RTM.

NOTE The management tools for Exchange RTM, which you traditionally can install on a variety of different systems in your network to administer Exchange without physically having to be present at the server, will not work on Server 2008 or Vista. However, the SP1 version of the tools can be installed on both.

The following operating systems are possible with Exchange 2007 RTM:

- Windows 2003 Server 64-bit Standard, Enterprise, or Datacenter with SP1 or higher (with or without the Multilingual User Interface Pack [MUI]).
- Windows 2003 Server 64-bit R2 Standard, Enterprise, or Datacenter (with or without the MUI).

The following operating systems are possible with Exchange 2007 SP1:

- The previously listed 2003 options, with SP2 installed.
- 64-bit edition of the Windows Server 2008 Standard operating system.
- 64-bit edition of the Windows Server 2008 Enterprise operating system.
- 64-bit edition of the Windows Server 2008 Datacenter operating system.

NOTE You cannot upgrade Exchange RTM to SP1 and upgrade to Server 2008. The supported method of installed Exchange 2007 SP1 on a server running 2008 is to perform a clean install of both.

Choose Your Exchange 2007 Version

Scenario/Problem: Exchange 2007 offers RTM and SP1 flavors that come in both Standard and Enterprise Editions. The RTM and SP1 options vary (with SP1 offering newer features) and the Standard and Enterprise editions contain differences in supported features.

Solution: If you are using a Server 2008 environment and do not wish to add a Server 2003 machine to the mix, you cannot use the RTM version of Exchange because it will not install on 2008. However, the SP1 version has more features and will install on both 2003 and 2008 servers.

NOTE Microsoft licenses Exchange as a Server/Client Access License (CAL) model. This means you purchase the server and receive a license, but also need to ensure you have a CAL for every user or device that accesses the Exchange Server.

We assume you will probably look at the SP1 flavor of Exchange, so we focus the rest of this book on that version only. Ninety-five percent of the information and steps will still work fine with the RTM version, aside from some of the alterations to the features and GUI we mentioned previously with SP1.

That brings us to the Standard or Enterprise differences:

- Standard Edition—Enables the creation of up to five storage groups and a maximum of five databases per Mailbox server role. In addition, there is a 16TB per database storage limit (same as the Enterprise edition) with support for Local Continuous Replication (LCR) and Standby Continuous Replication (SCR) only.

- Enterprise Edition—Enables the creation of up to 50 storage groups with a maximum of 50 databases per Mailbox server role. In addition, there is a 16TB per database storage limit with support for all four flavors of high availability including LCR, SCR, Cluster Continuous Replication (CCR), and Single Copy Clusters (SCC). Keep in mind though that Server has different editions as well, and if you want to use clustering, you need clustering services, which lean toward the Enterprise Edition of Server.

Choose the Right Hardware for the Role

Scenario/Problem: Initially, you might make decisions regarding the planning of your Exchange deployment, but eventually you have to include hardware into the discussion. With each of the server roles mentioned previously, you have different functionality, and by extension, different hardware requirements.

Solution: The solution begins with the processor. You then need to determine memory and hard disk needs per role. The interesting thing is that you might already have a system in place that you can use for your Exchange Server. You might not have to purchase anything.

The Processor

There are two primary processor options for you to consider, and you might have already guessed from looking at your server operating system choices that they are both 64-bit processors.

You can use:

- A processor that supports Intel's Extended Memory 64 Technology (EM64T)
- AMD 64 platform processors

The AMD Opteron or the Intel Xeon 64-bit processors are good choices, but there might be others that work fine. Keep in mind that the Intel Itanium (IA64) doesn't work with Server 2003 64, so that would hinder its use under those circumstances. Microsoft generally provides a list of approved servers and processor types that you can check ahead of time before you purchase to ensure you have compatibility with their processor requirements.

You might consider a multicore processor for your Exchange server because tests have shown that there is a performance benefit.

The Memory

Several theories regarding the memory needed depending on the server role exist. With the Typical installation where you have all the roles on one system, Microsoft recommends 2GB of RAM with 5MB added per user (with the number of storage groups also considered, as you'll soon see).

On the Mailbox servers where you have your storage groups, you are wise to include 2GB of RAM for every one to four groups. So, if you have five to eight groups, you would make sure you have 4GB and so on.

In terms of necessity, your Edge and HT servers do not require a substantial amount of memory to perform well. Per processor core, 1GB of memory with a 2GB minimum should suffice.

Disk Space

Installing Exchange requires about 1.2GB of space. If you are working with Unified Messaging language packs, you need to consider 500MB for each one. Make sure you have 200MB on your system drive.

Note that all disk volumes for Exchange 2007 should be NTFS formatted.

Edge Transport and HT servers store the message queue database and should therefore have at least 500MB of free space for Exchange 2007 SP1.

Obviously, your biggest disk sizes are needed on the servers that handle the mail repositories—your Mailbox role. How does one determine the amount of storage needed? Often it depends on the server configuration. Are you using a form of fault tolerance or high availability? How many users per mailbox? How many storage groups and databases and so forth? Remember, you aren't just looking at providing the proper capacity here; you need to ensure performance is looked after, too.

There is a requirements calculator located on the MS Exchange Team's site that is somewhat complicated but worth playing with, as shown in Figure 1.3. The site is located at: http://msexchangeteam.com/files/12/attachments/entry438481.aspx.

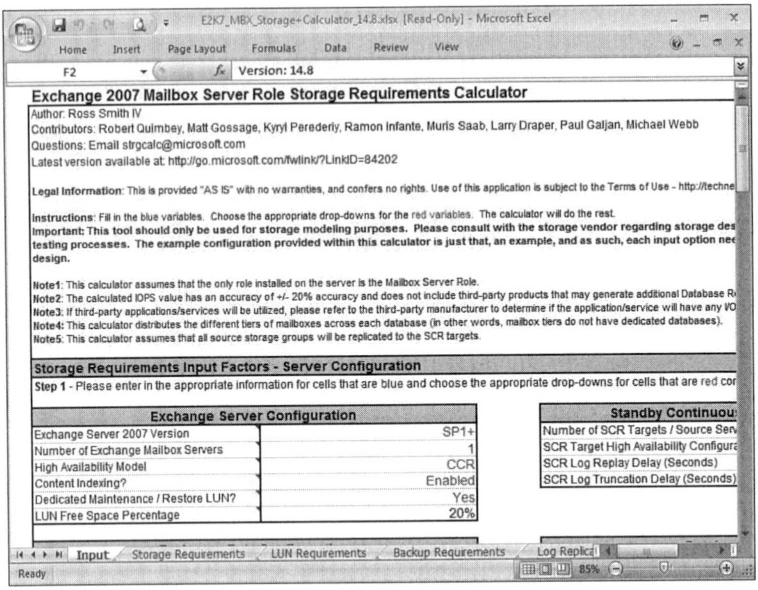

FIGURE 1.3
The Exchange 2007 Mailbox Server Role Storage Requirements Calculator spreadsheet.

With the Mailbox server, several considerations beyond the mailbox space itself exist. Imagine that each user is allowed 1GB of space, and you have 500 user mailboxes on that server. All 500 users might not have mailboxes that are full, but you have to be prepared for that level of mail. In addition to the database, there are transaction logs that are growing each day for which you need to be prepared (and you might prepare by moving those to other drives). You have deleted item and deleted mailbox retention to think about. Full text indexing uses about 25 percent of the total size of the mailbox database! Translation: Lots of disk space is a good thing on those mailbox servers. Faster, reliable disk technologies are always the wiser choice when putting together your Exchange servers.

NOTE For more detailed information regarding the processor, memory, and hard-disk configuration that will best suit your environment, consider Microsoft's technical site at http://technet.microsoft.com/en-us/library/bb124558(EXCHG.80).aspx, as well as the Exchange Team's blog site at http://msexchangeteam.com/.

Ensure the Needed Software Is Installed First

Scenario/Problem: There are three software installations that you have to perform prior to installing any of the server roles. These include the following:

- .NET Framework 2.0 or 3.0
- Microsoft Management Console 3.0
- Windows PowerShell

Solution: When attempting to perform the installation from the ISO file or the DVD, you are presented with a graphic screen that indicates whether those first three items are installed before proceeding to Step 4, which is Install Microsoft Exchange. One way to install those options is to click the links from the installation screen, or, you can seek out and install these features personally. In some cases, you might not need to install them.

.NET Framework v. 3.0 or 2.0 with Hotfix or SP1

On Server 2008, perform the following steps:

1. Select Start, and then click the Control Panel.
2. From Control Panel, double-click Administrative Tools.
3. From Administrative Tools, double-click Server Manager.
4. From within the Server Manager console tree, choose Features, and then select Add Features.
5. Using the Add Features Wizard, select .NET Framework 3.0, and then finish the wizard.

On Server 2003, you are welcome to download the 3.0 Framework and install. If you are already running 2.0, you will be prompted that there has been an update to this version for download before the installation of Exchange will take place. Or, you can simply download the .NET Framework 2.0 SP1 (which includes the update).

Make sure you use the 64-bit version of the .NET Framework.

Microsoft Management Console (MMC) 3.0

If you run Server 2003 R2 or Server 2008, the 3.0 Microsoft Management Console (MMC) is already installed, and you do not need to do anything else. If you work with Server 2003 (pre-R2), you might need to install the MMC 3.0, which can be downloaded either from the installation portal link or by downloading it directly from Microsoft at http://support.microsoft.com/?kbid=907265.

PowerShell 1.0

Installing PowerShell from Server 2008 is done in the following way:

1. Select Start, and then click Control Panel.
2. From Control Panel, double-click Administrative Tools.
3. From Administrative Tools, double-click Server Manager.
4. From within the Server Manager console tree, choose Features, and then select Add Features.
5. Using the Add Features Wizard, select PowerShell, and then finish the wizard.

If you are working with Server 2003, you need to download and install PowerShell. This can be done through the installation portal link or by going to the download site (http://support.microsoft.com/?kbid=926139) for PowerShell and performing the download and install manually.

Ensure Components Are Installed Per Server Role

Scenario/Problem: Depending on the server role, there might be components that should be enabled to provide specific functionality to that role.

Solution: Ensure you have all the components needed for the role you are working on installing. Otherwise, the installation will not succeed and the installation wizard will assist you by reminding you to turn on certain components you need.

The following components are necessary for the roles you install:

Mailbox Role:

- Internet Information Services (IIS)
- COM+ access (IIS 6.0 component)
- World Wide Web Publishing Service (W3SVC)

These can all be installed through Add or Remove Programs in Control Panel on Server 2003, or through Programs and Features in Server 2008.

The Client Access Server Role:

- World Wide Web Service
- ASP.NET
- For Outlook Anywhere: Remote Procedure Call (RPC) over HTTP Proxy

These can all be installed through Add or Remove Programs in Control Panel on Server 2003, or through Programs and Features in Server 2008.

The Edge Transport Role:

Must not be a member of an Active Directory domain, but must have the following:

- On a Server 2003: Active Directory Application Mode (ADAM) installed to provide functionality that is needed.
- On a Server 2008 with Exchange 2007 SP1: Active Directory Lightweight Directory Services (AD LDS)

The Hub Transport Role:

Because Exchange 2007 Hub Transport servers use their own implementation of the Simple Mail Transfer Protocol (SMTP), you need to avoid installing the IIS SMTP services. This goes for the Edge Transport server as well.

The Unified Messaging Role:

- Microsoft Exchange Speech Service—This is installed automatically when you choose to install Exchange 2007 with the UM role. However, if you have a server that runs Microsoft Speech Server, you have to remove the Speech Server services because UM relies on its own set of services.
- Windows Media Encoder 9 Series x64 Edition.
- Windows Media Audio 9 Voice codec for x64.
- Microsoft Core XML Services (MSXML) 6.0.

Plan Your Exchange Storage Architecture

Scenario/Problem: In the planning stages, before you install your first Exchange Server, you need to understand the way the storage architecture works. Understanding this can help you in planning and in simply understanding overall what happens within your Exchange world when messages come and go.

Solution: Let's take a look at how a message is handled by the Mailbox Server in terms of storage groups, databases, and transaction logs.

When you install Exchange, by default, a First Storage Group is created with a single database. You can add more storage groups (up to 5 for the Standard Edition or up to 50 for the Enterprise Edition) and within each one of those storage groups, you can add databases (up to 5 for the Standard Edition or up to 50 for the Enterprise Edition). Each database you add has the *.edb extension. If you create a mailbox and place it within a database within a storage group, when that mailbox receives mail, the Exchange Server adds it to the database. Understandably, these databases grow as more mail is added.

NOTE The default database size limit for Exchange 2007 Standard Edition is 50GB. There is no limit for the Enterprise Edition. It is possible, however, to use the Registry Editor to modify the database size limit. To learn how, visit this site: http://technet.microsoft.com/en-us/library/bb232092(EXCHG.80).aspx.

When an email message enters the Mailbox server, it goes through the memory and is written to transaction logs. Each log is 1MB in size (a reduction from 5MB in previous versions of Exchange). Depending on the amount of traffic coming into the Exchange Server, the data is also written to the database. Now the email message has been written to two locations: the database where the user will check in using his email client and retrieve his mail, and the transaction logs where the email is broken up, depending on its size, into 1MB chunks.

Transaction logs are created in a log stream; in other words, they follow a sequential manner. Although the current log written to might look like an E00.log, additional logs might look more like E000000002E (as you can see in Figure 1.4). There can be up to 2,147,483,647 log files in a log stream. The current log is not committed to the database and does not have its name changed until after it is filled to the full 1MB capacity. Then, it is closed out.

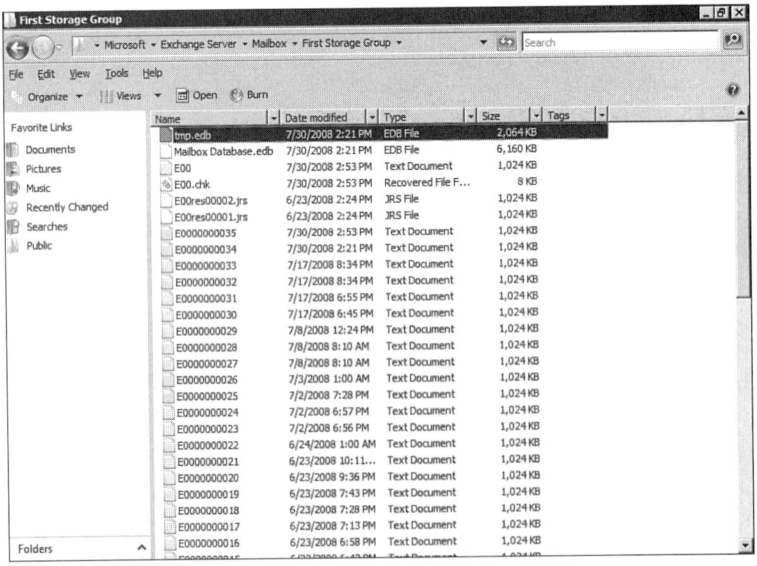

FIGURE 1.4
Your Exchange Database and transaction logs.

There is a check file to keep track of which transaction logs have been added to the database so that none are missed. A couple of reserve logs also exist, just in case the disk space runs out and you need a little extra space (although 2MB of extra transaction log space won't buy you much).

NOTE Each storage group can handle multiple databases; however, it is recommended that you place one database in one storage group. One key element to keep in mind is that the transaction logs are intertwined with a storage group. In the event you have three databases in the same storage group, the transaction logs will continue to use the log stream approach for all three at once. This might have a negative impact on performance and disaster recovery at some point, which is why the recommendation to use one database for each storage group exists.

The goal with transaction logs is to provide redundancy for your database. This can be a protection for you, but only if you separate the transaction logs from your database.

Consider the following scenario: You perform nightly backups of your Exchange database. It's Thursday, around 4:00 p.m., and the disk handling your database crashes (or your database corrupts) and you need to restore the database from backup. No problem, you have last night's backup handy. However, what about the mail from that day? It's not going to be in the backup of the database, right? However, it will be located in those transaction logs. So, you restore the database, and the transaction logs replay themselves into the newly restored database. Obviously, this works only if the transaction logs are not ruined along with the database. The obvious point is to separate the two onto different disks.

Overall, the best practice is to move your database and transaction logs off the drive that holds the system files and then separate the database from the transaction logs. To go one step further, if you can place your databases on a form of striped volume (if redundancy is provided some other way) or a striped volume with parity (a RAID 5 setup) to enable fault tolerance, and if you can mirror your transaction logs, you can achieve the best-practice level of storage for your mailbox servers.

CHAPTER 2

Consider Deployment Scenarios

IN THIS CHAPTER

- Make Heads or Tails of Upgrade Terminology
- Upgrade from Exchange 2007 RTM to SP1
- Transition from Exchange 2000/2003 to Exchange 2007
- Migrate from Exchange 5.5
- Migrate from Lotus Domino
- Migrate from Novell GroupWise
- Evaluate Third-Party Solutions

Make Heads or Tails of Upgrade Terminology

Scenario/Problem: In working with and researching the upgrade process from non-Exchange messaging systems as well as Exchange 5.5, 2000, and 2003, the terminology seems to be confusing and inconsistent. What is the proper view of the process?

Solution: The key to the problem is understanding the way Microsoft words things. To start with, there is no in-place upgrade to Exchange 2007 from a previous version. You cannot take an Exchange 2003 system and upgrade it to 2007. The reason for this is that Exchange 2007 didn't run on the 64-bit platform for Server 2003, so you are required to set up a new server with the proper 64-bit operating system. After you have the new server, you can *transition*; that is, you can move your mailboxes and configuration.

You can upgrade from Exchange 2007 RTM to SP1, as we discuss shortly. This is the only true in-place upgrade that can be performed, but only under specific circumstances.

However, transitions are not for all circumstances. The only transitions you can perform with Microsoft tools are transitions from Exchange 2000 or 2003 over to 2007. Some of the articles or books you read might use the word *upgrade* when they are actually referring to a transition.

Anything other than what we've just described is considered a *migration*. This implies a change in the messaging infrastructure. In this case, the data, (the mailbox data), is migrated over. However, the configuration data is not carried over as it would be in a transition.

NOTE It might surprise you to learn that Exchange 5.5 doesn't allow for a transition model of upgrade. Even more shocking should be the fact that you cannot install your first Exchange 2007 server unless all Exchange 5.5 servers are removed and the Exchange mode is raised to a native level (which indicates all Exchange 5.5 servers are out of the mix).

Note in discussions of transitions that coexistence is unavoidable. This refers to the time period in which your Exchange 2000/2003 servers reside in the same organization as your Exchange 2007 server.

Upgrade from Exchange 2007 RTM to SP1

Scenario/Problem: In the event you have Exchange 2007 RTM on a server running Server 2003 and you want to upgrade this server to SP1, how would you do it?

Solution: The first part of the solution requires you to prepare your system and your Active Directory (AD) for the changes that are coming with SP1. Consider the following:

1. You need to make sure you meet the minimum requirements, which starts with making sure you have SP2 installed on the server (one of the prerequisites).
2. Begin the upgrade process with the servers that are your firsts for roles. It's recommended that you begin with your Client Access Server (CAS) and Hub Transport (HT) servers in a larger organization, where your servers may be broken up into their individual roles.
3. A Schema update is required, which you can perform separately or during the install process. However, in either case you need to be a member of the Schema and Enterprise Admins group. If you haven't prepared the domain, you can do so separately through a command prompt, or you can do so through the install process, but in both cases, you must be logged on with a user that is in the Enterprise Admins group.
4. Make sure you have the proper permissions to perform the upgrade. On an internal Exchange server (Hub, Mailbox, CAS or UM), you should use the account that is delegated the Exchange Organization Administrators role (if it's the server that is your first in your organization). You should also be a Local Administrator on that system.
5. If you want to upgrade the Edge Transport server, you need to be a member of the local Administrators group for that system.
6. It's recommended you stop and restart the Remote Registry service.

Be aware of the following caveats to the process before you attempt to proceed:

- If you are working with a clustered mailbox server, you can perform only the upgrade through the command line interface (CLI), which we demonstrate shortly.
- Do not attempt to upgrade your Server 2003 running Exchange 2007 RTM over to Server 2008 first and then attempt to upgrade from the RTM to SP1. This can create havoc. Instead, you can uninstall Exchange and then perform the upgrade to 2008, then reinstall Exchange SP1 (keeping in mind that RTM doesn't install on Server 2008). Again, to place SP1 on a server running 2008, there is no upgrade. It's a direct install.

Perform the upgrade using the GUI or the CLI. From the GUI, begin the process by inserting the DVD or mounting the ISO file you might have. After you see the introduction Start page from the wizard, perform the following:

1. Under Install, select Install Microsoft Exchange Server 2007 SP1.
2. Click Next at the Introduction page.
3. Select I Accept for the License Agreement.
4. After the Readiness Check comes back with green lights saying you have met the prerequisite checks, you can select the Upgrade option to begin the upgrade.
5. From the Completion page, select Finish.

In the event you will use the CLI, you need to open a command prompt and perform the following:

1. Make sure the DVD is in the drive or the ISO file you have is mounted and you know the drive letter.
2. From the command prompt, navigate to the location of the setup.com file.
3. Then type **`setup.com /mode:upgrade`**.

Transition from Exchange 2000/2003 to Exchange 2007

Scenario/Problem: You have a preexisting Exchange organization that runs one or more Exchange 2000 or 2003 servers. You want to include Exchange 2007 into the mix, coexist for a period, and eventually transition over to Exchange 2007 completely.

Solution: The methodology to transitioning must be handled in stages. Each stage requires a certain amount of planning and decision making. Overall, however, you need to install Exchange 2007 servers to take over for your existing ones, move mailboxes and Public Folders over to the Exchange 2007 servers, and eventually phase out the 2000/2003 servers.

Let's look at the following stages:

- Deciding which servers to replace first
- Preparing AD
- Moving over mailboxes
- Using 2007 as a Public Folder replica
- Phasing out 2000/2003

Deciding Which Servers to Replace First

Scenario/Problem: Your existing 2000/2003 infrastructure might be one server and might be easy to transition. Or, it might be an entire organization with bridgehead servers and front-end servers.

Solution: The methodology to transitioning must be handled in stages. Each stage requires a certain amount of planning and decision making. Overall, however, you need to install Exchange 2007 on at least one system using the Typical installation with the three main server roles (Client Access, Hub Transport, and Mailbox).

In the event you replace a much larger Exchange 2000/2003 organization in pieces that includes roles such as bridgehead servers and front-end servers along with mailbox servers, the following are important to the process:

- Client access servers—Replace the front-end servers
- HT servers—Replace the bridgehead servers
- Mailbox servers—Eventually replace the mailbox servers

Table 2.1 Server Role Comparison Chart to Exchange 2003

Exchange 2000/2003	Exchange 2007	Comments
Mailbox servers	Mailbox Server role	Hosts mailboxes and public folders Can coexist with other server roles Only role supported on 2007 clusters
Front-end servers	Client Access Server (CAS) role	HTTP/S (OWA, ActiveSync Outlook Anywhere*), IMAP4 and POP3
Bridgehead servers	Hub Transport Server role	Routes mail, applies policies, and transports rules
—	Edge Transport Server role	Routes mail to/from Exchange organization Typically resides in perimeter networks
—	Unified Message Server role	Provides a universal Inbox for email, voice mail, and incoming faxes. Allows for Outlook Voice Access and an AutoAttendant

A logical reason exists for this order. You can install them out of order; however, the Mailbox server(s) is your most important one. It's the server(s) that eventually takes on all the mailboxes and Public Folders. It cannot function without the CAS and HT servers in place already. In addition, if you work in stages for your preparation and installation of Exchange 2007 into the environment, you can certainly combine the CAS and HT together if you like, but if you have to start with one, the CAS is what Microsoft recommends first.

Preparing AD

Scenario/Problem: Whenever moving from one version of Exchange to another, starting with Exchange 2000, configuration changes must be made in AD. These include changes to the schema and to the forest and domain configurations. How should these be handled?

Solution: The simplest solution is to simply begin the installation of your first server (be it a Typical installation, which will install the Client Access Server, Hub Transport, and Mailbox server roles all together, or a customized solution where you install one or some of those options) because this automatically runs all the behind-the-scene switches.

However, company policies might require a step-by-step approach to the process. Usually this is due to the replication traffic that might be caused in a larger organization when changes are made to AD.

NOTE Exchange is designed to be installed on a 64-bit server, and so some have wondered how to prepare AD if they don't have the 64-bit server. Well, there is a 32-bit training version that you can use. However, you must have both the .NET Framework and PowerShell on the server first. You shouldn't try to run the switches on servers that run Exchange 2000/2003 currently or you will see failure messages.

Switches and their meanings:

- /PrepareLegacyExchangePermissions—Microsoft recommends you run this switch in the root domain of the forest and on the intended Exchange 2007 server. You run this command to ensure the Recipient Update Service functions correctly after you perform the update of the schema for Exchange 2007. To learn more about the reasoning behind this, check http://technet.microsoft.com/en-us/library/aa997914(EXCHG.80).aspx.
- /PrepareSchema—This connects to the Schema Master role (or you can run on the Schema Master role) and makes changes to the Schema.
- /PrepareAD—This makes several helpful changes, such as creating Universal Security Groups in both the root and existing domain. It also, for the sake of preparing to coexist, creates an Administrative Group named Exchange Administrative Group (FYDIBOHF23SPDLT) and a Routing Group called Exchange Routing Group (DWBGZMFD01QNBJR). Note: You won't be able to see the groups through the Exchange Management Console in Exchange 2007; you can only see the groups through the System Manager in E2K or E2K3.

However, you can make changes through PowerShell. To learn more about this, see http://technet.microsoft.com/en-us/library/aa997292(EXCHG.80).aspx. Note: If you run this switch before the other two, it runs the others automatically.

- /PrepareDomain and /PrepareAllDomains—These switches configure permissions on a container called Domain for your Exchange servers, Organization Administrators, Authenticated Users, and Mailbox Administrators. It creates the System Objects container, establishes proper permissions, configures a new domain Global Group, and adds that group into the Universal Security Group.

Keeping all the previous in mind, the easiest way to prepare AD short of installing Exchange 2007 directly is to perform the following:

1. Open a command prompt.
2. Type **`setup.com /PrepareAD`**.
3. Wait for the preparation to complete, which includes the /PrepareLegacyExchangePermissions and /PrepareSchema switches.
4. Upon completion, type **`setup.com /PrepareAllDomains`**.

In the event you truly need to perform each step in its own time slice, begin with /PrepareLegacyExchangePermissions and continue with each one when the time is right until you are ready to perform the actual installation of your first Exchange 2007 Server.

NOTE The installation process is covered in Chapter 3, "Install Exchange 2007."

Moving Over Mailboxes

Scenario/Problem: After your organization has an Exchange 2007 Mailbox Server in place, the goal is to move over mailboxes. This can be a slow process where you coexist for quite some time with both environments, or it can be a quick process that reduces the coexistence period.

Solution: To begin with, note that all users on Exchange 2000/2003 Mailbox Servers are easily located within the Exchange Management Console. To see this, perform the following:

1. Open the Exchange Management Console on an Exchange 2007 server (or from another system that has the Exchange 2007 management tools installed).
2. In the console tree, locate and select the Recipient Configuration node.
3. Note that next to the names of users, there is a column titled Recipient Type Details that indicates whether a user is a legacy user, meaning the user has a mailbox on a legacy Exchange server, or whether the user is simply a user, as shown in Figure 2.1.

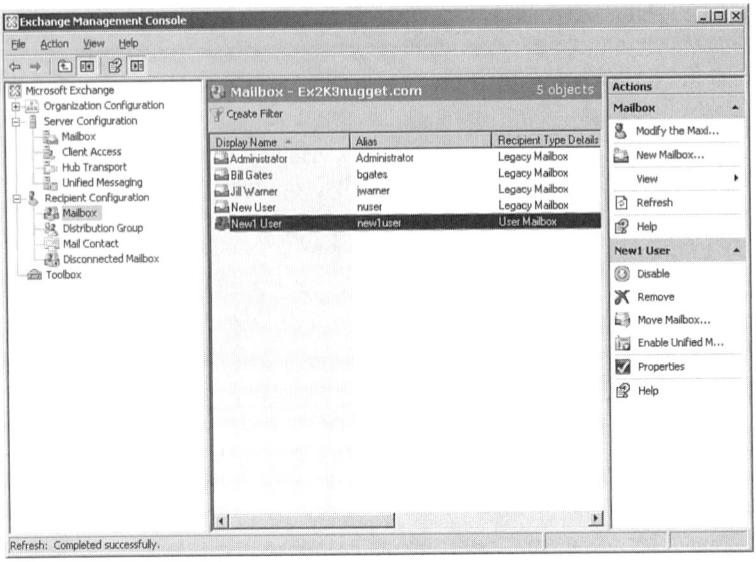

FIGURE 2.1
Viewing legacy mailboxes.

To move a mailbox or multiple mailboxes in the same forest, you can use the Move-Mailbox wizard from within the Exchange Management Console. You can also use the Move-Mailbox cmdlet from within PowerShell.

To use the Exchange Management Console to move a mailbox or collection of mailboxes, perform the following:

1. Open the Exchange Management Console on an Exchange 2007 server (or from another system that has the Exchange 2007 management tools installed).
2. In the console tree, locate and select the Recipient Configuration node.
3. Select the mailbox or mailboxes you wish to move.
4. From the Actions Pane (or by right-clicking your selection), choose the Move Mailbox option and the wizard will begin.
5. From the Introduction screen, you have to select the Browse button and choose the destination of the mailbox (to a different server or different mailbox database on the same server). Then choose Next.
6. Under the Move Options tab, shown in Figure 2.2, you can choose what happens if corrupted messages are found. You can skip the mailbox completely or you can skip the corrupted messages (and determine the maximum number of messages to skip). You can usually just skip corrupted messages because your goal is to move that mailbox over for the transition, so you don't have a choice—corrupted or not, that mailbox has to move. You can personally select

the Global Catalog and Domain Controller for the move; if you don't, the wizard automatically handles this (and that is easiest and best). There is also a checkbox for moving toward Exchange 2003 or 2000 (but we aren't doing that, so that option is unnecessary in this case). When finished, click Next.

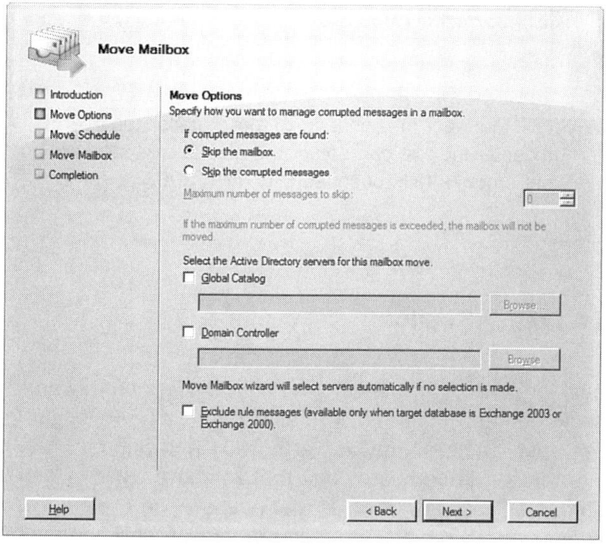

FIGURE 2.2
The Move Mailbox Wizard options.

7. You're taken to the Move Schedule tab, which enables you to move the mailbox immediately, or at a time of your choosing (in the event you want to wait until after work hours or the weekend, which is usually wise if you are dealing with a production environment). Choose the date and time and click Next.
8. You are presented with the Move Mailbox tab, which is a summary of your entire request. It shows you all the mailboxes available for the move and what options you've selected. If you feel it is ready, select Move.
9. Ultimately you end up on the Completion tab, where you are shown the results of your requests to move the mailbox or mailboxes. Select Finish and you should be set.

Using the Exchange Management Shell can be slightly more complicated, especially if you haven't had experience with the shell or don't prefer the command-line approach. The wizard works just fine. However, if you want to work with the move-mailbox cmdlet, you type in the following:

```
Move-Mailbox OrganizationName\UserName -TargetDatabase
"StorageGroupName\MailboxDatabaseName"
```

For example, for an organization named PrimaTech that has a user, Jenny, to move over to the UsersTwo Storage Group under the MBTwo Mailbox Database, it would look like this:

```
Move-Mailbox PrimaTech\Jenny -TargetDatabase "UsersTwo\MBTwo"
```

For more cmdlet parameters, visit http://technet.microsoft.com/en-us/library/aa997961(EXCHG.80).aspx.

NOTE You cannot use the System Manager in Exchange to move mailboxes over to Exchange 2007. It begins the process, and you can select the new server, storage group, and database. However, the process fails because Exchange 2003 doesn't recognize this as a valid step.

Using 2007 as a Public Folder Replica

Scenario/Problem: Previous versions of Exchange use Public Folders heavily and pre-2007 versions of Outlook require a Public Folder store to function. Although Public Folders are not relied upon as heavily in Exchange 2007 and Outlook 2007, clients do not require them. The odds are good that you have legacy clients in place and an extensive Public Folder store that needs to be moved over to 2007 before you remove the 2000/2003 servers from your environment.

Solution: For starters, on your Mailbox Server, you need to ensure a Public Folder database is installed. If, during the installation, you indicated that there were legacy clients in your environment, the Public Folder store would have been added automatically. If not, however, you need to perform the addition of the database manually. To do this, perform the following:

1. On the Exchange 2007 Mailbox Server role for which you want the Public Folder database, open your Exchange Management Console.
2. In the console tree, locate and select the Server Configuration node.
3. Choose the Mailbox option.
4. Under the Database Management tab, notice the listing of your storage groups and databases. After you decide which storage group you want to place the Public Folder in (or if you decide to create a new storage group specifically for the database), select the database and choose New Public Folder Database from the Actions Pane.
5. The New Public Folder Database wizard displays, and you are asked to provide a name for the database (as shown in Figure 2.3). The name is your choice. You are also asked to provide a Database file path. This enables you the opportunity to place the database file in a safe location (one that has some form of fault tolerance included).

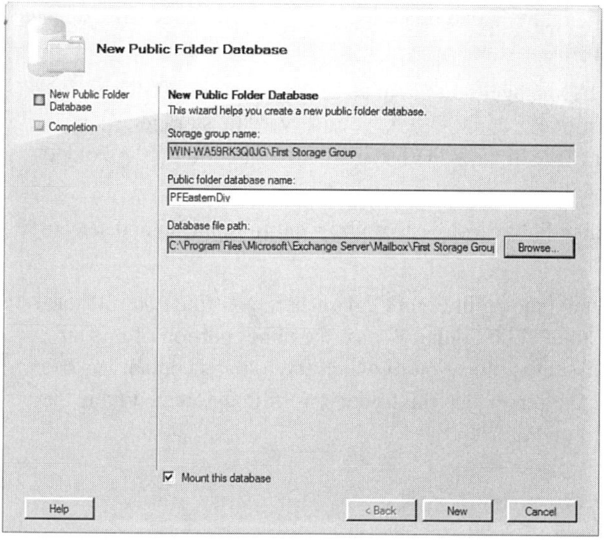

FIGURE 2.3
Creating a new Public Folder database that is mounted automatically.

6. Note the Mount This Database checkbox at the bottom of the screen that says it ensures that the database is not only created, but mounted (making it accessible) immediately after creation. It's checked by default, and we usually leave it as such.
7. When you are ready, select New.
8. After the database is created and mounted, select Finish.

Now that you have a Public Folder database in place on your Exchange 2007 MB server, you want to create a replica of your Public Folder data in your Exchange 2000/2003 organization onto that server.

Prior to Exchange 2007 SP1, there was no graphic tool for managing Public Folders in Exchange 2007 and so the encouragement for creating replicas was to use the tools that existed in Exchange 2000/2003, working with the System Manager. With SP1, however, you can open the EMC and select the Toolbox node. From there you can choose the Public Folder Management Console. This actually opens an entirely different console for you to work with.

NOTE We discuss Public Folders in-depth in Chapter 4, "Manage Storage and Databases."

You need to create your replica now. To do this with the System Manager in Exchange 2000/2003, perform the following:

1. Open Exchange System Manager and navigate to Administrative Groups. Expand your administrative group, Servers, your server, the storage group, and then the Public Folder Store to view the Details Pane of all the Public Folders contained in the store.
2. Right-click the Exchange Public Folder that you want to replicate and select Properties.
3. Go to the Replication tab (shown in Figure 2.4), where you find controls that allow you to replicate the Public Folder. Notice the upper portion of this tab contains an area that lists every location to which the folder's content has been replicated. By default, the server that the folder was initially created on is the only location displayed on the list.

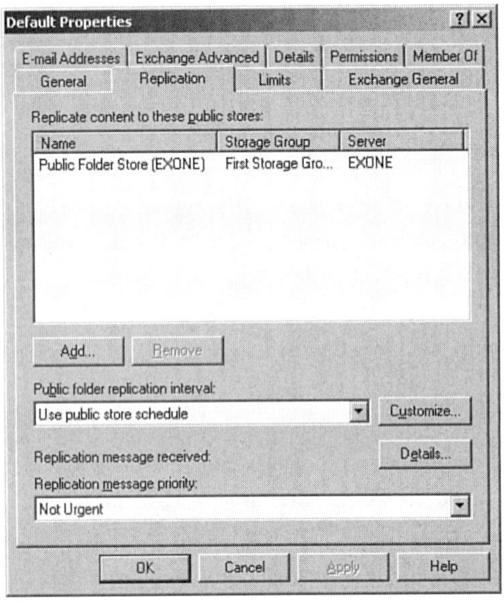

FIGURE 2.4
The Replication tab enables you to add replicas of your Public Folders to other servers.

4. You can replicate the chosen Exchange Public Folder to stores on other servers by clicking the Add button, and then selecting the Public Folder store on which you want to create the replica. You can remove a Public Folder replica from a store by selecting the replica that you want to delete and clicking the Remove button.
5. Notice the Public folder replication interval. This setting refers to the length of time that passes before an Exchange Public Folder is replicated to its associated Public Folder stores. By default, the replication interval is set to use the public store schedule. However, the Public folder replication interval dropdown list

enables you to set the replication interval to two hours, four hours, or you can use a custom schedule by selecting Customize.

6. Next, you'll notice text that says, "Replication Message Received." You can click the Details button to the right of this text to view replication statistics. Clicking the Details button reveals the Replication Status dialog box. This dialog box provides you with information such as replication status, the last time that replication occurred, and the average transmission time. You can use this information both for troubleshooting and for performance-monitoring purposes.
7. The last setting on the Properties sheet is the Replication Message Priority option. By default, the replication message priority is set to Normal. You have the option of setting a high-priority folder to Urgent or setting low-priority folders to Not Urgent.

To create the replicas using the Public Folder Management Console in Exchange 2007 SP1, perform the following:

1. Open the Exchange Management Console.
2. Select Tools and then select Public Folder Management Console (shown in Figure 2.5), which opens an entirely different console to work with.

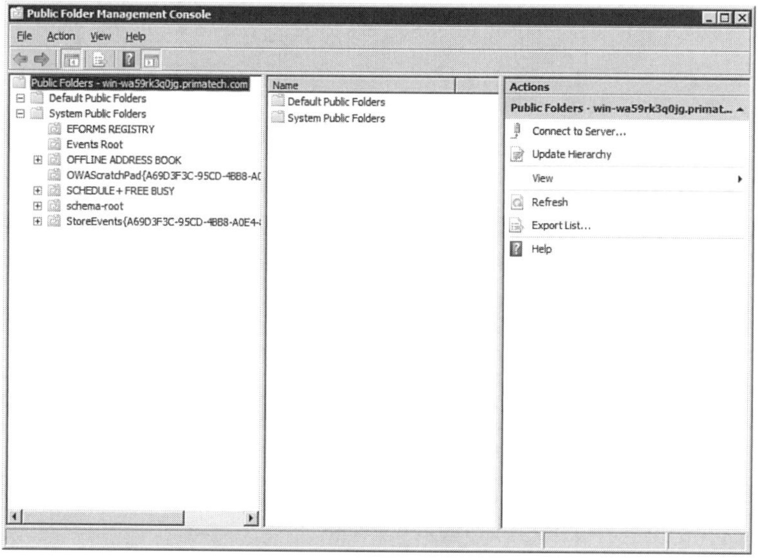

FIGURE 2.5

A first look at the Public Folder Management Console.

3. From the Action pane, select the Connect to Server option and locate the server with Public Folders you wish to add replicas.
4. After you see the server and the Public Folders listed, you can go into the Properties of the folder and select the Replication tab.

5. On the Replication tab, select the Add button to create replicas. You can select the X to delete replicas.
6. By default, the checkbox is selected for Use Public Folder Database Replication Schedule. You can uncheck the box and use a preselected schedule by clicking the down arrow, or you can create a custom schedule by selecting the Customize option. You can also determine the local replica age limit in days.
7. After this is complete, click OK.

After you allow enough time for the replicas to be formed on your Exchange 2007 Server and you are confident that no data will be lost, you can return to the Public Folder management tools and remove the legacy Exchange servers from the list.

NOTE An excellent Knowledge Base article from the Microsoft Exchange Team entitled "Moving Public Folder Replicas from Exchange 2000 to Exchange 2007" can be found at http://msexchangeteam.com/archive/2007/10/30/447339.aspx.

Another interesting method for moving Public Folders involves the use of a script in the Exchange Management Shell. These scripts can be found in the Exchange server's c:\temp\scripts folder. The one we want is MoveAllReplicas.ps1. For example, if we want to move all Public Folder replicas from Server1 to Server2, we would run the script this way:

```
MoveAllReplicas.ps1 -Server Server1 -NewServer Server2
```

Phasing Out 2000/2003

Scenario/Problem: There are always concerns and issues to follow up on before the final transition is complete and the state of coexistence ceases. What more should you be worried about before you uninstall the last of your legacy Exchange servers?

Solution: One concern you might have is your Offline Address Book or Schedule+ Free Busy folders, which are important for pre-2007 versions of Outlook to function. However, this need not be a worry because they are automatically replicated to your Exchange 2007 servers to ensure connectivity to your legacy clients.

Other concerns might include the following:

- DNS configuration—Ensure you have your internal and external DNS configured properly for the new servers.
- Connectivity—Ensure you can connect through your Client Access Servers to your Outlook Web Access, Outlook Anywhere, ActiveSync, and so on.
- Testing internal and external mail—Ensure persons can send mail to mailboxes on the same server, on other servers, and to external servers.

After you are convinced you have everything functioning properly in your Exchange 2007 environment, you can begin the process of removing the last of your legacy servers. This is done using the Add/Remove Programs tool from the Control Panel.

NOTE Before you can remove the last of all of your legacy Exchange servers, you must assign the Recipient Update Services (RUS) over to an Exchange 2007 server. This is done through the System Manager on the legacy server, shown in Figure 2.6. Expand Recipients, and then select the Recipient Update Services folder. Go into the Properties of the RUS services, and on the General tab, change the server to an Exchange 2007 server. Any Exchange 2007 server is fine, even though in reality Exchange 2007 no longer uses RUS. Moving the services is meant to satisfy the legacy Exchange services so that it allows itself to be uninstalled.

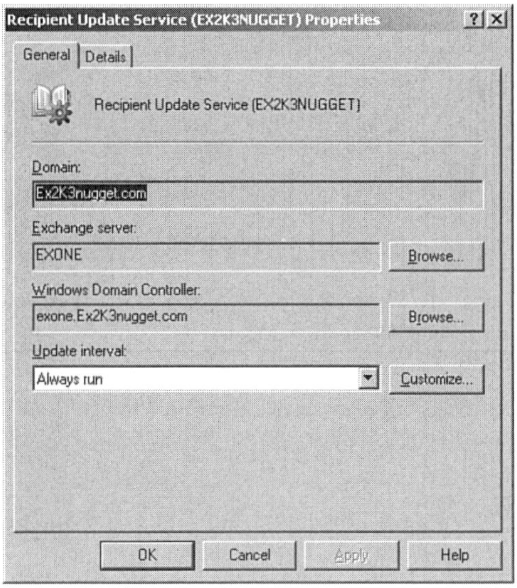

FIGURE 2.6
Changing RUS before decommissioning your last Exchange 2000/2003 server.

Migrate from Exchange 5.5

Scenario/Problem: In the event you have an organization that is still using Exchange 5.5, how can it move mailboxes over to Exchange 2007?

Solution: There are no Microsoft tools that support the migration of mailboxes directly from 5.5 to 2007. However, it is possible to migrate mailboxes to an Exchange server running Exchange 2000 or 2003 and then move those over to 2007.

The simplest solution is to install an Exchange 2003 server in its own organization, separate from the Exchange 5.5 organization. Use the Migration Wizard and move the mailboxes to Exchange 2003.

After completion, install Exchange 2007 into the same organization as the Exchange 2003 and use the Move-Mailbox Wizard to move those same mailboxes over to 2007.

NOTE There are third-party solutions that might be worth considering when attempting a migration from 5.5 to 2007. For example, Quest Software (www.quest.com) has a Migration Manager that performs the Exchange 5.5 to 2007 migration. CommVault Systems (www.commvault.com) offers an archiving tool called QiNetix, which can archive Exchange 5.5 content and restore it back to an Exchange 2007 server. Logically, there are other tools to consider.

Migrate from Lotus Domino

Scenario/Problem: If my organization uses Lotus Domino and we want to move to Exchange 2007, would we have to start at the beginning and lose all that we currently have built?

Solution: Microsoft has provided the Microsoft Transporter Suite for Lotus Domino, which consists of the following five components that you can use:

- Directory Connector—Synchronizes objects between the Domino Directory and AD in much the same way the Microsoft Connector for Lotus Notes does in Exchange 2003.
- Free/Busy Connector—Gives users running the Outlook and Lotus Notes clients the capability to perform calendar free/busy queries across the two systems.
- Directory Migration—Enables you to create new AD user accounts for the Domino Directory users.
- Mailbox Migration—Performs the actual migration of user data from Domino mail databases to Exchange 2007 mailboxes.
- Application Migration—Enables the migration of Domino applications to Microsoft SharePoint.

You can learn more about these tools and download them directly from Microsoft at http://www.microsoft.com/downloads/details.aspx?FamilyID=35fc4205-792b-4306-8e4b-0de9cce72172&displaylang=en.

Migrate from Novell GroupWise

Scenario/Problem: If my organization uses Novell GroupWise and we want to move to Exchange 2007, is there a Transporter Suite for GroupWise?

Solution: Unfortunately, Microsoft did not release a suite of tools for GroupWise migration to 2007. However, you can consider tools provided with Exchange 2003. They include the following:

- Connector for Novell GroupWise—Provides the capability to route mail to the GroupWise system and for Exchange to understand the GroupWise address space. After configuration, it also enables the two directories to be synchronized to ensure that there is a consistent address book across both systems.
- Calendar Connector—Enables users from both systems to see each others' scheduling information.
- Migration Wizard—Includes an option to migrate from Novell GroupWise.

To use these tools, you need to install an Exchange 2003 server first because you cannot install an Exchange 2003 server into a pure Exchange 2007 organization. Install the 2003 server, use the tools to move over everything you need, and then you can move those items over to your Exchange 2007 server.

Evaluate Third-Party Solutions

Scenario/Problem: Would I fare better with transitioning or migrating by going with a third-party solution, such as Quest Software, for my needs?

Solution: Not always. For one, Quest isn't free, nor are any of the other third-party solutions. We highlight Quest because it has long been the master of Exchange migrations among professionals in the field. However, there are several factors to consider.

If you can perform the transition or migration with native tools and you are provided with all that you need, why seek a third-party solution?

If the third-party solution offers you something you cannot obtain through the tools Microsoft natively supplies and these are features you need, it might be worth your consideration.

For example, with Novell GroupWise migrations, the Migration Wizard compares with Quest pretty evenly with users email, folders and subfolders, attachments, calendars, and tasks. However, Quest can pull over address books and contacts (the Migration Wizard cannot). It can also pull over shared folder permissions and archives and GroupWise distribution lists and memberships (again, the Migration Wizard cannot).

So, the key is to investigate your options and evaluate your needs before you stray from the native tools Microsoft provides. Count the cost, so to speak.

CHAPTER 3

Install Exchange 2007

IN THIS CHAPTER

- Perform a Readiness Check Using the Exchange Best Practices Analyzer
- Perform a Typical Installation of Roles
- Perform a Custom Installation
- Install an Edge Transport Server
- Perform a Mailbox Active/Passive Installation
- Work with the EMC and the Exchange Management Shell

Perform a Readiness Check Using the Exchange Best Practices Analyzer

Scenario/Problem: Whether you are preparing your existing organization for a transition to 2007 or performing a clean installation in a pristine environment, you should make sure you are ready. You can perform a mental check to ensure you have all your pieces in order (Active Directory [AD] preparations, hardware and software prerequisites, and so forth). However, to truly be sure that your system is ready, you need to use a tool called the Exchange Best Practices Analyzer, which includes a Readiness Check.

Solution: Using the Best Practices Analyzer after Exchange is installed is simple because it is located in your Toolbox within your Exchange Management Console (EMC). However, on a system that doesn't have Exchange, you need to download and install the tool. Here are the steps, from beginning to end.

1. To begin with, because the tool is not installed, go to www.exbpa.com and download the latest version of the tool onto the server you wish to install Exchange on.
2. Install the tool.
3. After installation, click Start, and then click Best Practices Analyzer Tool.
4. The first thing the tool does is check for updates from Microsoft. The tool might have updates, or the configuration files might have updates. The configuration file is what contains all the properties that the tool retrieves and the rules it uses to analyze those properties. You can select Cancel This Check or allow it to complete. We recommend you allow it to complete.
5. If a new version of the tool or configuration file is found, you are asked whether you want to download the latest updates or continue without making any updates. We recommend you download the latest updates.
6. After the download is complete, you see the Welcome screen. From here, you can perform a new scan by choosing Select Options For a New Scan or view a preexisting scan by choosing Select a Best Practices Scan To View. In this case, you want to have a new scan performed.
7. You are asked to connect to an Active Directory Server. Ordinarily one is already in the box, but you can change it if you like. You can also select the Show Advanced Login Options down arrow to make adjustments. Or, simply click Connect to the Active Directory Server.
8. First network and permissions are checked. Then you are taken to the options for the New Best Practices scan.
9. Enter an identifying label for the scan. You can name it something simple like Scan1.

10. Scroll down to the Select The Type Of Scan To Perform section. Note that this tool can be useful for other tests later on and throughout the lifetime of your Exchange organization. However, you want to select the last option, Exchange 2007 Readiness Check, as seen in Figure 3.1.

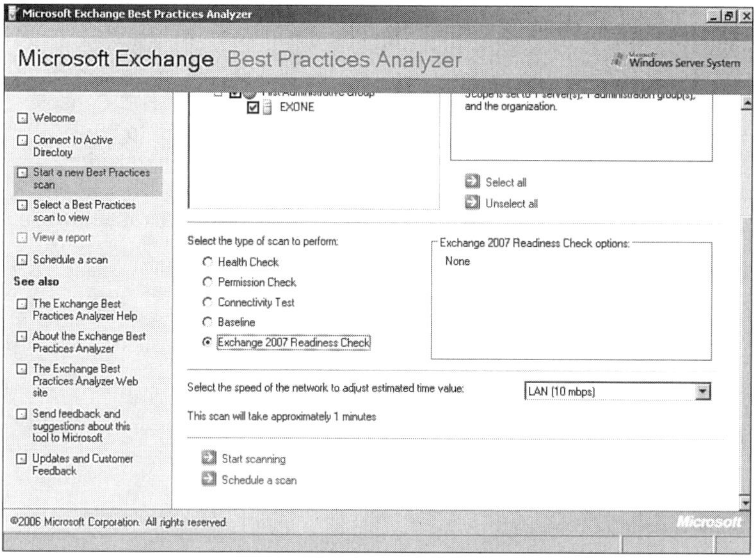

FIGURE 3.1
The Exchange Best Practices Analyzer getting ready to perform a Readiness Check.

11. You can choose the speed of the network (although this is usually determined automatically). Then select the Start scanning option unless you wish to schedule a scan time.

12. After scanning completes, you are offered the option to view a report of this Best Practices scan. The report is easy to read, with a tab for Critical Issues (that is, issues that will prevent the installation from going forward), All Issues (includes both warning and informational items), and Informational Items.

13. Based upon any critical issues that come back, make the needed and recommended adjustments so that you can go forward with the installation process.

The Exchange Best Practices Analyzer Readiness Check is prepared to perform a host of checks against your Active Directory, the system you are trying to install Exchange on, and, in the case of a transition, checks on the existing legacy Exchange organization. Here are a few checks that might cause problems for installation if you aren't prepared:

- Checks to ensure the Schema Master is Windows 2003 SP1 or later.
- Checks to make sure AD domains are in native mode, not mixed mode.
- Checks to make sure the Global Catalog servers run Windows 2003 SP1 or later.

Perform a Typical Installation of Roles

Scenario/Problem: You've prepared your AD. Service Packs are installed where they belong. All hardware and software prerequisites have been met. You have a single, new 64-bit server running Server 2008. You wish to install a Typical installation of Exchange 2007 SP1. How do you do it?

Solution: Assuming the installation of the .NET Framework, the 3.0 MMC Console and Windows PowerShell are taken care of when you place the DVD into the machine. or begin the installation from a mounted ISO file and the installation wizard begins and the opening splash screen already has you at the point where you must select Step 4: Install Microsoft Exchange Server 2007 SP1 (as shown in Figure 3.2). At this point you will perform the following:

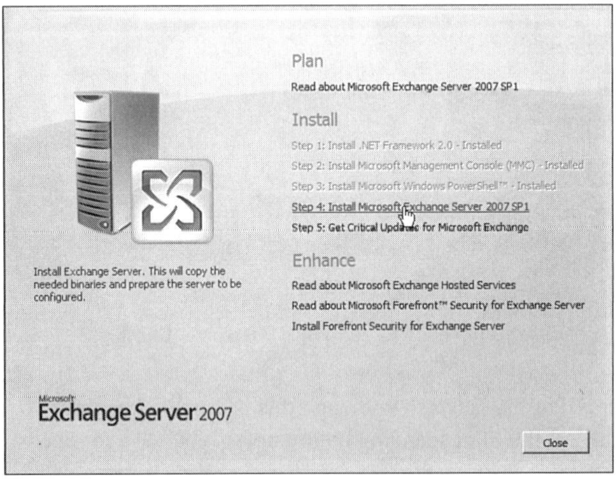

FIGURE 3.2
The installation wizard with five steps toward installation.

1. Select the link from Step 4 to begin the installation wizard.
2. You are taken to the Introduction screen, which provides information regarding some of the new features and functionality included with SP1. After reading the information provided, select Next.
3. You are taken to the License Agreement screen where you can scroll down and read the entire agreement if you like. You can choose Print to get a portable, easy-to-read version of the agreement. There are two options. You either choose I accept the terms in the license agreement or I do not accept the terms in the license agreement. Note, if you do not accept, you cannot continue with the installation process. After you choose, select Next.

4. You are taken to the Error Reporting screen. Here you are asked to participate in a group effort with Microsoft to determine why certain errors occur on systems. If you choose Yes (Recommended), errors that occur automatically send reports to Microsoft without further permission. The other option is No. Choose one and then select Next.

5. This brings you to the Installation Type screen shown in Figure 3.3; here, you can choose either a Typical or Custom Exchange Server installation. In this case, we select Typical Exchange Server Installation, which installs the Hub Transport server role, the Client Access server role, the Mailbox server role, and the Exchange Management tools on the server. Confirm the path for the Exchange Server installation files and choose Next.

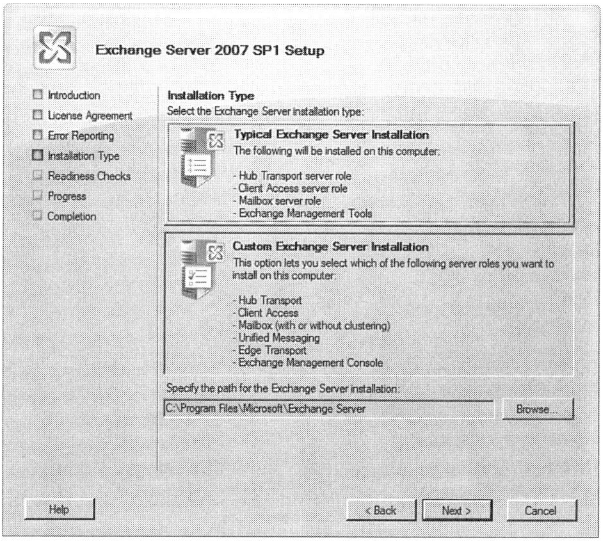

FIGURE 3.3
Choose a Typical or Custom installation type.

6. If it is the first server in the organization, you are taken to the Exchange Organization screen, where you are asked to provide a name for your Exchange organization. When that is done, choose Next.

7. You are now taken to the Client Settings screen, which asks a simple yes-or-no question regarding the type of clients you use. If you use only Outlook 2007 clients, choose No. If you have Outlook 2003 or Entourage clients, choose Yes. Choosing Yes indicates that you have a need for a Public Folder database to be set up (because this is part of the requirements for legacy clients). After you choose, select Next.

8. You are taken to the Readiness Checks screen, where the system is checked to see whether Exchange is ready to be installed or if something is missing. First, the Organization Prerequisites are checked and then the Hub Transport, Client Access, and Mailbox roles, as shown in Figure 3.4, are checked. When the checks are complete, select Install.

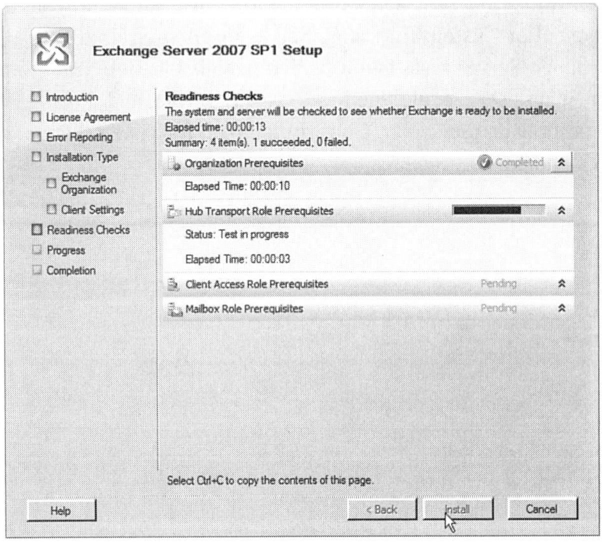

FIGURE 3.4
The Exchange installation Readiness Checks.

9. You are taken to the Progress screen, where you are shown the progress and elapsed time for the installation procedure to take place. Barring any unforeseen issue at this point, you simply need to give it a little time and it completes the installation.

10. You are shown a Completion screen, as shown in Figure 3.5, with a view of which items completed installation (hopefully all of them), and there is a checkbox (Finalize Installation Using The Exchange Management Console) at the bottom that is checked by default. Select Finish.

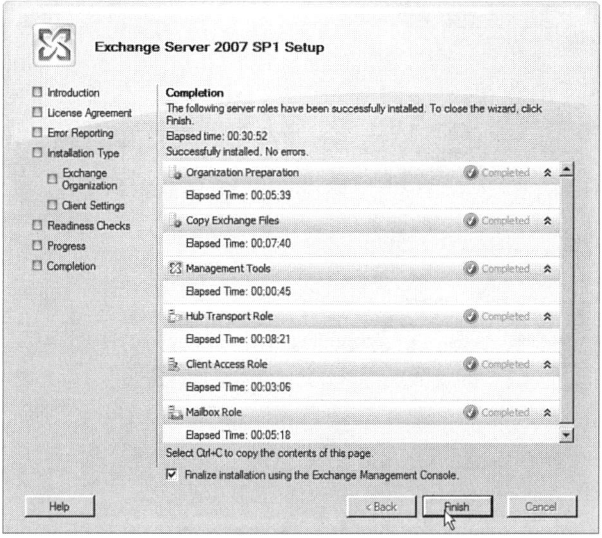

FIGURE 3.5
The completion of your Typical installation.

At this point, you can do one of two things. You can go back to the installation disk and perform Step 5, "Get Critical Updates for Microsoft Exchange." Or, you can move forward with the EMC and follow the prompts prepared for you in Finalize Deployment, shown in Figure 3.6. This includes items such as Enter the Exchange Server Product Key, Run the Microsoft Exchange Best Practices Analyzer, and on, with instruction provided for each server role.

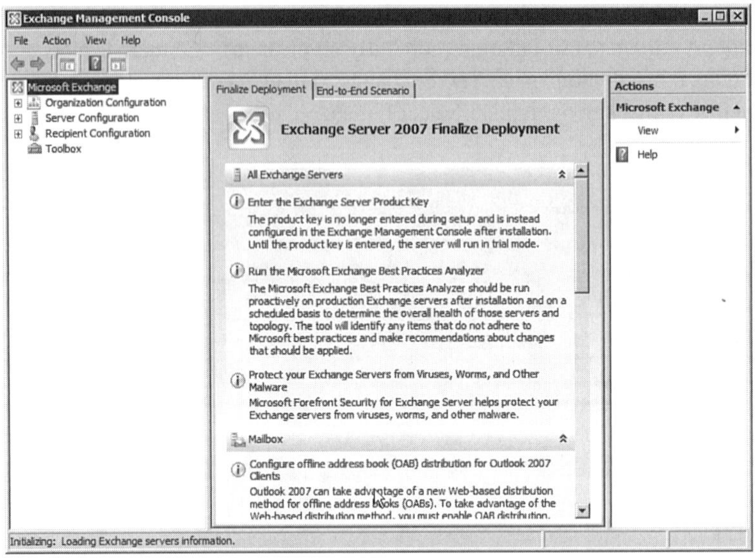

FIGURE 3.6

Finalize the deployment from the EMC.

Perform a Custom Installation

Scenario/Problem: You want to install a server that includes the Unified Messaging role. Or you wish to have a Client Access and HT server only. Maybe you want to have a simple Mailbox server added to your organization. How do you do this?

Solution: Following all of the same prerequisite rules for installing any Exchange 2007 server, you begin the installation in the same way you would the Typical installation, by performing the following:

1. Insert the DVD or mount the ISO for the Installation screen to display. Select the link from Step 4 to begin the installation wizard.
2. You are taken to the Introduction screen, which provides information regarding some of the new features and functionality included with SP1. After reading the information provided, select Next.
3. The License Agreement screen displays; scroll down and read the entire agreement if you like. You can choose Print to get a portable, easy-to-read version of the agreement. There are two options. You either choose I Accept The Terms In The License Agreement or I Do Not Accept The Terms In The License Agreement. Note that if you do not accept, you cannot continue with the installation process. Accept the agreement and select Next.

4. You are taken to the Error Reporting screen. Here you are asked to participate in a group effort with Microsoft to determine why certain errors occur on systems. If you say Yes (Recommended), errors that occur automatically send reports to Microsoft without further permission. The other option is No. Choose and then select Next.

5. This brings you to the Installation Type screen, where you can choose either a Typical or Custom Exchange Server installation. In this case, select Custom Exchange Server Installation. You are taken to the Server Role Selection screen shown in Figure 3.7.

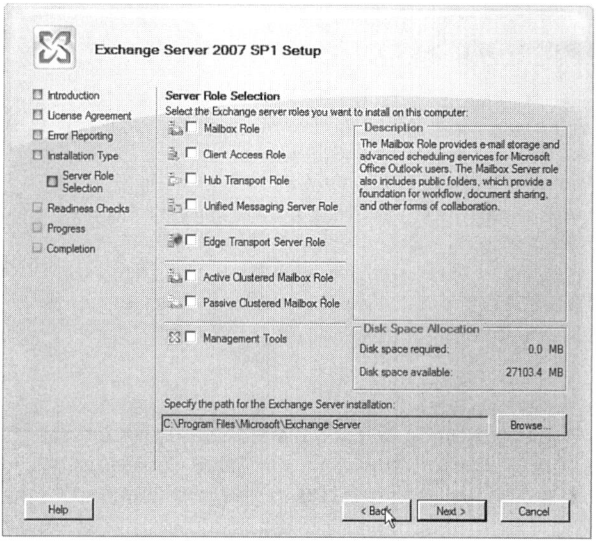

FIGURE 3.7
The Server Role Selection screen.

6. As you can see in Figure 3.7, the four main internal roles (the roles you can install together on the same machine if you wish but are all installed on a system connected to AD) are at the top. You can select one, some, or all four roles. Next is the Edge Transport Server role, which we save for the next section. You also have the two clustered Mailbox roles, which we discuss later. These are not the same as the standard Mailbox role because they work in harmony with clustering services provided by the server itself. Additionally, you have Management Tools (which you are welcome to install on your own, too). Select your options and choose Next.

7. The Readiness Checks screen checks to make sure your system is ready for the installation of the server options you've chosen. After you are clear to move forward, choose Install.

8. The Progress screen walks you through the process of the actual installation. When complete, it takes you to the Completion screen and shows you what has been installed successfully. Click Finish.

Additional servers to your organization show up within the EMC and you can manage them from a central location.

NOTE Installing Exchange from the command line in unattended mode is also a possibility. You use the setup.com command with a variety of switches, such as /mode, /roles, and so forth. You have quite a bit of flexibility and a ton of options. To learn about this, visit http://technet.microsoft.com/en-us/library/aa997281(EXCHG.80).aspx.

Install an Edge Transport Server

Scenario/Problem: Your organization has a perimeter network. That is, it has a firewall between the internal network (where most of your servers reside as well as all your client systems) and you have another firewall that extends out to the Internet. Between these two firewalls is what we call the Demilitarized Zone (DMZ) and servers such as your Internet Security and Acceleration (ISA) Server 2006 or, in this case, your Edge Transport server, reside here. The Edge Transport server provides antispam and antivirus support for all mail going in and out of the organization. The question is, how do we set one up?

Solution: Because the server with the Edge Transport role doesn't have access to the internal AD, configuration and recipient information is stored within the Active Directory Application Mode (ADAM) directory service (on pre-2008 Servers) and Active Directory Lightweight Directory Services (AD LDS) on a server that runs 2008.

So, for starters, ADAM or AD LDS must be installed. You should configure the Domain Name System (DNS) suffix on the Edge Transport server, too. Then the Edge Transport server must be installed. Finally, a connection must be made between a HT server and the Edge Transport server.

Preparing the Edge Transport Directory Service

If you use Server 2003, you will need to install ADAM. To do this, perform the following:

1. Select Start, Control Panel, and then click Add or Remove Programs.
2. Select Add/Remove Windows Components.
3. Select Active Directory Services under Components, and then select Details.
4. Select the Active Directory Application Mode (ADAM) check box under Subcomponents of Active Directory Services, and then select OK.
5. Select Next on the Windows Components page.

6. Read and review the message that displays. Then do one of the following:
   a. Select Finish if the message, "You have successfully completed the ADAM Setup Wizard" displays.
   b. If an error message displays, make a note of the error, select Finish, and then review the ADAM event messages in Event Viewer.

If you plan to use Server 2008, you need to install AD LDS. To do that, perform the following:

1. Select Start, Server Manager.
2. From the console tree, right-click Roles, and then select Add Roles.
3. Review the information on the Before You Begin page of the Add Roles Wizard, and then select Next.
4. On the Select Server Roles page, in the Roles list, select the Active Directory Lightweight Directory Services checkbox, and then click Next.
5. Finish adding the AD LDS server role by following the instructions in the wizard.

Configuring the DNS Suffix and Adding a Host Record for the Edge Servers

The Edge Transport server, because it doesn't have a connection to the AD and resides in the perimeter network, requires a manual intervention on a variety of configuration options that would ordinarily occur automatically if it were part of the AD. The configuration will fall on the administrator's shoulders. To begin with, you should configure the DNS suffix for the server by performing the following:

1. Select Start, Control Panel, and then double-click System to open the System Properties.
2. Select the Computer Name tab.
3. Click Change.
4. From the Computer Name Changes page, click More.
5. In the Primary DNS Suffix Of This Computer: field, type a DNS domain name and suffix for the Edge Transport server.
6. Click OK three times and you are done.

> **NOTE** Your Edge Transport server, depending on your configuration, might have two network connections: one to the outside firewall and one to the internal. The internal connection should be configured to use two internal DNS servers as the preferred and alternative DNS servers.

Creating a Host record requires work on the DNS server side. This is done on an internal DNS server. Perform the following:

1. Select Start, Administrative Tools, and from the expansion of tools, select DNS.
2. Expand Forward Lookup Zones and right-click the name of your domain. Select New Host (A).
3. From the New Host dialog, enter the name of the server in the Name field and the IP address in the IP Address field.
4. Check the Create Associated Pointer (PTR) Record box.
5. Select Add Host and then click Done.

Installing the Edge Server

The installation procedure is the same for the Edge as it is for the other server roles. However, unique factors include that it rests on the perimeter of the network, that you cannot install the Edge Transport role with other roles, and that you have to ensure another directory services is in place and that a connection is made to the HT afterward.

To perform the installation graphically, do the following:

1. Insert the DVD or mount the ISO for the Installation screen to display. Select the link from Step 4 to begin the installation wizard.
2. You are taken to the Introduction screen. Click Next.
3. You are taken to the License Agreement screen, where you can scroll down and read the entire agreement if you like. Choose I Accept The Terms In The License Agreement and select Next.
4. You are taken to the Error Reporting screen. Here you are asked to participate in a group effort with Microsoft to determine why certain errors occur on systems. If you say Yes (Recommended), errors that occur automatically send reports to Microsoft without further permission. The other option is No. Choose an option and then select Next.
5. This brings you to the Installation Type screen, where you can choose either a Typical or Custom Exchange Server installation. In this case, select Custom Exchange Server Installation.
6. Select Edge Transport Server Role, and then select Next.
7. The Readiness Checks screen checks to make sure your system is ready for the installation of the server options you chose. After you are clear to move forward, choose Install.
8. The Progress screen walks you through the process of the actual installation. When complete, it takes you to the Completion screen and shows you what has been installed successfully. Click Finish.

After the installation is complete and the EMC displays, as shown in Figure 3.8, you will notice the difference in the console immediately. Your finalization needs are different from the other server roles, but you will notice that the navigation console on the left is sparse. This is because the Edge Transport server can be installed alone only, so that the console is not cluttered with additional pieces that are not needed.

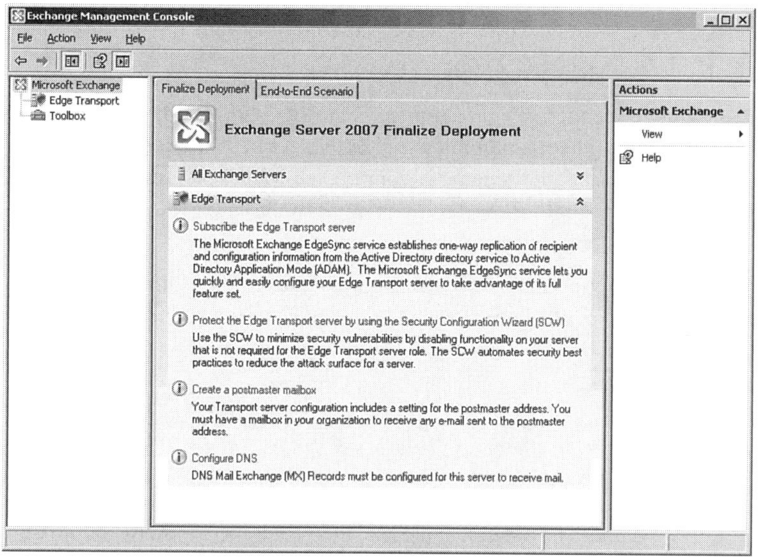

FIGURE 3.8
The Edge Transport management tools in the EMC.

> **NOTE** To avoid the graphic installation completely, you can put the DVD in and type **`setup /mode:install /roles:ET`** as a command prompt. As long as all the prerequisites are met, the installation should proceed without a problem.

Making the Connection with an HT Server

The process of linking an HT server and ET server together is known as the EdgeSync process. The process begins with exporting the EdgeSync subscription file and then taking the file and importing it on an HT server. The purpose of this process is to establish a one-way replication of recipient and configuration information from Active Directory to either ADAM or AD LDS (depending on the type of server you are using). The connection with the HT servers and the Edge Transport server(s) is a unique one of trust, so that the HT servers can route messages going to the Internet through the Edge Transport server that has been configured and is associated with the HT server.

To begin, you want to log on to the Edge Transport server and perform the following:

1. Open the Exchange Management Shell.

2. Type **`New-EdgeSubscription -FileName "c:\edgesubscriptioninfo .xml"`** (note that the filename and location is completely your choice, this is just an example).

After the file is complete, copy it over to the HT server. Make sure you have fully qualified domain name (FQDN) connectivity between the servers by performing simple ping tests by name. On the HT server, perform the following:

1. Open the Exchange Management Shell.
2. Type **`New-EdgeSubscription -filename "C:\EdgeSubscriptionInfo .xml" -CreateInternetSendConnector $true -site "Default-First-Site-Name"`**. (Note that the filename is your choice when you create the file, so enter the name you gave it. The default site name might have been changed, so make sure the site is correct, too.)
3. The synchronization process usually takes places at four-hour intervals. If you want to immediately begin the process of synchronization, you can type **`Start-EdgeSynchronization`**.

NOTE You can use the Test-EdgeSynchronization cmdlet to determine whether there is a problem between the Edge Transport servers and the HT servers. This is an Exchange 2007 SP1-only cmdlet. Simply typing in the cmdlet retrieves plenty of information; however, you can use switches that enable you to tailor your test. You can find these at http://technet.microsoft.com/en-us/library/aa996925(EXCHG.80).aspx.

Perform a Mailbox Active/Passive Installation

Scenario/Problem: You've no doubt noticed that there are two installation types for the Mailbox role that are unique: the Active Clustered Mailbox role and Passive Clustered Mailbox role. Ordinarily, we would cover these in Chapter 10, "Design and Deploy High Availability for Exchange 2007." However, because they are technically part of the installation features, we discuss them here.

Solution: It's not so much that the installation of the Active and Passive Mailbox servers is any different from other installations we've performed. Rather, you must consider the preparation before you install these two.

First, you cannot install the Active or Passive Clustered Mailbox roles with any other roles. They must reside alone.

Second, they function properly only if you have installed the proper clustering services on either Server 2003 or Server 2008. You must ensure you have two servers configured with failover clustering and a File Share Witness. To learn more about this, see Chapter 10.

Third, those clustering services function only if you have the Enterprise Edition of Server running.

Install the Active Side on Server 2003

This can be done using the command line, but the Setup Wizard tends to be easier. To install, perform the following:

1. Insert the DVD or mount the ISO for the Installation screen to display. Select the link from Step 4: Install Microsoft Exchange 2007 SP1 to begin the installation wizard.
2. You are taken to the Introduction screen. Click Next.
3. You are taken to the License Agreement screen, where you can scroll down and read the entire agreement if you like. Choose I Accept The Terms In The License Agreement and select Next.
4. You are taken to the Error Reporting screen. Here you are asked to participate in a group effort with Microsoft to determine why certain errors occur on systems. If you say Yes (Recommended), errors that occur automatically send reports to Microsoft without further permission. The other option is No. Choose an option and select Next.
5. This brings you to the Installation Type screen, where you can choose either a Typical or Custom Exchange Server installation. In this case, select Custom Exchange Server Installation.
6. From the Server Role Selection screen, select Active Clustered Mailbox Role, and then select Next. (Note that the path you allow for the active installation files must match the path for the passive installation files.)
7. You are taken to the Cluster Settings screen. Here, you can choose Cluster Continuous Replication or Single Copy Cluster, depending on the type of cluster you have configured.
8. Next, specify the Clustered Mailbox Server Name and the path for the Clustered Mailbox Server database files. Then click Next. (Note that clustered mailbox server [CMS] names must be 15 characters or less.)
9. On the Cluster IP Address Configuration, enter a static IP address (IPv4 address) and click Next.
10. The Readiness Checks screen checks to make sure your system is ready for the installation of the server options you chose. After you are clear to move forward, choose Install.
11. The Progress screen walks you through the process of the actual installation. When complete, it takes you to the Completion screen and shows you what has been installed successfully. Click Finish.

After the CMS is online and functioning, you can install the passive side.

Install the Active Side on Server 2008

Without going through each step again, note that you can do more on the Cluster IP Address Configuration page. For example, you can choose to leave the IPv4 network option selected. You can choose to use a dynamic IP address for the CMS. You can also select an IPv6 network. If you are installing the cluster into a multiple subnet arrangement, you can choose the Second Subnet checkbox and configure the second subnet according to your configuration needs.

Install the Passive Side on Server 2003/2008

Installing the passive side to the clustered mailbox role is the easiest part. It's as simple as installing a standard Mailbox server, although you select passive instead. To perform the installation on both Server 2003 and 2008, do the following:

1. Insert the DVD or mount the ISO for the Installation screen to display. Select the link from Step 4: Install Microsoft Exchange 2007 SP1 to begin the installation wizard.
2. You are taken to the Introduction screen. Click Next.
3. You are taken to the License Agreement screen, where you can scroll down and read the entire agreement if you like. Choose I Accept The Terms In The License Agreement, and then select Next.
4. You are taken to the Error Reporting screen. Here you are asked to participate in a group effort with Microsoft to determine why certain errors occur on systems. If you say Yes (Recommended), errors that occur automatically send reports to Microsoft without further permission. The other option is No. Choose an option and select Next.
5. This brings you to the Installation Type screen, where you can choose either a Typical or Custom Exchange Server installation. In this case, select Custom Exchange Server Installation.
6. From the Server Role Selection screen, select Passive Clustered Mailbox Role, and then select Next. (Note that the path you allow for the active installation files must match the path for the passive installation files.)
7. The Readiness Checks screen checks to make sure your system is ready for the installation of the server options you've chosen. After you are clear to move forward, choose Install.
8. The Progress screen walks you through the process of the actual installation. When complete, it takes you to the Completion screen and shows you what has been installed successfully. Click Finish.

Work with the EMC and the Exchange Management Shell

Scenario/Problem: New tools can be overwhelming. The EMC might not be as difficult, being a GUI, but the Exchange Management Shell (EMS) might challenge you. However, it shouldn't. Both tools have been designed to make your life as an Exchange administrator easier. Throughout this book, you see instructions to help you navigate the console and the shell. To understand those instructions, we provide a little introduction to both tools to help you adjust.

Solution: Let's review the interface options of the EMC and the command syntax behind the EMS.

The Exchange Management Console

Note from Figure 3.9 that the console layout is easy to work with. Many who have worked with System Manager in Exchange 2003 are quite pleased with the changes, which make it easier for us to locate and access those dialog boxes we need.

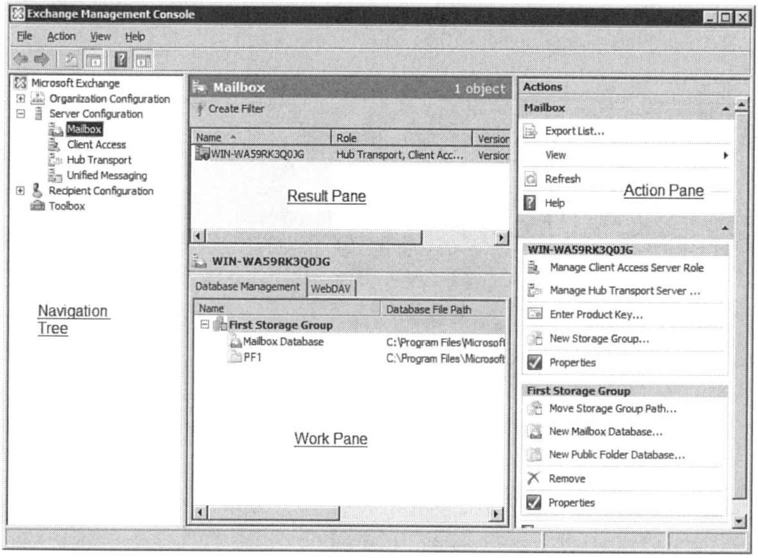

FIGURE 3.9
The EMC.

Note the Navigation Tree on the left hand side. We refer you to this tree often by instructing you to locate one of the four work centers, which include the following:

- Organization Configuration
- Server Configuration

- Recipient Configuration
- Toolbox

Note also the Result pane, the Work pane, and the Action pane. When being given instruction on how to locate a certain dialog or action, you are instructed to navigate the console initially, through the work centers and static containers. Then, you might need to select items in the Result or Work pane before choosing your action.

Up near the top, there is a Show/Hide Action Pane button that you can use to turn off the Action pane. At that point, you can right-click items in your other panes to see what actions are available or you can use the Action menu. You can also Show/Hide the Console Tree.

From the View menu, you can Add/Remove Columns. You can also select Customize and turn on or off various features of the console.

The Exchange Management Shell

The EMS is not designed to confuse you or make your life harder. In fact, many situations occur where you won't need to even consider the EMS, but for those times that you do, you'll find that a simple line of code is going to pack a lot of power.

When you first open the EMS, you are presented with a Welcome, some basic commands to get you started, and a Tip of the Day (as shown in Figure 3.10).

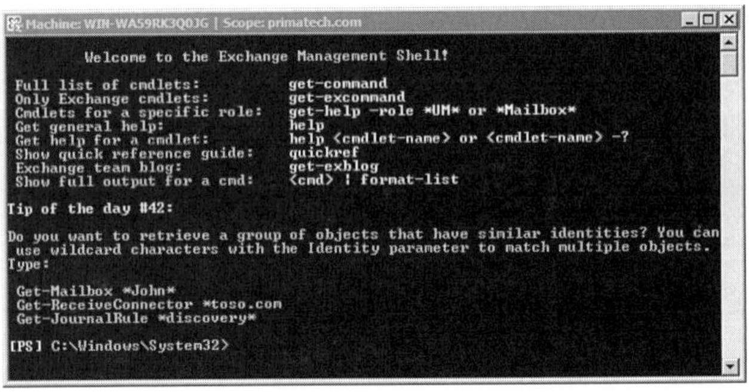

FIGURE 3.10
The EMS.

Commands are created through verb-noun pairings called *cmdlets*. Consider using simple ones such as get-mailbox, move-mailbox, get-storagegroup, and so forth.

There are only 26 different verbs at your disposal, so it shouldn't take you too long to catch on. These include the following:

Add	Clean	Clear	Connect	Copy	Disable
Dismount	Enable	Export	Get	Import	Install
Mount	Move	New	Remove	Restore	Resume
Retry	Set	Start	Stop	Suspend	Test
Uninstall	Update				

To see a full list of commands, you can type **`get-command`** at the EMS prompt. To see only the Exchange commands, you can type **`get-excommand`**. For help with any of these, you just type **`help`** and the cmdlet name. It provides you with information on the cmdlet and the parameters that go along with it to make that cmdlet more helpful. Those parameters might be **`-Identity`**, **`-WhatIf`**, **`-SortBy`**, and so on.

If you recall the verb part but not the noun, you can always type the verb and then press the Tab key. It continues to scroll through your options alphabetically until it reaches your cmdlet.

You are able to direct the output of your initial command to another command. This is called *pipelining* and the pipe symbol (|) is used to accomplish this. The second part of the command might process the results even further by filtering, sorting, grouping, or enabling aspects on the results of the first part of the command.

The primary goal of this section is not to overwhelm you, but is simply to get you started with PowerShell and the Exchange Management Shell. The majority of our lessons show you the EMC side to Exchange administration, but sometimes the CLI is unavoidable, as noted earlier when we performed the EdgeSync process.

CHAPTER 4

Manage Storage and Databases

IN THIS CHAPTER

- Manage Storage Groups
- Create Mailbox Databases
- Mount/Dismount Mailbox Databases
- Manage MB Database Properties
- Manage Public Folder Databases
- Configure a Best-Practice Disk Strategy

Manage Storage Groups

Scenario/Problem: A Mailbox server is responsible for handling storage groups. The Standard Edition can hold 5 (with 5 databases) and the Enterprise Edition can handle 50 (with 50 databases). It's recommended that you put one database inside one storage group if possible. The question is: How does one handle the management of a storage group and create and remove storage groups?

Solution: We work through the following scenarios:

- Create a new storage group
- Remove a storage group
- Move a storage group path
- Enable or disable circular logging for a storage group
- Storage group properties from the EMS

Create a New Storage Group

To create a new storage group, make sure you are logged in as an Exchange Server Administrator role and as part of the local Administrators group and perform the following:

1. Open the Exchange Management Console (EMC).
2. From the Navigation Tree, expand the Server Configuration work center and click Mailbox.
3. From the Result pane, choose the server on which you want to create a new storage group.
4. Now, either right-click in the white space within the Work pane or look at the Actions pane, and choose the New Storage Group option.
5. The New Storage Group Wizard displays, as shown in Figure 4.1. You can supply the storage group name. Then you can browse for locations other than the default for the log files and the system files. The default location is C:\Program Files\Microsoft\Exchange Server\Mailbox\<*name of storage group*>.
6. When ready, select New.
7. The Completion screen should show you that the wizard was successful and you have the storage group you want. Click Finish.

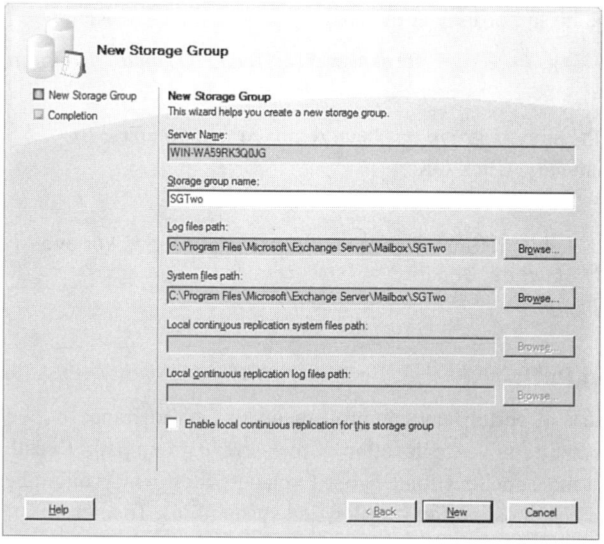

FIGURE 4.1
The New Storage Group Wizard.

NOTE You might have noticed while completing the New Storage Group Wizard steps that there was an option to enable local continuous replication for this storage group, which we chose to ignore at this time. We discuss this setting and its purpose and use in Chapter 10, "Design and Deploy High Availability for Exchange 2007."

PS NOTE The cmdlet through the Exchange Management Shell (EMS) used to create the storage group is `New-StorageGroup <Name of Storage Group> -Server <Name of Server>`. You can take advantage of other parameters. In fact, if you press Ctrl+C when the wizard is complete, you are given the exact command for creating the storage group you created. You can then paste that into Wordpad or Notepad to learn more about how PowerShell works.

Remove a Storage Group

Keep in mind that you cannot remove a storage group that still contains databases. To remove a storage group, perform the following steps:

1. Open the EMC.
2. From the Navigation Tree, expand the Server Configuration work center and click Mailbox.
3. From the Result pane, choose the server from which you want to remove the storage group.
4. Select the storage group you want to remove from the Work pane.

5. Right-click the storage group, or look at the Actions pane and choose Remove.
6. A warning displays asking, "Are you sure you want to remove *<name of storage group>*?" Select Yes.
7. You are notified that the storage group has been removed, but you have to remove the log file manually. Click OK.

> PS NOTE The cmdlet through the EMS used to remove a storage group is `Remove-StorageGroup "Name of Storage Group."`

Move a Storage Group Path

There are times, either because of performance improvements or fault tolerance concerns, when you might want to move the location of the storage group path. Recall that the default location is in the same location as your Exchange files, which might be your c: drive. This is not the best location for your log and system files. To alter this, perform the following:

1. Open the EMC.
2. From the Navigation Tree, expand the Server Configuration work center and click Mailbox.
3. From the Result pane, choose the server that you want to move the storage group paths to.
4. In the Work pane, select the storage group.
5. Right-click the storage group or look at the Actions pane and choose Move Storage Group Path.
6. The Move Storage Group Path Wizard displays with the current location for the log and system files. You can choose the Browse buttons next to either one to select new locations for each. (Note: If Local Continuous Replication [LCR] is enabled for the storage group, you are also given the opportunity to move the location of the LCR files.)
7. After you choose the new locations, click Move.
8. You are warned that to move the files, the databases need to be dismounted, so they are inaccessible for a short period of time. To continue, click Yes.
9. You are taken to the Completion screen, where you can see whether the operation completed successfully.
10. Click Finish.

PS NOTE The cmdlet through the EMS used to move a storage group path is `Move-StorageGroupPath -Identity "Name of Storage Group" -LogFolderPath:"New Location Path" -SystemFolderPath:"New Location Path."`

Enable or Disable Circular Logging for a Storage Group

By default, circular logging is disabled on storage groups. The purpose of circular logging is to reduce disk storage requirements by limiting the number of transaction log files. As you learned in Chapter 1, “Introduction to Exchange 2007 SP1,” transaction logs help to ensure recoverability of data in the event of a failure of the disk holding the database or the database corrupts in some way. By enabling circular logging, you reduce your chances of being able to completely recover because circular logging enables Exchange to overwrite transaction logs after the data within the log file has been committed to the database.

NOTE Within a production environment, it's rare to use circular logging. However, there are times when you might not be as concerned about recoverability so much as disk space. You might also use circular logging temporarily when moving large amounts of mailboxes to a target server because traditionally you need to ensure you have on the transaction log drive 20 percent more space than the total size of the mailboxes you move. If you don't have that space, turn on circular logging until you can get the space worked out.

To enable circular logging (or disable it by deselecting the checkbox), perform the following:

1. Open the EMC.
2. From the Navigation Tree, expand the Server Configuration work center and click Mailbox.
3. From the Result pane, choose the server.
4. In the Work pane, select the storage group.
5. Right-click the storage group or look at the Actions pane, and then choose Properties.
6. Notice that you can change the name of the storage group, and you can see from Figure 4.2 that there is an Enable Circular Logging option that you can select. Select the checkbox.

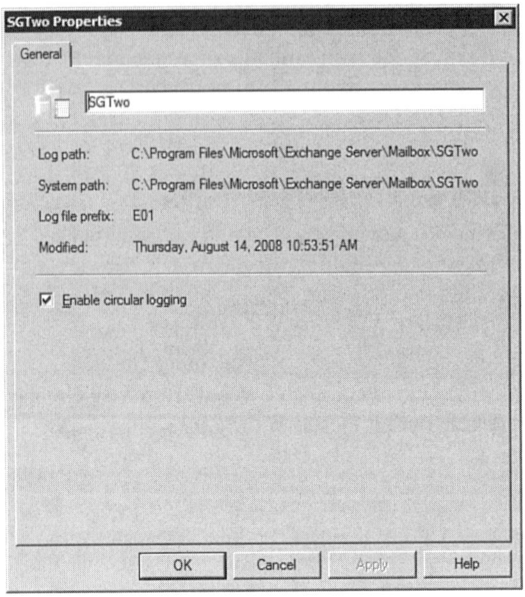

FIGURE 4.2
Enabling circular logging on a storage group.

7. Click OK.

> **PS NOTE** The cmdlet through the EMS used to enable circular logging is `Set-StorageGroup "Name of Storage Group" -CircularLoggingEnabled:$True`.

Storage Group Properties from the Exchange Management Shell

By going into the properties of a storage group from within the EMC, you are presented with a bare minimum in terms of information about that storage group. You can find a lot more information through the EMS.

To do so, you need to use the `Get-StorageGroup` cmdlet, but you also need to pipeline it as a format list (`fl` for short).

If the name of the storage group is SGTwo, the command you would type is:

```
Get-StorageGroup "SGTwo" | fl
```

As you can see from Figure 4.3, the information returned is quite extensive. Ordinarily you might not need that depth of information, but in the event you do, it is available.

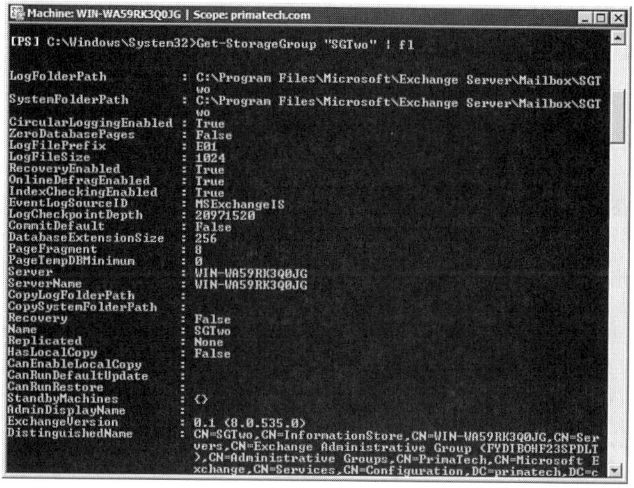

FIGURE 4.3
Using the Get-StorageGroup cmdlet with a format list.

Create Mailbox Databases

Scenario/Problem: After you have a storage group in place, your next step is to create a mailbox database. The goal is to place only one database in any one storage group. How do you create mailbox databases?

Solution: To create a new mailbox database, perform the following:

1. Open the EMC.
2. From the Navigation Tree, expand the Server Configuration work center and click Mailbox.
3. From the Result pane, choose the server.
4. In the Work pane, select the storage group where you want to place the mailbox database.
5. From the Actions pane select New Mailbox Database, which begins the New Mailbox Database Wizard.
6. Enter the following information:
   a. Mailbox Database Name—Up to 64 characters without using characters like \ /, ", =, and ;.
   b. Database File Path—Here you can click Browse and choose a new location for the .edb file that will be your database. Otherwise, it goes into the default location.

   c. Mount This Database—Selected by default, but you can deselect it if you want to wait on having this database become available for use.

   d. Note—If you have LCR enabled for the storage group, you see another dialog for the LCR path for the database.

7. Click New.
8. When complete, you are taken to the Completion screen.

> PS NOTE The cmdlet through the EMS used to create a new mailbox database is `New-MailboxDatabase -Name <name of database> -StorageGroup ServerName\ StorageGroupName`. To mount the database type: **`Mount-Database -Identity <name of database>`**.

Remove a Mailbox Database

If you decide you no longer need a certain database and want to remove it, first ensure you have moved all your mailboxes over to an available database. Then perform the following:

1. Open the EMC.
2. From the Navigation Tree, expand the Server Configuration work center and click Mailbox.
3. From the Result pane, choose the server.
4. In the Work pane, select the storage group that holds the mailbox database and select the database you want to remove.
5. From the Actions pane, select Remove.
6. You will be warned and asked if you want to continue. Select Yes.
7. When the dialog displays telling you the database has been removed, you should note the location of your .edb file because you have to delete it manually.
8. Click OK.

> PS NOTE The cmdlet through the EMS used to remove a mailbox database is `Remove-MailboxDatabase -Identity <name of database>`.

Mount/Dismount Mailbox Databases

> **Scenario/Problem:** Every database can be mounted or dismounted, which determines whether the Microsoft Exchange Information Store Service can access that database.
>
> Databases can be automatically dismounted during certain operations. For example, if you move the database path, certain backup types (called offline backups) exist where you have to dismount the database before backing it up.

Solution: To dismount a database, perform the following:

1. Open the EMC.
2. From the Navigation Tree, expand the Server Configuration work center and click Mailbox.
3. From the Result pane, choose the server.
4. In the Work pane, select the storage group that holds the mailbox database and select the database you wish to dismount.
5. From the Actions pane, select Dismount Database.
6. Click Yes when you receive a warning message that says, "Are you sure you want to dismount database <*name of database*>?"

To remount that database, you perform the same actions as stated previously except this time you select Mount Database.

> PS **NOTE** The cmdlet through the EMS used to mount or dismount databases is `Dismount-Database "Name of Database"` or `Mount-Database "Name of Database"`.

Manage MB Database Properties

> **Scenario/Problem:** In managing your mailbox database, properties can be involved. Everything from journaling to setting storage limits and even client settings is included.

Solution: To understand the various settings within the properties of a mailbox database, we are going to break it down into tabs and sections as follows:

- General
- Limits: Storage Limits and Deletion Settings
- Client Settings

To locate the properties of a database, perform the following:

1. Open the EMC.
2. From the Navigation Tree, expand the Server Configuration work center and click Mailbox.
3. From the Result pane, choose the server.
4. In the Work pane, select the storage group that holds the mailbox database and select the database you wish to view the properties of.
5. From the Actions pane, select Properties.

The General Tab

The General tab initially shows you a lot of dynamic information, as you can see in Figure 4.4. In addition to seeing the name of your database and the database path (and copy path if there is one), you see items such as your last full backup and your last incremental backup, indicating whether transaction logs were purged and when. Status shows you the mounted or dismounted state of your database. Additionally, you can see when the last time database properties in Active Directory (AD) were changed.

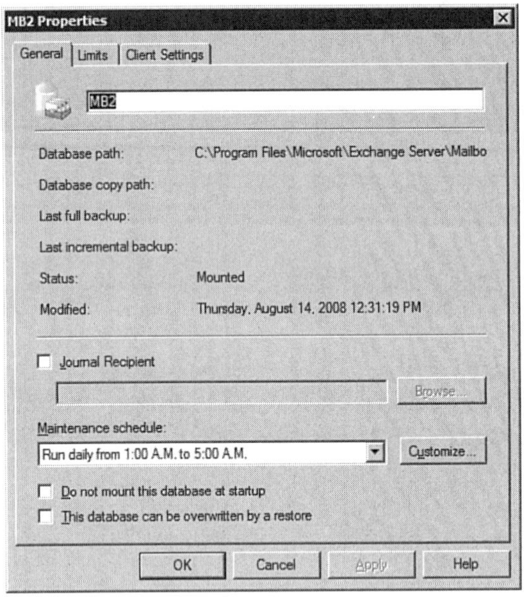

FIGURE 4.4
The General tab of your database properties.

You should also take note of the two checkboxes at the bottom of the screen. The first is Do Not Mount This Database At Startup, which prevents the database from being mounted with the startup of the Information Store. This is helpful if an administrator wants to bring databases back online in a certain order rather than all at once.

The other checkbox is This Database Can Be Overwritten By a Restore, which is used when you need to restore from an offline backup. This occurs if the database is backed up by making a copy, not with an online backup of the database.

How Do I Create a Copy of All Mail Going In and Out of This Database?

Scenario/Problem: You want to have a copy of all mail sent to a journal recipient. How would you accomplish this? Noting that we are in the properties of the database on the General tab, the solution is clear.

Solution: Notice the Journal Recipient checkbox. If you select this and choose a recipient (that is, a mailbox specifically set up to be the journal recipient for this database), mail going to and from all mailboxes in this database is copied and that copy is sent to the journal recipient.

How Do I Schedule Maintenance on My Databases?

Scenario/Problem: A daily schedule is automatically configured to run on your database for the purpose of purging deleted items permanently, purging mailboxes that have been deleted, verifying everything is in order in terms of mailboxes and folders, and cleaning up white space. All this occurs online (that is, while the database is mounted). How do you make adjustments to this schedule?

Solution: On the General tab of the database properties, note the Maintenance Schedule option from which you can select the down arrow and choose from a variety of different time schedules provided. Or, you can choose the Customize option and configure a schedule that better suits the needs of your organization.

The Limits Tab

Under the properties of the database, the second tab is the Limits tab, shown in Figure 4.5. Here, we have two sections: Storage Limits and Deletion Settings. Each has a unique purpose and poses unique scenarios to consider.

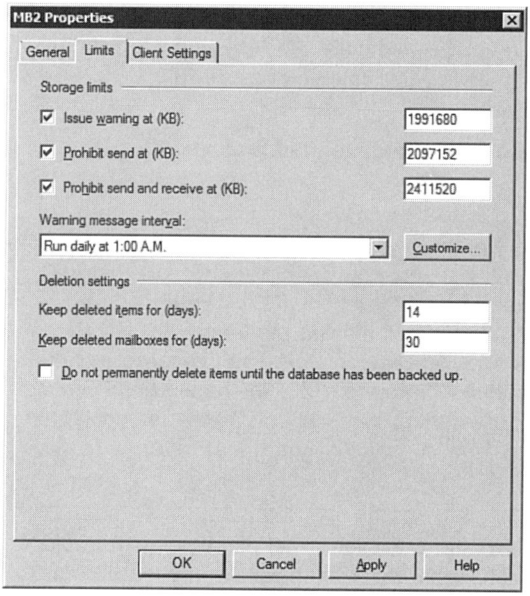

FIGURE 4.5

The Limits tab of your database properties.

How Do I Configure Storage Limitations and What Types Can I Configure?

Scenario/Problem: By default, the storage limitations per mailbox, according to the database storage limits, is more than 2GB. Although you would like to provide that size mailbox limit for each person, it's not possible yet. Rather, you want to provide a 500MB limit. How do you do this? And what else can you enforce at this level?

Solution: On the Limits tab, as you can see from Figure 4.5, you have a warning issued to the user at close to 2GB. Shortly thereafter, the user is no longer able to send email. Then at the final limit, the user cannot send or retrieve email.

A warning message interval sends a message to users when they reach these milestones of limitations. Users receive simple messages explaining that they either are getting close to their limits and should delete a few items to reduce the size of their mailbox or, if the size continue to grow, they are told they cannot send (or cannot send and receive). You can alter the warning interval by selecting the down arrow or choosing the Customize option.

It might be difficult as an administrator to know exactly how much disk space you need. There are calculators to assist so that you can determine the number of users, the amount of space left for deleted items and mailbox retention, and so on. However, just as a simple example plan, let's say you wanted every user to have 500MB of space. If you have 1,000 users, you are looking at 500,000 MB, or roughly 488GB. That is just for the standard mailbox sizes. Now you need to consider if you have some people (such as the CEO of the company) you wish to give larger mailboxes to.

With a 500MB mailbox size, you might try a warning at 400MB, with a prohibition of sending at 450MB and prohibition of sending and receiving at 500MB.

How Do I Alter the Default Deleted Item and Deleted Mailbox Retention Times?

Scenario/Problem: When a user deletes a message, it goes in the Deleted Items folder. The message isn't truly deleted, and you have to explain that to your users. They must delete it from the Deleted Items folder. However, even then it is not truly deleted just yet. By default, there is a 14-day retention period during which Exchange holds onto the messages until the maintenance period begins after the 14 days are up. Administrators might delete mailboxes because workers have left, but those mailboxes also have a default 30-day retention time during which they can be retrieved. How do you configure these settings or readjust them to better suit your needs?

Solution: The real benefit of deleted item or mailbox retention times is to avoid getting backup tapes. Imagine a scenario in which you have a database with 100 mailboxes. All 100 people within that database have about 100MB of mailbox space. They are temporary workers or document processors and they do not require a great deal of email real estate. By extension, if they delete something and say,

"Excuse me, but 10 days ago I deleted an important email," you might not feel obligated to go looking to restore that email. If the deleted item retention time is still at 14, you can tell them how to retrieve their own email. However, in the interest of saving disk space, you might decide to lower the amount of time here. With persons of great importance, you might, in the interest of job security and a positive evaluation, increase the time to 30 days on deleted items so that a CEO can quickly retrieve messages he may have accidentally deleted.

As for deleted mailboxes, it depends on how often you delete a mailbox and need to restore it. You could always use backups, so you might want to lower this number.

The checkbox Do Not Permanently Delete Items Until the Database Has Been Backed Up is a good one to turn on; however, ideally you perform backups more often than once every 14 days. The odds of an item not being backed up should be small if you perform regular (daily) backup routines.

The Clients Settings Tab

Under the properties of the database, the third tab is the Clients Settings tab shown in Figure 4.6. This tab enables you to configure two settings: the default Public Folder database, which is where mailbox clients within this database first go to retrieve the information about the Public Folder store, and the offline address book, which is where you specify which offline address book (OAB) a client should download. The default configuration (and one that is usually sufficient for small- to medium-sized companies) is the default offline address list.

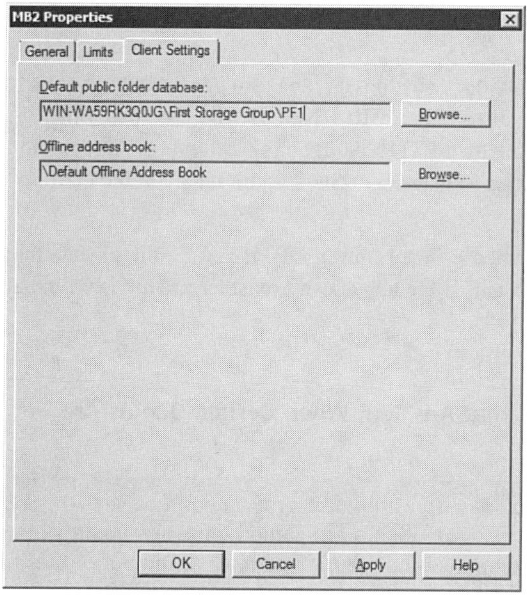

FIGURE 4.6
The Clients Settings tab of your database properties.

> **PS NOTE** The cmdlet through the EMS used to view the properties we just considered from the EMC is `Get-MailboxDatabase "Name of Database" | fl`.

Additional MB Database Management Issues

There are always little things that we need to do to enhance our working experience or change the way certain defaults work. For example, consider the following scenarios.

How Do I Modify a Database Size Limit?

> **Scenario/Problem:** Your mail databases will grow. Technically, in Exchange 2007, they can keep growing, but that isn't true. The Standard Edition has a 50GB limit on the database size. The Enterprise Edition does not have a limit. This limit is "for your own good" in the interest of keeping your databases manageable, considering the size of your server and organization. However, what if you want that limit removed?

Solution: First, Microsoft doesn't mind if you make this change (although it encourages you to be careful editing your Registry). In fact, Microsoft tells us how to do it in the TechNet Center. To modify the database size limit, perform the following on the Exchange Server:

1. Click Start, Run.
2. Open your Registry Editor by typing **`regedit`** and pressing Enter.
3. Navigate to the following key: `HKEY_LOCAL_MACHINE\SYSTEM\CurrentControlSet\Services\MSExchangeIS\<SERVER NAME>\Private-<database GUID>` (Note: If you aren't sure the GUID of your database, run the `Get-MailboxDatabase "Name of Database" | fl` command in the Exchange Management Shell and it tells you the `GUID` to look for.)
4. Look for the `DWORD` called Database Size Limit in GB. If you find it, change the subkey value to the size you want. If the key doesn't exist, create a key with that name and put the value in.

How Do I Modify the Messages That Are Sent When Certain Quotas Are Reached?

> **Scenario/Problem:** As a mailbox fills up with email, first a user receives a warning message with some instructions, then a prohibition message about sending the email, and finally, a message that all mail coming in and out of the mailbox is disabled. Those messages are generic, but you can customize them to your organization. How do you do it?

Solution: It would be nice if you could type these in easily in the EMC, but unfortunately, these are some of the features they left for the EMS. The cmdlets you want to use are `New-SystemMessage`, `Get-SystemMessage`, `Set-SystemMessage`, and `Remove-SystemMessage`.

To create the correct message, use the WarningMailbox message (for mailboxes that are exceeding their warning threshold), the ProhibitSendMailbox message (for mailboxes that can no longer send email), and the ProhibitSendReceiveMailbox message (for mailboxes that have completely maxed out and can no longer send or receive). Logically, there are more parameters you can use in relation to mailboxes or Public Folders. There are plenty of messages; however, for now, we focus on the ones that relate to the database.

Let's say you want to customize the WarningMailbox quota message. You could open the Exchange Management Shell and type the following:

```
New-SystemMessage -QuotaMessageType WarningMessage -Language EN
-Text "Your mailbox is almost full and you should consider deleting
items from your mailbox as well as your deleted items folder."
```

Now, this message is close to the real message, but it's just an example of what you could use. You have to determine what you want. To learn more about managing quota messages, visit http://technet.microsoft.com/en-us/library/bb232089(EXCHG.80).aspx.

How and Why Do I Monitor Online Defragmentation?

Scenario/Problem: We mentioned earlier that you can configure the maintenance schedule for your mailbox database to have cleanup work done on it. Part of that cleanup work is an online defragmentation. You might want to know how long the real process takes because you might have three or four hours slated, but you can reduce that time and perhaps schedule things differently among your databases. How can you perform the monitoring?

Solution: The answer is through the Event Viewer and Performance Monitor. You need to enable certain counters in the Registry. To start with, perform the following:

1. Click Start, Run.
2. Open your Registry Editor by typing **`regedit`** and pressing Enter.
3. Navigate to the following key: `HKEY_LOCAL_MACHINE\SYSTEM\CurrentControlSet\Services\ESE\Performance`.
4. Right-click the word Performance and select New, and then select DWORD Value.
5. Call the new **`DWORD`** value **`Show Advanced Counters`**.
6. After it is created, double-click the new Show Advanced Counters and enter the value data field as 1.
7. Close the Registry Editor.

You can use the Event Viewer, as well as the Reliability and Performance Monitor (or simply the Performance Monitor in Server 2003), to search for online defragmentation information.

Within Event Viewer, you want to perform searches in the Application log for Event ID: 703.

You want to filter the log and look for online defragmentation completion at least every two weeks on every database on the server.

To filter events in Event Viewer in Windows Server 2008 for Event 703, perform the following:

1. Open Event Viewer. (Click Start, point to Administrative Tools, and then select Event Viewer.)
2. In Event Viewer, look at the left Navigation Tree, expand Windows Logs, and then expand Application to view the Application log.
3. To filter for Event 703, look at the Actions pane and click Filter Current Log. The Filter Current Log dialog box displays.
4. From the Filter Current Log dialog box, on the Filter tab, in the Includes/Excludes Event IDs box, type **`703`**, and then click OK. All events with an ID of 703 display in the Result pane.
5. To view the event description, right-click the event, and select Event Properties.

The monitoring aspect through the Performance Monitor can be performed with standard counters and/or the counters you enable through the Registry. In either case, what are we looking for?

For starters, SP1 added some counters to look at, such as the following example:

`MSExchange Database—Instances \Online Defrag Pages Freed/Sec and \Online Defrag Data Moves/Sec`

In addition, there are a handful of other Online Defrag counters that you can utilize. For more information, go to http://technet.microsoft.com/en-us/library/bb691410(EXCHG.80).aspx.

Manage Public Folder Databases

Scenario/Problem: Either to allow pre-Outlook 2007 clients to connect to your Exchange environment or to use the benefits of a Public Folder environment, you need to begin somewhere. If that Public Folder database doesn't already exist, you need to create one. Then, you have to worry about management.

Solution: The following sections cover:

- Creating a new Public Folder database
- Creating and removing Public Folders

- Mail-enabling Public Folders
- Configuring Public Folder database settings
- Configuring Public Folder settings

Creating a New Public Folder Database

To accomplish the creation of a new Public Folder database, perform the following:

1. Open the EMC.
2. From the Navigation Tree, expand the Server Configuration work center and click Mailbox.
3. From the Result pane, choose the server on which you want to create a new Public Folder database.
4. From the Work pane, choose the storage group in which you want to create the new Public Folder database.
5. From the Actions pane (or by right-clicking the storage group), click New Public Folder Database. The New Public Folder Database Wizard displays.
6. Type the name of the new Public Folder database in the Public Folder Database Name box.
7. You can specify the location of the Public Folder database files by clicking Browse, and then entering the path for the Exchange database file (.edb) for the Public Folder. (This is optional.)
8. Leave the Mount This Database option selected.
9. Click New, and after the database is created, the Completion page displays.

> **PS NOTE** The cmdlet through the EMS used to create a new Public Folder database is `New-PublicFolderDatabase -Name "Name of Database" -StorageGroup "Name of Storage Group"`.

Creating and Removing Public Folders

Creating and removing Public Folders initially could be done only through the Outlook client (if a person had the correct permissions) or through the EMS. There was no GUI for working with Public Folders beyond the creation of the database itself. That has changed with the inclusion of the Public Folder Management Console tool found in the Toolbox options.

To create Public Folders from within SP1, perform the following:

1. Open the EMC.
2. From the Navigation Tree, expand the Toolbox work center, and from the Result pane, select Public Folder Management Console. You can double-click the tool or choose Open Tool from the Actions pane.

3. The SP1-added Public Folder Management Console displays separately from the EMC.
4. Select Default Public Folders, and you might note that there are currently no folders in your system.
5. Click New Public Folder, and the wizard begins.
6. All you are asked for is a name. Provide a name and click New.
7. After the folder is created, you are shown the Completion screen and a green circle. Click Finish.

To remove a Public Folder, you need to select it and choose Remove from the Actions pane. A warning displays and you need to confirm that you wish to remove it.

> PS **NOTE** The cmdlet through the EMS used to create a new Public Folder is `New-PublicFolder -Name "Name of Folder"`. You can also place a new Public Folder in other folders that are already in place using the `-Path` parameter. So, if you want to place a folder named Research within a folder named Legal, type **`New-PublicFolder -Name "Research" -Path \Legal -Server "ServerName"`**.

Mail-Enabling and Disabling Public Folders

By default, public folders do not receive email until you mail-enable them. They can receive posts from persons that have permission in the company, but not emails. To mail-enable a public folder, perform the following steps:

1. Open the EMC.
2. From the Navigation Tree, expand the Toolbox work center and from the Result pane, select Public Folder Management Console. You can double-click the tool or choose Open Tool from the Actions pane.
3. In the Navigation Tree of the Public Folder tool, expand Default Public Folders.
4. Find the folder you want to mail-enable. Then right-click on it or look in the Actions pane for the Mail Enable option.
5. You should note that the icon for the Public Folder changes. Now a small letter is shown next to the folder (whereas ordinarily it is inside the folder).
6. To disable the folder, select it again and choose Mail Disable.

> **NOTE** After you mail-enable a public folder the properties will change. If you check a public folder that is not mail-enabled and one that is, you'll notice that they both still retain their Public Folder settings, but the mail-enabled folder has settings that relate to email addresses, mail flow, and so forth, just like a regular mailbox would.

PS NOTE The cmdlet through the Exchange Management Shell to mail-enable a public folder is `Enable-MailPublicFolder -Identity "\Name of Public Folder"`.

Configuring Public Folder Database Settings

Public Folders can be managed as one entity under the database properties, or individually as folders. Often you establish your settings at the database level and not the folder level because it is easier to manage in bulk.

You'll notice that some of the settings are similar on the database level. To look at the properties, perform the following:

1. Open the EMC.
2. From the Navigation Tree, expand the Server Configuration work center and click Mailbox.
3. From the Result pane, choose the server with your Public Folder database.
4. In the Work pane, select the Public Folder database.
5. Either right-click and choose Properties or select Properties from the Actions pane.

Note that all the information on the General tab, including the maintenance options, is the same as what we saw on the mailbox database earlier.

The Replication tab (shown in Figure 4.7) contains only a few settings:

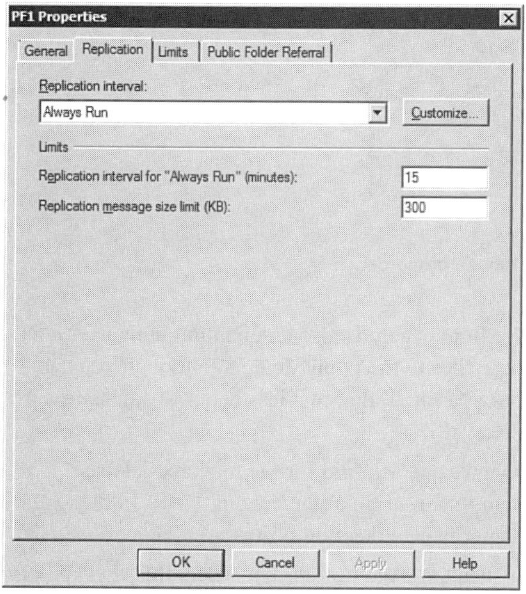

FIGURE 4.7

The Replication tab of your Public Folder database properties.

- Replication Interval determines when the replication of Public Folders occurs when content updates are made. The default is for it to Always Run, but you can turn it off completely or change the time frame, even customize the replication schedule.
- Replication Interval For "Always Run" (Minutes) shows the time interval that replication can occur.
- Replication Message Size Limit (KB) shows the size limit of a replication message. Smaller items can be grouped together into a single replication message, while larger ones are handled differently.

The Limits tab is slightly different from its mailbox database counterpart, as you can see in Figure 4.8.

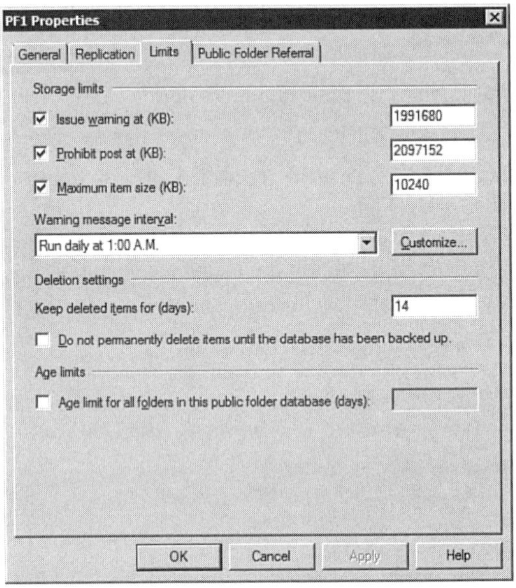

FIGURE 4.8
The Limits tab of your Public Folder database properties.

There is a still a warning and prohibit limit. There is also a maximum item size (KB) that prevents people from posting huge files to the public folders (although you can adjust this depending on the need, but you might find that it is better to adjust on a per folder basis, rather than at a database level).

The warning message interval works the same as it did for the mailbox database. Notice that there is only a deleted item retention time (the default is still 14 days) and the checkbox is still available for the permanent deletion of items.

There is an extra checkbox under the heading Age Limits. You select this checkbox to limit the age of all folders in the database. You can set a value of 0 to 24,855 days. After the items in the folder reach the specified age, Exchange deletes them and frees up the space automatically.

NOTE The big question you might have is why would you want to limit the age of a public folder? Well, you might use a public folder for a variety of reasons—perhaps to collect automated messages or spam. Or you might simply want to ensure that, beyond a certain number of years, the age limit is up.

The final tab is the Public Folder Referral tab. Here you can do one of two things: the default is to use Active Directory site costs, or you can create a custom list to use.

The purpose of this is to configure the folder replica that ultimately is accessed by the client application. The way referrals work is that a client tries to open a public folder and the server has to determine where the contents should come from. Ordinarily, you have several replicas of your public folders (although in a smaller environment you might only have a single location). After the server determines the best replica to offer, it gives the client a referral. If the replica exists on the server itself, it uses the local replica; if not, it tries to look in the same AD site (by default) unless you specify otherwise on this tab.

Configuring Public Folder Settings

Public Folder settings on individual folders require you to go back to the Public Folder Management Console. Select the Default Public Folders, and then look for the individual folder you wish to make changes to in the Results pane. When you find the folder, select it, and click Properties from the Actions pane.

You see three tabs:

- General—Shows you standard information such as the total number of items, the size of the folder, when it was last modified, and so forth. There is one checkbox, Maintain Per-user Read and Unread Information For This Folder, which is selected by default. This enables a user to see whether a message has been read or unread in Outlook.
- Replication—Here is where you can choose other servers, if you have them, to hold replicas of your public folders. Imagine several branch offices around the world that have people who want to access the same information. If it all resides in one location, that creates extra traffic. However, if you can create replicas in appropriate locations (not necessarily of every folder if you don't want or need to, but those that are more interesting on the global level), it reduces traffic and improves performance. You can adjust the replication schedule or simply go with the one already established on the database. You can also determine a local replica age limit (in days).
- Limits—This tab enables you to either use the database quota, item retention, and age limits or choose to use a different set of limits on this particular folder. You might decide a particular folder requires more of a maximum item size for posts, depending on the content in it. You might decide it requires a shorter age limit before content expires. Whatever the case, you configure those limits here.

Configure a Best-Practice Disk Strategy

Scenario/Problem: Storage groups, databases, transaction logs—it's a lot to consider when looking at maximizing both performance and fault tolerance. What are some recommended methods of accomplishing both?

Solution: First, your operating system is installed somewhere, traditionally on the c: drive. The entire hard drive is constantly read from and written to in an effort to keep your operating system up and running and functioning smoothly. No matter how good the drive is, how much memory you have, how fast your processor is, or how many cores you have, the fact is the operating system needs to be alone. You might install Exchange on the same drive (or on a different drive altogether, which would separate the calls made into two drives and speed up performance slightly), but you absolutely should keep all storage groups and databases off of the system drive.

Let's say you put your transaction logs and database files on their own hard drive. That is a good step. However, keep in mind that messages come into the memory and are written to the transaction logs and the database almost simultaneously depending on the queue of traffic and the size of the messages. Having the transaction logs and system files on the same drive as the databases is going to affect performance. Not to mention that if that drive crashes, you might be able to restore from a backup, but your backup is only as good as the night before, which is hopefully when you performed the backup.

The transaction logs can replay into the database if you have to restore from a failed disk or a corrupted database. So, you are better off separating your transaction logs and database files onto separate disks, too.

Now we have performance increasing and fault tolerance, too. What more can we do? Earlier solutions for your logs and database were to create a mirror set for your transaction logs to ensure an immediate backup of all your logs. Your database was recommended to be placed on a RAID 5 Striped Set with Parity configuration. These are not bad practices, but you might try something a little more modern.

You can still create a mirror of your transaction logs. You might place your database on a striped volume with no parity (because that takes up disk space). Instead, you can use LCR to get an online copy of your database.

Using LCR, which we show you how to configure in Chapter 10, provides a duplicate of your database, where the log files (immediately or through a timed delay of your specification) can replay themselves over to the copy of the database. In this case, you always have your logs and database separate (upping performance and fault tolerance). You have your database on a fast disk arrangement (which improves performance even more although without the fault tolerance) and you have an LCR high availability solution that provides the fault tolerance to your database.

You might decide, going forward, to provide more in terms of fault tolerance and high availability and go with a cluster (and Cluster Continuous Replication) or with SP1 a Standby Continuous Replication. All these options are explained in greater detail in Chapter 10.

Keep in mind, no solution is best. However, by understanding what affects performance and fault tolerance, considering ways to avoid disaster recovery scenarios, and keeping in mind your individual budget, you can come up with solutions that improve performance, tolerance, availability, and recovery (if needed).

CHAPTER 5

Manage Recipients

IN THIS CHAPTER

- Modify Recipient Configuration
- Create User Mailboxes
- Create a Linked Mailbox
- Create Resource Mailboxes
- Manage Resource Mailboxes
- Create Mail-Enabled Contacts and Mail-Enabled Users
- Create Distribution Groups and Dynamic Distribution Groups
- Configure Expansion Servers

Modify Recipient Configuration

Scenario/Problem: At times, you might have difficulty locating the recipients you know exist. This could be due to a scope setting or a governor on the number of recipients to display. How do you correct this problem?

Solution: By default, Exchange displays the recipient scope from the domain-level perspective. If you alter the scope, you change the set of recipients displayed.

To change the recipient scope, perform the following:

1. Open the Exchange Management Console (EMC).
2. From the Navigation Tree, select the Recipient Configuration work center.
3. On the Actions pane, the option Modify Recipient Scope brings up the Recipient Scope dialog, as shown in Figure 5.1.

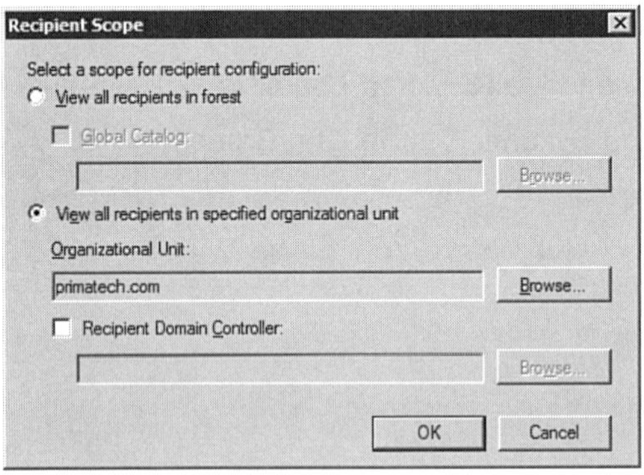

FIGURE 5.1
The Recipient Scope dialog box.

4. You can make the following changes:

- View All Recipients in Forest—This shows you more than the recipients within a specified Organizational Unit (OU), which is the default setting. If you want to use a specific Global Catalog, you can select the checkbox and choose Browse to locate it. If none is selected, Exchange chooses one for you.
- View All Recipients in Specified Organizational Unit—This enables you to choose an OU and all OUs beneath it. If you wish, you can select the Recipient Domain Controller (DC) option and choose the DC you want. If not, Exchange chooses one for you.

If, instead, your problem is that you cannot see all of your recipients (let's say you have 1,500 but you see only 1,000 in your Results pane), you need to adjust the Maximum Number of Recipients to Display option. Perform the following:

1. Open the EMC.
2. From the Navigation Tree, select the Recipient Configuration work center.
3. On the Actions pane, select the option Modify the Maximum Number of Recipients to Display.
4. Note that the maximum number by default is 1,000. You can alter this to no less than 1 and no more than 1,000,000.

NOTE You might be responsible for the entire organization and want to see as much as possible. However, if you are responsible for a section of the organization, you might want to adjust the scope to your particular OU and adjust the number of recipients shown to the level that benefits you, rather than seeing everything.

Create User Mailboxes

Scenario/Problem: After your server is configured and ready to send and receive mail, the next logical step is to provide recipients. Those recipients can come from users that already exist in Active Directory (AD) or you can create them as you create their mailboxes. Let's consider both approaches.

Solution: In this section, we look into the creation of a mailbox for an existing user and for a new user. Then we review how you remove a mailbox or simply disable one temporarily.

NOTE To create recipient mailboxes, you need to be a member of the Exchange Recipient Administrator role. You must also have the Account Operator role for the AD portions that apply.

Create a Mailbox for an Existing User

To create a mailbox for a recipient named Joe User who already exists within AD, do the following:

1. Open the EMC.
2. From the Navigation Tree, select the Recipient Configuration work center.
3. From the Actions pane, select New Mailbox and the New Mailbox Wizard opens.

4. On the Introduction screen, shown in Figure 5.2, you are presented with the several different mailbox types that we discuss throughout this chapter. The first is User Mailbox, which is selected by default; keep this mailbox type selected. Click Next.

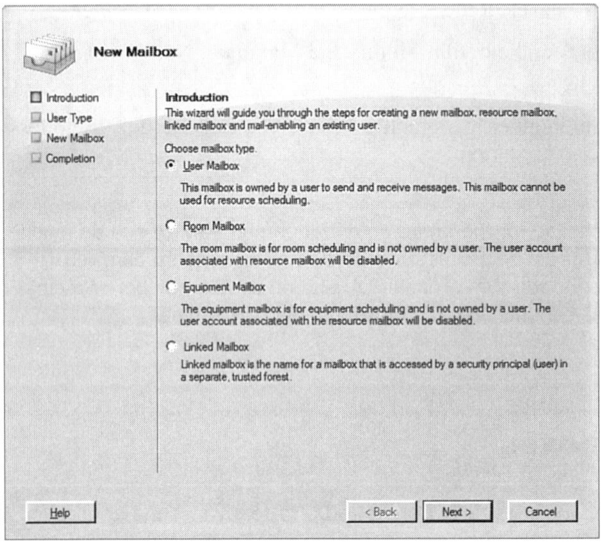

FIGURE 5.2
The New Mailbox Wizard Introduction screen.

5. You are asked if you want to create a mailbox for a new user or existing user. In this case, choose Existing Users, and then click the Add button. You are shown only those users who do not currently have mailboxes; locate the user Joe User. After you select the user, click Next.
6. You are taken to the Mailbox Settings screen, shown in Figure 5.3. You are shown the Alias for the user, which you can change. You are also asked to provide the following:
    a. Mailbox Database—Browse to the location of the database you want this mailbox to be a part of.
    b. Managed Folder Mailbox Policy—If you have a policy you would like to enforce, you can choose it now; if not, you can add this policy later.
    c. Exchange ActiveSync Mailbox Policy—This might not apply and depends on whether the user has a mobile device you allow to connect to the Exchange organization and if you have a policy you wish to apply.

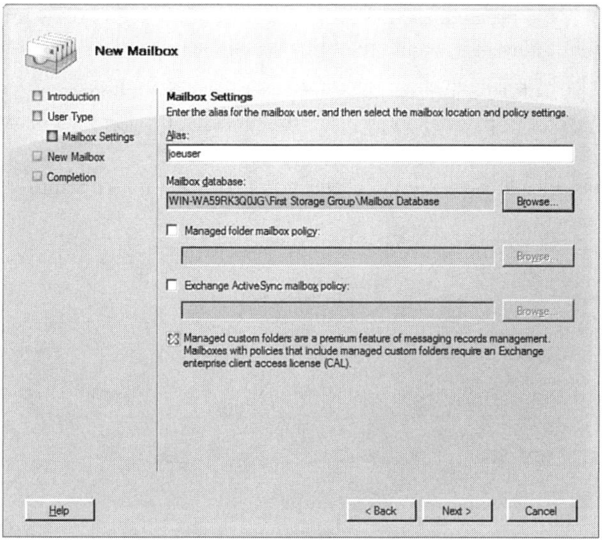

FIGURE 5.3
The New Mailbox Wizard's Mailbox Settings screen.

7. After you have the information provided, click Next.
8. You can review the summary of your configuration and then click New.
9. After the mailbox is created, a Completed checkbox displays, and you can click Finish.
10. Note that you should now have another recipient in the Recipient Configuration Results pane.

PS NOTE The cmdlet through the Exchange Management Shell (EMS) used to enable a user that already exists, such as Joe User, would be `Enable-Mailbox joeuser@primatech.com -Database "ServerName\StorageGroupName\MailboxDatabaseName"`.

Create a Mailbox for a New User

If your goal is to create a new user (in our example, Jane User) at the same time you create a new mailbox for that user, perform the following:

1. Open the EMC.
2. From the Navigation Tree, select the Recipient Configuration work center.
3. From the Actions pane, select New Mailbox and the New Mailbox Wizard opens.
4. On the Introduction screen, User Mailbox is selected by default; keep this selected. Click Next.

5. You are asked if you want to create a mailbox for a new user or existing user. In this case, leave the default New User, and then click Next.

6. You are taken to the User Information screen, shown in Figure 5.4 where you are asked to provide the OU to place the new user, the name and logon information, and the password with confirmation. You can select a checkbox that says User Must Change Password at Next Logon. After you fill in this information, click Next.

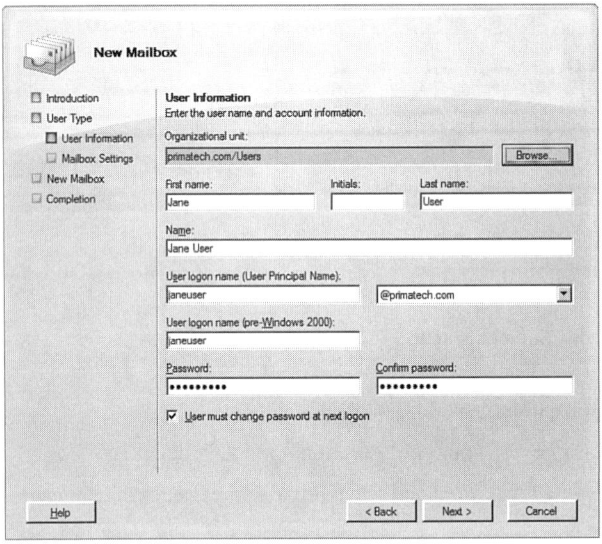

FIGURE 5.4
Creating a new user and mailbox.

7. You are then presented with the Mailbox Settings options, which include the database, managed folder mailbox policy, and ActiveSync mailbox policy. We describe these in the last scenario. Choose your options and click Next.

8. You are presented with a configuration summary that is somewhat longer than when you create a mailbox and the user is already created. Confirm your options and select New.

9. After the wizard completes, you see a Completed green check mark and you can click Finish.

PS **NOTE** The cmdlet through the EMS used to create and mail-enable a user is the `New-Mailbox` cmdlet, with a variety of different parameters you can locate at http://technet.microsoft.com/en-us/library/aa997663(EXCHG.80).aspx.

Remove a Mailbox

If you have a person leave the company and you need to remove a mailbox, perform the following:

1. Open the EMC.
2. From the Navigation Tree, select the Recipient Configuration work center.
3. Select Mailbox.
4. From the Results pane, find the mailbox you wish to remove.
5. From the Actions pane, choose Remove.
6. You are presented with a warning message that asks if you are sure you want to remove that user's mailbox. Select Yes.

NOTE The default deleted mailbox retention time is 30 days. In the event the person returns within the 30-day period, you can restore the mailbox without seeking backup tapes for that user's mailbox.

PS NOTE The cmdlet through the EMS used to remove a mailbox for a user is `Remove-Mailbox`.

Disable a Mailbox

At times, you might want to disable, not remove, a mailbox, so that other users cannot send mail to or receive mail from it. The mailbox still exists, but it is unusable. To do this, perform the following:

1. Open the EMC.
2. From the Navigation Tree, select the Recipient Configuration work center.
3. Select Mailbox.
4. From the Results pane, find the mailbox you wish to disable.
5. From the Actions pane, choose Disable.
6. You are given an informational message that says, "Disabling the mailbox will remove the Exchange properties from the Windows user object and mark the mailbox in the database for removal. Are you sure you want to disable 'UserName'?" Click Yes.

At this point, if you want to re-enable the mailbox (that is, connect the mailbox back up to the user account in AD), you need to go to Disconnected Mailbox, select the mailbox, and click Connect.

NOTE If you create a user and disable the mailbox before the user logs in and accesses his mail once, when you disable the mailbox, it does not go into the Disconnected Mailbox location.

PS **NOTE** The cmdlet through the EMS used to disable a user like janeuser@primatech.com is `Disable-Mailbox janeuser@primatech.com`.

Create a Linked Mailbox

Scenario/Problem: Linked mailboxes are user mailboxes (they are exactly the same as any other mailbox) that are accessed by users in a separate, trusted forest. The reason for a mailbox of this sort is that when you have Exchange deployed in a resource forest, the resources are in one forest, whereas the user accounts are in another trusted forest. It's a complicated form of scenario, but regardless, you still have the ability to create mailboxes that can be accessed by users in the trusted forest.

Solution: To create a linked mailbox, perform the following:

1. Open the EMC.
2. From the Navigation Tree, select the Recipient Configuration work center.
3. From the Actions pane, select New Mailbox, and the New Mailbox Wizard opens.
4. On the Introduction screen, select Linked Mailbox. Click Next.
5. On the User Type screen, you are asked if you want to have a New User or Existing User. You want to create a New User. Even if the user account exists in the trusted forest, you still need to associate this mailbox with an account in this forest. In the end, it is associated with a disabled user account that is associated with this linked mailbox. Click Next.
6. Fill in the user information on the User Information screen, but remember that these fields are for the disabled account, not the real user account for the user that he uses to log on. Click Next.
7. From the Mailbox Settings screen, you have to choose the Alias, the location of the database, and you have to indicate if you have policies (managed folder or ActiveSync) that you want to use. Click Next.

8. You are taken to the Master Account screen, as shown in Figure 5.5. The fields you have to complete include the following:
    a. Trusted Forest or Domain—Select Browse to open the dialog and select the domain that has the master account. Then click OK. This enables the Linked Domain Controller field.
    b. Use the Following Windows User Account to Access Linked Domain Controller—This is useful if you want to access the domain controller with credentials other than those you currently use. You can select the checkbox and put in the username and password of the other account.
    c. Linked Domain Controller—Select Browse and from the dialog, you can select the linked domain controller and then click OK. This enables the Linked Master Account field.
    d. Linked Master Account—Select Browse and you can choose the user account you want to use for the master account for the linked mailbox. Then click OK.
9. Select Next and review the configuration summary. Then click New.
10. When complete, a green checkbox displays and you can click Finish.

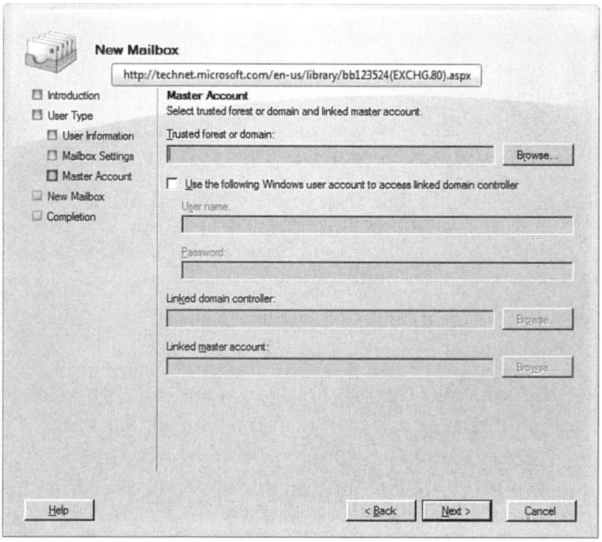

FIGURE 5.5
The Master Account screen for creating a linked mailbox.

Create Resource Mailboxes

Scenario/Problem: The calendar and scheduling features in Exchange are excellent and often used to keep track of more than people; it also tracks rooms and equipment (such as projectors and other equipment). Can we create mailboxes that are not for sending and receiving mail, but for scheduling purposes?

Solution: Absolutely. These are called resource mailboxes. You can create two different kinds: a room mailbox and an equipment mailbox. With the room mailbox, you can assign it to a conference room, auditorium, training room, and any other room that people share ordinarily. With an equipment mailbox, you can assign these to items that are usually shared among workers such as a projector, laptops, company cars, and equipment.

NOTE When you create a resource mailbox (room or equipment), an account is also created for those resources in AD. However, the accounts are disabled by default. This prevents a person from logging in to the network with a resource account.

Create a Room Mailbox

To create a room resource mailbox, perform the following steps:

1. Open the EMC.
2. From the Navigation Tree, select the Recipient Configuration work center.
3. From the Actions pane, select New Mailbox and the New Mailbox Wizard opens.
4. On the Introduction screen, select Room Mailbox and click Next.
5. You are asked if you want to create a mailbox for a New User or Existing User. In this case, leave the default New User, and then click Next.
6. You are taken to the User Information screen, where you are asked to provide the OU to place the new user, the name and logon information, and the password with confirmation. There is also a User Must Change Password at Next Logon checkbox that you can select. (Note: This might seem odd considering that this is a room and not a person you are creating the mailbox for. So, fill in the information accordingly. Call it literally Conference Room 1 or CF1. The password ensures someone can take ownership of the schedule of that room.) After this information is complete, click Next.
7. You are then presented with the Mailbox Settings options, which include the database, managed folder mailbox policy, and ActiveSync mailbox policy. Choose your options and click Next.

8. You are presented with a configuration summary. Confirm your options and select New.
9. After the wizard completes, you see a Completed green check mark and you can click Finish.

Create an Equipment Mailbox

The procedure for creating an equipment mailbox is a duplicate of what you would do when creating a room mailbox. The only difference is in choosing equipment rather than a room. To create an equipment mailbox, perform the following:

1. Open the EMC.
2. From the Navigation Tree, select the Recipient Configuration work center.
3. From the Actions pane, select New Mailbox and the New Mailbox Wizard opens.
4. On the Introduction screen, select Equipment Mailbox, and click Next.
5. You are asked if you want to create a mailbox for a New User or Existing User. In this case, leave the default New User, and then click Next.
6. You are taken to the User Information screen, where you are asked to provide the OU to place the new user, the name and logon information, and the password with confirmation. You can also select a User Must Change Password at Next Logon checkbox. (Note: This might seem odd considering you are creating the mailbox for equipment and not a person. Fill in the information accordingly. Call it literally Projector 1, Laptop 10, or whatever acronym and numerical order you wish to put in place. The password ensures someone can take ownership of the schedule of that piece of equipment.) After this information is filled in, click Next.
7. You are then presented with the Mailbox Settings options, which include the database, managed folder mailbox policy, and ActiveSync mailbox policy. Choose your options and click Next.
8. You are presented with a configuration summary. Confirm your options and select New.
9. After the wizard completes, you will see a Completed green check mark and you can click Finish.

Configure Resource Mailbox Properties

You can configure many properties, and to do so properly takes command-line work. For starters, look at the Resource Information tab that is added in with a resource mailbox. To do this, perform the following steps:

1. Open the EMC.
2. From the Navigation Tree, select the Recipient Configuration work center.

3. Select Mailbox.
4. From the Results pane, locate the resource mailbox you want to view (room or equipment). Right-click the mailbox and choose Properties or locate it from the Actions pane.
5. Note the Resource Information tab. You can specify the Resource Capacity and the Custom Properties.
6. The Resource Capacity is simply an indication of the number of people that can use the resource. For example, if it is a room, you indicate the number of people the room can handle.
7. The Resource Custom Properties enables you to click the Add button and select from a list of certain features that are unique to that particular room. For example, you might select the room that includes the projector or other AV equipment, or the room with the cappuccino maker.

The difficult part for those who dislike the command-line work is that the options you can choose for the Resource Custom Properties have to be input through the EMS using the cmdlet Set-ResourceConfig.

In the example shown in Figure 5.6, you see the Resource Custom Properties with a variety of options included in the EMS using the following command:

```
Set-ResourceConfig -ResourcePropertySchema ("Room/Projector",
"Room/CappuccinoMaker", "Room/AV")
```

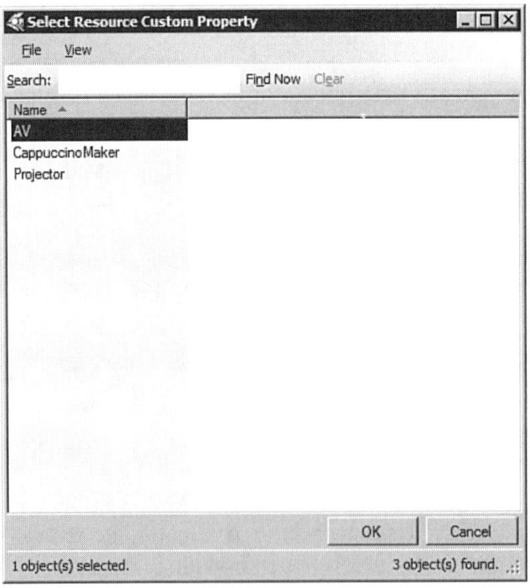

FIGURE 5.6
Adding custom resource properties to a room resource mailbox.

Manage Resource Mailboxes

Scenario/Problem: Managing resources given mailboxes is a key element that is best given to someone else to worry about. As an administrator you don't want to be responsible for every room, projector, laptop, and so forth your company might have.

Solution: You want to allow permission for another user to have control over the resource mailbox. You can do this through the EMC (new in SP1) or the Exchange Management Shell. To perform the task through the EMC, do the following:

1. Open the EMC.
2. From the Navigation Tree, select the Recipient Configuration work center.
3. Select a resource mailbox in the result pane.
4. From the Actions pane, select the option Manage Full Access Permission.
5. To add a user and provide him with control, select the Add button.
6. Locate the user you wish to add, select the user, and click OK.
7. Click Manage.
8. When the task is complete, click Finish.

You might perform the same task through the EMS by typing the following command:

```
Add-MailboxPermission -Identity <Resource-Mailbox> -User <user> -
AccessRights <Access Allowed> -InheritanceType <Inheritance's Type>
```

For example, to allow Jane User to have full access over ConferenceRoom1, you type:

```
Add-MailboxPermission -Identity 'ConferenceRoom1' -User 'Jane User'
-AccessRights FullAccess -InheritanceType All
```

After permissions are granted to the user, there are a few ways to manage the resource. One way is to go through Outlook Web Access. Log on using the account that has permission and then perform the following:

1. From within Outlook Web Access (OWA), select the drop-down arrow next to the user name you are logged in as in the top-right corner.
2. The Open Other Mailbox displays. Type the name of the resource mailbox and click OK.
3. Now your user account mailbox is open in one browser window and the resource mailbox is open in another.
4. Select the Options button from the top-right toolbar.
5. Some of the first things you might want to adjust are the Calendar Options. You can determine which days of the week a certain resource is made available to others.

6. Notice an option called Resource Settings, shown in Figure 5.7. This option exists only for resources, not for users. You have a variety of different settings you can configure.

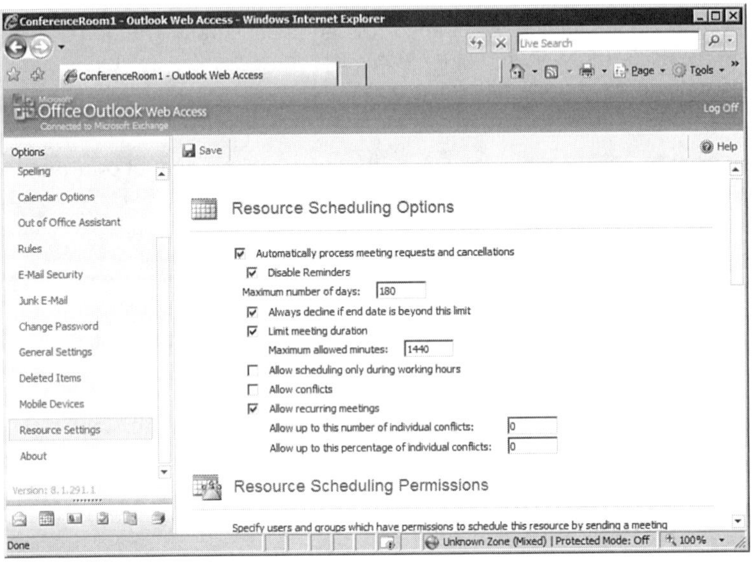

FIGURE 5.7
Resource Settings for a resource mailbox.

Resource Settings

Configuring resource settings can be done from the Exchange Management Shell, but it is much easier to do it from within the Outlook Web Access or Outlook tools. Under the Resource Settings, three sections of settings include the following:

- Resource Scheduling Options
- Resource Scheduling Permissions
- Resource Privacy Options

Resource Scheduling Options

To enable these settings, you have to first click the checkbox Automatically Process Meeting Requests and Cancellations. These settings determine how the resource mailbox can be used and scheduled and how conflicts should be resolved, as shown in Table 5.1.

TABLE 5.1 **Resource Scheduling Options**

Setting	Description
Disable Reminders	Selecting this box prevents the mailbox from receiving reminders for meetings.
Maximum Number of Days (default 180)	Number of days a resource can be booked in advance.
Always Decline If End Date Is Beyond This Limit	Selecting this box prevents meeting requests if the end date occurs after the maximum number of days limit.
Limit Meeting Duration Maximum Allowed Minutes: (default is 1440)	Places a tourniquet on the duration of a meeting or use of a resource in minutes.
Allow Scheduling Only During Working Hours	This option works in harmony with the Calendar Work Week settings under Calendar Options. If selected, people are not able to schedule time with the resource beyond working hours.
Allow Conflicts	Allows the resource to be scheduled by more than one person at the same time.
Allow Recurring Meetings: Allow Up to This Number of Individual Conflicts (default 0)	Allows a person to schedule a recurring meeting for those meetings that are known to take more than one timeframe to complete the agenda.
Allow Up to This Percentage of Individual Conflicts (default 0)	The number of conflicts or percentage of conflicts allows the meeting to be scheduled in spite of conflicts. The default is set to 0.

Resource Scheduling Permissions

Logically, the resource can be reserved or scheduled by anyone by default. However, you might streamline that. You might have a specific room with specialized equipment that only a handful of executives can schedule the use of. In that case, permission settings need to be changed. Note the following permission settings in Table 5.2.

TABLE 5.2 **Permission Settings**

Setting	Description
These users can schedule automatically if the resource is available.	Default is Everyone. However, you can select Users and Groups instead that have permission to automatically schedule a resource.
These users can submit a request for manual approval if the resource is available.	The default is Select Users and Groups, which must be configured. The request for approval is sent to the mailbox itself or to a delegate of the mailbox. If you change this to Everyone, everyone needs to submit a request for approval. Less of an automatic way of handling the schedule but certainly more hands-on for the person(s) in charge of resources.
These users can schedule automatically if the resource is available and can submit a request for manual approval if the resource is unavailable.	The default is Select Users and Groups, which must be configured. Therefore, if the resource is available, a person can reserve it. If it isn't, the person can request it anyway in the event something changes. The request goes to the resource mailbox or to the person(s) in charge of the resource. If you change this to Everyone, this is the case for all users.
For requests requiring approval: Always Forward to Delegates	If the Always Forward to Delegates checkbox is selected, which is the default setting, requests that require approval are forwarded to users who are delegates of the resource.
Always Tentatively Accept These Requests	If the Always Tentatively Accept These Requests checkbox is selected, which it is by default, meeting requests that require approval are accepted tentatively.

Resource Privacy Options

These settings help control what information is included in meeting requests and cancellations. They are checkboxes that are somewhat self-explanatory:

- Always Add the Organizer Name to the Meeting Subject
- Always Remove the Private Flag On an Accepted Message
- When Declining Meeting Requests
  - Include Detailed Information About Conflicting Meetings in Response
  - Include Organizer's Name in Conflict Information

- Always Delete the Following When Sent to This Resource:
    - Email Messages
    - Attachments From Meeting Requests
    - Comments From Meeting Requests
    - Subject of Meeting Requests

Response Message

You can select the Add Additional Text That Will Be Included in Responses to Meeting Requests checkbox. Then, type the information into the box and format it using the tools provided.

Create Mail-Enabled Contacts and Mail-Enabled Users

Scenario/Problem: First off, what is the difference between a mail contact and a mail-enabled user? Second, how do we create them? Finally, how are they used in our organization?

Solution: You might have a person who requires an email address in your company and you create a mail contact, which is an AD object with full information about the person, although the person is not able to access internal resources.

A mail-enabled user account is similar, but as a user account, these persons can log on to the network and can access resources if given permission.

Both a contact and a mail-enabled user can be shown in the Global Address List (GAL), both have external email addresses, and both involve users that do not usually work within company walls.

Create a New Mail Contact

To create a new mail contact, perform the following steps:

1. Open the EMC.
2. From the Navigation Tree, select the Recipient Configuration work center.
3. Select Mail Contact.
4. From the Actions pane, select New Mail Contact.
5. The New Mail Contact Wizard opens and begins with the Introduction screen that asks if you want to create a New Contact or work from an Existing Contact. Choose New Contact and click Next.

6. In Figure 5.8, note that some items are familiar, whereas others appear to be missing. Supply the following information:
   a. Organization Unit—By default, this is the Users container, but you can place the contact wherever you like in AD.
   b. First Fame, Initials, Last Name—All self-explanatory to provide some details about the contact.
   c. Alias—The alias automatically fills in as you enter the other information about the person. You can alter this, however, to provide whatever you like for the alias.
   d. External E-mail Address—If the address is a simple SMTP address, click Edit and provide the email address for the external client. However, if the person has an X.400, GroupWise, or Lotus Notes address, you can select the arrow next to Edit and choose Custom Address and supply the email address and the type.

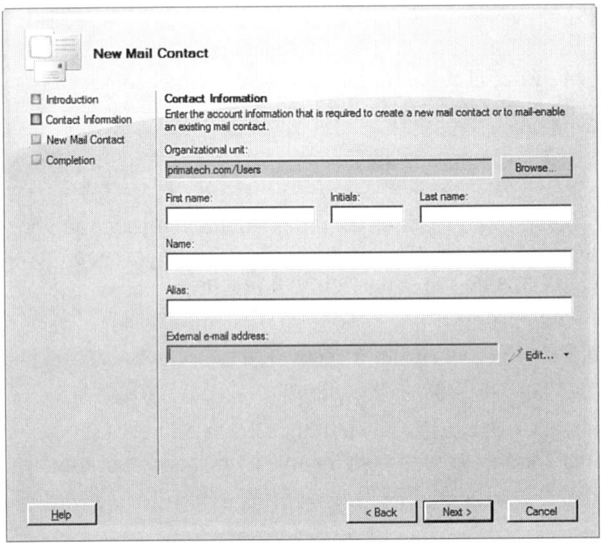

FIGURE 5.8
Creating a new contact mailbox.

7. After the Contact Information has been filled in, click Next.
8. On the New Mail Contact screen, review the Configuration Summary, and if it's satisfactory, click New.
9. When complete, you are taken to the Completion screen and shown a green Completed sign. Click Finish.

Notice that the user is created in AD. If you open Active Directory Users and Computers, you find that the user exists but is listed as Type: Contact. There is no way to log on with this account because it doesn't have any account logon information or a password. If you open the properties of the account, you find only a handful of tabs including General, Address, Telephones, Organization, and Member Of. Most of this is to allow contact information to be added to the object.

In the properties of the contact from within the EMC, you can see the same information, only it has spread across different tabs. Also note a couple of extra tabs:

- E-mail Addresses—Allows you to add more email addresses and determine which one is the external address and which one is the Set as Reply email address.
- Mail Flow Settings—Here you can configure message size restrictions. You can also configure message delivery restrictions (for accepting and rejecting messages from different senders).

You can disable or remove any of these contacts by simply locating them in the Mail Contact Results pane, selecting the account or accounts, and choosing the Disable option or the Remove option.

Create a New Mail User

Creating a new mail-enabled user also creates an object in AD. However, it does not create a mailbox. Messages sent to the user are forwarded to the external address. To create a new mail user, perform the following:

1. Open the EMC.
2. From the Navigation Tree, select the Recipient Configuration work center.
3. Select Mail Contact.
4. From the Actions pane, locate and select New Mail User.
5. The New Mail User Wizard opens and the Introduction screen asks if you want to create a New User or work from an Existing User. Choose New User and click Next.
6. The information you must provide is the same user and account information you would provide for a standard mailbox, including a password. Enter that data and click Next.
7. You are taken to the Mail Settings screen, which asks only for two pieces of information. The first is an alias for your mail-enabled user. The second is the external email address. If the address is a simple SMTP address, click Edit and provide the email address for the external client. However, if the person has an X.400, GroupWise, or Lotus Notes address, you can select the arrow next to Edit and choose Custom Address and supply the email address and the type. When complete, click Next.
8. On the New Mail User screen, review the Configuration Summary and if it's satisfactory, click New.

9. When complete, you are taken to the Completion screen and shown a green Completed sign. Click Finish.

Note in Figure 5.9 that both users are located in the Mail Contact and have different icons depending on their types.

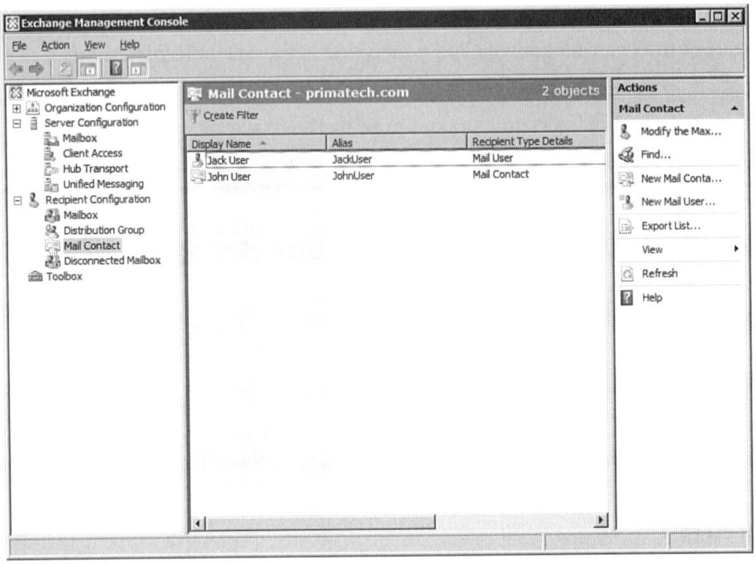

FIGURE 5.9
Viewing mail users and mail contacts from the Mail Contact node.

Create Distribution Groups and Dynamic Distribution Groups

Scenario/Problem: At times, users want to email an entire group of people. They might want to create their own groups in Outlook, but they might also want to simply email a group that already exists in AD. How do you mail-enable a group, and what types of groups can you do this with?

Solution: For starters, sending a mass email to a group that is already established is a logical thing to do and easy to set up. These are called distribution groups.

- Distribution Group—This is a group that is mail-enabled and has its own email address. When you send an email to the group, it results in expansion of the group and the messages are delivered to all the members of the group.

- Dynamic Distribution Group—A group is usually managed by users being added or removed. Dynamic distribution groups are different in that they are populated by user attributes that are defined by filters.

Exchange supports the following types of distribution groups:

- Mail-enabled universal distribution groups
- Mail-enabled universal security groups
- Mail-enabled non-universal groups
- Dynamic distribution groups

Create a New Distribution Group

To create a new distribution group (that is, a group that doesn't previously exist that you wish to mail-enable but is an entirely new group), perform the following:

1. Open the EMC.
2. From the Navigation Tree, select the Recipient Configuration work center and click Distribution Group.
3. On the Actions pane, note the option to create a New Distribution Group or New Dynamic Distribution Group. Choose New Distribution Group to open the wizard.
4. From the Introduction screen, you are asked if you want to create a Distribution Group for a new or existing group. In this situation, choose New Group.
5. On the Group Information screen shown in Figure 5.10, you are asked for the following information:
    a. Group Type—Leave as Distribution.
    b. Organizational Unit—The default is Users, but you can browse and select another location.
    c. Name—Provide the group name.
    d. Name (pre-Windows 2000)—Based upon legacy naming, this name is automatically populated by the Name field and should be fine.
    e. Alias—By default, this is also the name of the distribution group, but you can change that here.

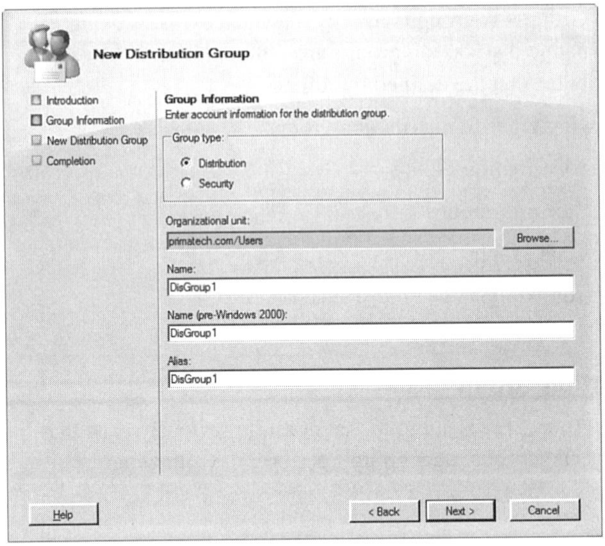

FIGURE 5.10
The Group Information screen when creating a new distribution group.

6. After you have the information added, click Next.
7. You'll be taken to the New Distribution Group screen, where you confirm the configuration summary and click New.
8. When the group is created, you are taken to the Completion screen and shown a green Completed checkmark. Click Finish.

Note that the group is now visible in your Recipient Configuration, Distribution Group node as well as from your Active Directory Users and Computers tool. If you open the group from the Active Directory Users and Computers tool, you will notice that it is a Universal distribution group. If you select the Members or Member Of tabs (in either location, the AD, or EMC), you will notice that these tabs are empty because this is a brand new group.

Mail-Enable a Distribution Group

To mail-enable a preexisting distribution group, perform the following:

1. Open the EMC.
2. From the Navigation Tree, select the Recipient Configuration work center and click Distribution Group.
3. Over on the Actions pane, choose New Distribution Group to open the wizard.
4. From the Introduction screen, you are asked if you want to create a Distribution Group for a new or existing group. In this situation, choose Existing Group.

5. Select Browse. Notice that the options presented are Universal groups. You might have Universal distribution or security groups in place, both are presented but Local or Global groups are not shown.
6. Select the group you wish to have mail-enabled, and then click Next.
7. The Group Information screen is shown; however, in this scenario, the information is already filled out for you. The only item you can change is the Alias. Click Next.
8. Review the Configuration Summary before clicking New.
9. After the group is mail-enabled, you are notified with a green Completed checkmark. Click Finish.

NOTE To add or remove members of a Distribution Group, you can open the group from within the Recipient Configuration, Distribution Group node (or from within Active Directory Users and Computers), and you can select the Members tab and click the Add button. If you wish to remove members, you can select users and click the X to remove them.

Create a New Dynamic Distribution Group

Differing from the standard types of groups that are based upon memberships, dynamic groups are defined by filters and conditions each time a message is sent to the group. An individual might potentially be part of the group one moment and not part of the group the next moment if he falls out of the scope of the group.

To create a dynamic distribution group, perform the following:

1. Open the EMC.
2. From the Navigation Tree, select the Recipient Configuration work center and click Distribution Group.
3. Over on the Actions pane, choose New Dynamic Distribution Group to open the wizard.
4. From the Introduction screen, you are asked what OU you want the group placed in. The default is the Users container, but you can click Browse and adjust this. You are asked to provide a name and alias for the group, too. Provide the information and click Next.
5. From the Filter Settings screen, you are asked to select the recipient container where you want to apply this filter. The default is Users, but you can click Browse to locate a different container so that the group can be more narrowly defined to an OU. You are also asked if you want to include all recipient types or specific recipient types, such as the following:
    a. Users with Exchange mailboxes
    b. Users with external email addresses

   c. Resource mailboxes
   d. Contacts with external email addresses
   e. Mail-enabled groups

6. Select your options and click Next.
7. You are taken to the Conditions screen, shown in Figure 5.11. Note that the initial conditions are State or Province and Department or Company. However, then you have the various custom attributes that you can establish values for. You can select more than one condition, too. In Step 1, you select the condition, such as Recipient Is In a Department. Then you see a link in Step 2 that you click to specify the condition. For example, you might say Sales (for the Sales department).

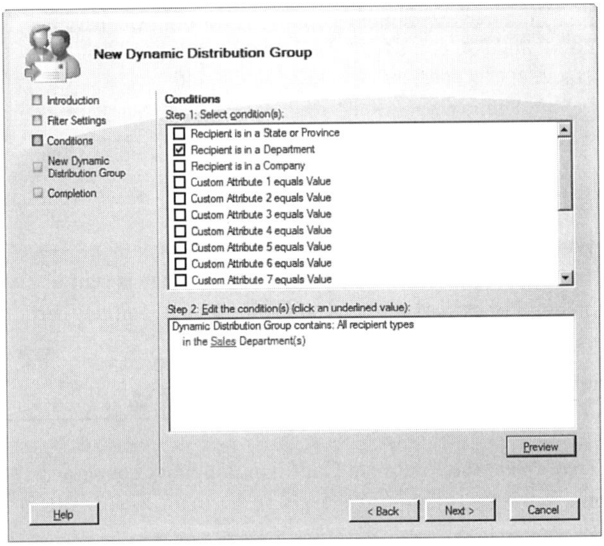

FIGURE 5.11
Creating conditions for your dynamic distribution group.

8. Before clicking Next, you can choose the Preview option, which shows you (based upon the filter settings and conditions you have established) what users are going to be in your Dynamic Distribution Group. After you are satisfied with the filter and condition settings, click Next.
9. Review the configuration summary and then click New.
10. After the group is created, you see a green checkmark and a Completed response. Click Finish.

After the group is created, you can always return to the properties of the group and change the filter and condition settings. The Dynamic Distribution Group has an object in AD and you can view it in the AD Users and Computers tool; however, you will find that because of the nature of the group, there are no properties you can configure within AD. It's simply a named object.

NOTE Creating a dynamic distribution group set of conditions that relate to custom attributes might have you curious about where these attributes are configured. If you go to the Recipient Configuration/Mailbox node and go into the properties of any of the recipients, right on the General tab is a box at the bottom that says Custom Attributes. Select this and you can see that you can put any information within those boxes that you choose.

PS **NOTE** The cmdlet through the EMS used to create a new distribution group or a new dynamic distribution group are `New-DistributionGroup` and `New-DynamicDistributionGroup`, with a variety of syntax and parameter information that can be added along with it.

Configure Expansion Servers

Scenario/Problem: The work involved for the server when an email is sent to a distribution group is causing a problem for your server. How can you balance the workload?

Solution: By default, a distribution group is simply expanded on any server in the organization. However, you can change this for the distribution group or dynamic distribution group by performing the following:

1. Open the EMC.
2. From the Navigation Tree, select the Recipient Configuration work center and click Distribution Group.
3. Select Distribution Group or Dynamic Distribution Group from the Results pane.
4. From the Actions pane, select Properties.
5. Go to the Advanced tab, shown in Figure 5.12.

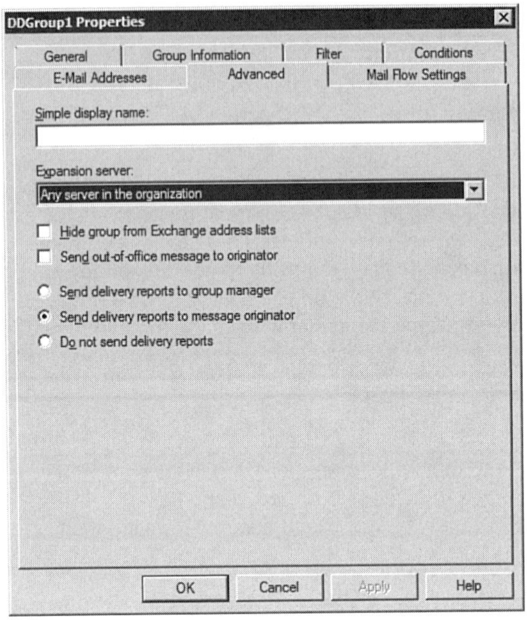

FIGURE 5.12
Configuring an Expansion server.

6. Notice the Expansion Server setting with the drop-down arrow. Use this list to select a Hub Transport (HT) server to handle the expansion list, or you can leave the default Any Server in the Organization. (Note: Extremely large distribution lists can affect performance on a production server, so it might be invaluable for you to offload this intense workload.)
7. Click OK to finish the process.

Advanced Distribution or Dynamic Distribution List Properties

In determining your expansion server, you might have noticed that you can configure a few important settings from here, including the following:

Checkboxes:

- Hide Group From Exchange Address Lists—Users can still send messages to the group through the email address directly, but it does not show in the address lists.
- Send Out-Of-Office Messages to Originator—If you email the group and someone has the out-of-office message turned on and this checkbox is selected, you receive the out-of-office reply. If you don't want this extra traffic going through your server, leave this checkbox blank.

Radio Buttons for Non-Delivery Reports (NDRs):

- Send Delivery Reports to Group Manager—Sends the NDR only to the distribution group manager.
- Send Delivery Reports to Message Originator—This is the default.
- Do Not Send Delivery Reports—This option minimizes traffic that you might consider unnecessary.

CHAPTER 6

Manage Organization Permissions and Mailbox Settings

IN THIS CHAPTER

- Create Exchange Administrative Roles
- Work with Address Lists
- Work with Offline Address Books
- Use Managed Content Settings
- Configure Mailbox Properties and Settings

Create Exchange Administrative Roles

Scenario/Problem: Smaller Exchange environments might see only one person as the Exchange administrator handling all the roles and all the responsibilities. However, in larger scenarios you might need more help and those persons can be given permission to do only the job they are assigned. This involves assigning administrative roles to users. How is that done?

Solution: To begin with, open the Exchange Management Console and select the Organization Configuration work center. Notice in the Results pane that there is only one tab—Exchange Administrators. In that tab are five default objects, some of which are based upon Exchange Security Groups that are automatically created when you install Exchange. You can see these groups from within the Active Directory Users and Computers console:

- Exchange Organization Administrators
- Exchange Public Folder Administrators
- Exchange Recipient Administrators
- Exchange Servers
- Exchange View-Only Administrators
- ExchangeLegacyInterop

With the exception of the ExchangeLegacyInterop group, which is designed for interoperability with Exchange 2003 servers within the same forest, the other security groups directly relate to the roles that you can assign from within the Exchange Management Console.

The roles you can assign include the capabilities shown in Table 6.1.

TABLE 6.1 **Roles You Can Assign in Exchange Management Console**

Role	Permissions
Exchange Organization Administrator	This is the highest role you can assign and gives an individual the capability to configure and control all organization-wide settings, including the capability to handle Edge servers, Unified Messaging (UM) settings, Recipient objects, and so on.
Exchange Public Folder Administrator	Gives a person the capability to create and manage top-level folder objects, use the Public Folder Management Console, and run Exchange Management Shell (EMS) commands relating to Public Folders.
Exchange Recipient Administrator	Gives a person the capability to create and manage recipient objects such as users, contacts, distribution groups, dynamic distribution groups, and Public Folders.

Role	Permissions
Exchange View-Only Administrator	Enables a person to view items in the Exchange organization tree. Although it might seem like a basic set of permissions, other roles require these permissions to fulfill their requirements.
Exchange Server Administrator	Enables this person to handle server-related tasks such as storage group and database control, Client Access Server (CAS) settings, Hub Transport (HT), and UM settings. Note: The person must also be a member of the local Administrators group to grant these permissions.

To assign an administrative role to a user or group, perform the following steps:

1. Open the Exchange Management Console (EMC).
2. From the Navigation Tree, expand the Organization Configuration work center.
3. From the Actions pane, select Add Exchange Administrator.
4. The Add Exchange Administrator Wizard displays and the first screen has you select a user or group and choose a role and scope for the Exchange administrator (as you can see in Figure 6.1).

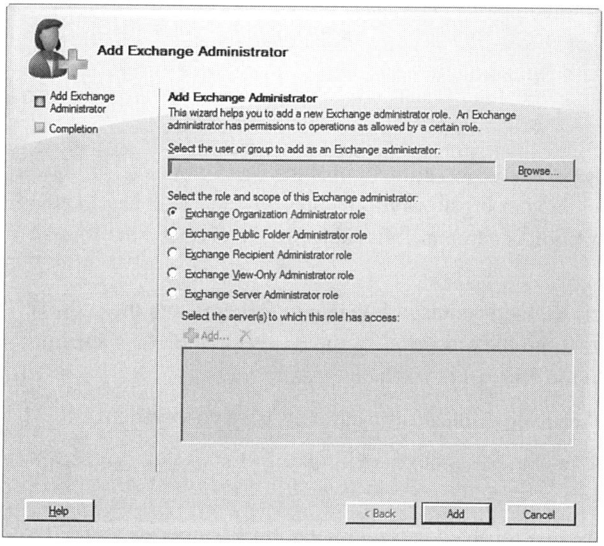

FIGURE 6.1
The Add Exchange Administrator Wizard.

5. Select the server(s) that the role has access to by selecting the Add option and choosing those servers you want the person or group to be able to control.

6. Click Add.
7. After the wizard is complete, you are taken to the Completion screen where a green checkmark and Completed affirmation is given and you can click Finish.

To remove any of the Exchange Administrators, you simply select the user or group from the Results pane and select Remove from the Actions pane.

> PS **NOTE** The cmdlet through the EMS used to create an Exchange Administrator is `Add-ExchangeAdministrator -Identity "Name of Person or Group" -Role (OrgAdmin, PublicFolderAdmin, RecipientAdmin, ServerAdmin, or ViewOnlyAdmin) -Scope "Server Names"`. To view all Exchange Administrators, type **`Get-ExchangeAdministrator`**.

Work with Address Lists

> **Scenario/Problem:** With each new recipient, it becomes more difficult to keep track of users, contacts, and other resources. There is one Global Address List, but how can address lists be created to break down the collection of recipient and Active Director (AD) objects so that it's more manageable for your users?

Solution: As a user, when you work with your client application (for example, Outlook or Outlook Web Access) and you attempt to send an email or select the Address Book icon, you are shown address lists that have been created by default. These include the following:

- Default Global Address List—Shows all mail-enabled users, contacts, groups, and resource mailboxes in your organization. Almost anything that has an email address in your organization is automatically added to the Global Address List (GAL).
- All Contacts—For mail-enabled contacts. You can hide these from the address lists if you like by going into the properties of the contact and on the General tab, selecting the option to Hide from Exchange Address Lists.
- All Groups—For mail-enabled groups (for example, distribution groups).
- All Rooms—For those resource mailboxes that relate to rooms that can be scheduled or reserved.
- All Users—Shows your mail-enabled users without all the extras you usually see in your GAL.
- Public Folders—Shows all the Public Folders in the organization.

As an administrator, you view your address list information through the Organization Configuration/Mailbox node under the Address Lists tab. From here, you can perform a variety of address list maintenance, editing, adding, and removing.

Create an Address List

You have the ability to structure your mail-enabled objects into customized address lists based upon specific attributes that can be populated dynamically. To create an address list, perform the following:

1. Open the EMC.
2. From the Navigation Tree, expand the Organization Configuration work center.
3. Select Mailbox and note the Address Lists tab.
4. From the Actions pane, select New Address List to begin the wizard.
5. On the Introduction screen, begin by providing a Name. Then you can choose a Container for your list. The \ indicates that it is a root list. If you select the Browse button, you can nest the list within another list.
6. For recipient types you can choose None, All Recipient Types, or the following specific types:
    - Users with Exchange mailboxes
    - Users with external e-mail addresses
    - Resource mailboxes
    - Contacts with external e-mail addresses
    - Mail-enabled groups
7. Make your selections and choose Next.
8. You are taken to the Conditions screen where, in Step 1, you can choose specific conditions (based upon state, province, department, or company) or custom attributes. Then, in Step 2, you can define those options.
9. You can select the Preview button to view a list of all those recipients who will be a part of your list based upon the criteria you've already established. Click Next when you are ready.
10. You now have the Schedule screen, where you specify when the address list should be applied and the maximum length of time it should run. The default setting is Immediately, but you can set a scheduled time. You can also select the checkbox Cancel Tasks That Are Still Running After (Hours) and specify a number of hours. Then click Next.
11. You are shown in the Configuration Summary that the list is both created and applied. When you are satisfied with the settings, click New.
12. When complete, click Finish.

NOTE If you begin to have difficulties with your address lists failing and you receive messages that say, "An Exchange 2007 server on which an address list service is active cannot be found," you might need to recheck your System Attendant to ensure it is started from within your Services console.

Apply Address Lists

An address list is usually "applied" when the filter rule has been edited, unless you make a request for the list to be applied manually. The idea of applying the list is that the membership is updated to include new recipients and remove those that are no longer in harmony with the criteria.

To apply an address list, perform the following steps:

1. Open the EMC.
2. From the Navigation Tree, expand the Organization Configuration work center.
3. Select Mailbox, and then click the Address Lists tab.
4. From the Actions pane, select Apply to begin the Apply Address List Wizard.
5. On the Introduction screen, you specify when the address list should be applied and the maximum length of time it should run. The default setting is Immediately, but you can set a scheduled time. You can also select the checkbox Cancel Tasks That Are Still Running After (Hours) and specify a number of hours. Then, click Next.
6. The Apply Address List screen provides you a Configuration Summary you can review, and then click Apply.
7. When complete, select Finish.

Edit Address Lists

To edit an address list after it has been created, perform the following steps:

1. Open the EMC.
2. From the Navigation Tree, expand the Organization Configuration work center.
3. Select Mailbox, and then select the Address Lists tab.
4. Select the address list you want to edit, and then click Edit from the Actions pane.
5. The screens are somewhat reminiscent of the creation screens for an address list, although certain items (such as the container) are not changeable. Make changes to the recipient types on the Introduction screen and click Next.
6. Adjust Conditions and Custom Attributes and click Next.
7. Review and adjust the schedule for the application of the list. Then click Next.
8. Review the Configuration Summary and click Edit.
9. When complete, click Finish.

Preview Members of an Address List

You can always review the members of an address list by editing the list and on the Conditions screen clicking the Preview button to see which objects are part of the list.

Another approach is through the EMS. For example, if you want to find the same list, you first need to retrieve some information from the Address List called the Distinguished Name. To do this for a list called Research in an organization called PrimaTech, you type the following:

```
Get-AddressList -Identity "Research" | fl DistinguishedName
```

You can see in Figure 6.2 that the response provided is quite long. You will need that response when typing in the `Get-Recipient` cmdlet using the Distinguished Name as the filter. To retrieve the list, you type:

```
Get-Recipient -Filter {AddressListMembership -eq 'CN=Research,CN=All
➥Address Lists,
CN=Address Lists Container,CN=PrimaTech,CN=MicrosoftExchange,
CN=Services,CN=Configuration,DC=primatech,DC=com'}
```

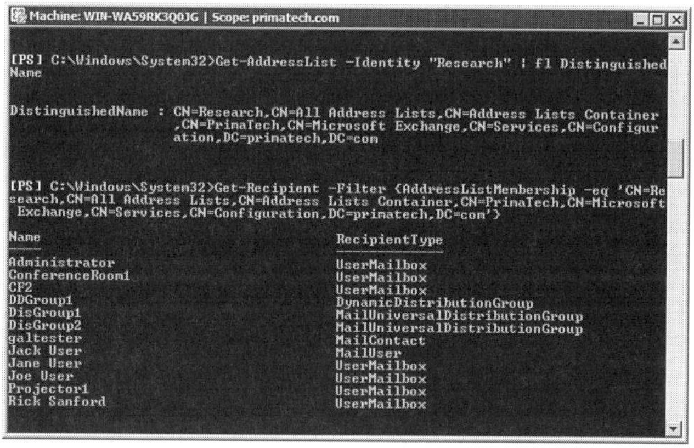

FIGURE 6.2
Previewing address list members in the EMS.

Multiple Global Address Lists

Ordinarily, the GAL, which houses all your email-enabled objects, is sufficient for your organization. Whether it is a small organization or a large one, rarely do you require more than one GAL. No matter how many you create, your users can see only one.

Possible reasons for creating additional GALs include the following:

- You have a single Exchange server organization hosting multiple companies within and users need to see only the GAL for the company for which they work.
- You have a large company that has multiple branch offices and you want to ensure users see only a subset of the organization based upon location.

Creating the additional GALs is done through the EMS. Creating them isn't difficult; the important part is to follow up with assigned permissions so that users will see the GAL you've created as opposed to the default GAL.

Create a Global Address List

To create additional GALs, perform the following steps:

1. Open the EMS.
2. Type **`New-GlobalAddressList -Name "Name of GAL"`**.

We have created a new GAL with the name we've chosen. This won't provide us any recipient or conditional filter properties for that GAL. So, let's say you specifically want to create a GAL called CompanyTwo and you want all mailbox users that have their Company condition set to CompanyTwo. To do this, type:

```
New-GlobalAddressList -Name "CompanyTwo" -ConditionalCompany "CompanyTwo"
➥ -IncludedRecipients "MailboxUsers"
```

Keep in mind that you can establish other conditions or include recipients using different parameters that you can research with the `New-GlobalAddressList` cmdlet. This is an example of creating a second GAL.

However, you might notice that the GAL does not update as quickly as you would like.

Update the Global Address Lists More Rapidly

If you want to speed up the process of the GAL updating its recipients, type the following:

```
Update-GlobalAddressList "Name of List"
```

Or, if you want all of your GALs to update (not that you would have too many of them), type the following:

```
Get-GlobalAddressList | Update-GlobalAddressList
```

Configuring Clients to Use One GAL or Another

Having your name be a part of a specially created GAL is one thing. If you meet the criteria, you are included in the list. However, for clients to see one GAL over another, some changes have to be made. By default, all clients choose the default GAL. To change this, we need to open the ADSI Edit tool. To do this, go to the Start button, click Administrative Tools, and then click ADSI Edit.

Imagine we have a secondary GAL called CompanyTwo. To ensure access to one GAL over another, we use permissions. You might want to create two security groups: one for the default GAL and the other for the C2 GAL that you can organize objects into each group.

From within ADSI Edit, if you enter the Configuration and navigate to Services, Microsoft Exchange, the Organization Name, Address Lists Container, All Global Address Lists, you can see in Figure 6.3 that in this case we have two GALs.

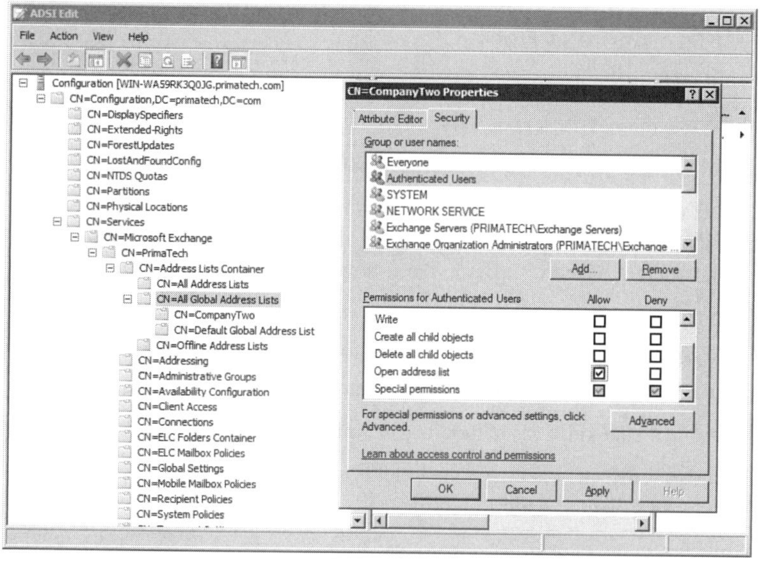

FIGURE 6.3
Using ADSI Edit to determine GAL permissions.

To configure access, you can right-click the GAL and go into the Properties. Select the Security tab. If you select Authenticated Users, you will see they have the Read and Open address list permissions. Clear these items for authenticated users and add the users or group to your permission settings with the Read and Open address list permissions.

Perform the same task for the default GAL. Clear all authenticated users, just assign the security group with the users you wish to have access.

Work with Offline Address Books

Scenario/Problem: Understandably, you cannot always be connected to the network and therefore cannot always be connected to your online address book. So, the offline address book (OAB) provides you with a copy you can use when not connected. How do you create, configure, and distribute offline address books to your users?

Solution: The purpose of an OAB is to provide access to the address information while offline, so there are a few things administrators can configure. They can create additional address books, they can choose which ones are made available, and they can determine the distribution method used (either web-based or Public Folder distribution).

Create an Offline Address Book

1. Open the EMC.
2. From the Navigation Tree, expand the Organization Configuration work center.
3. Select Mailbox and select Offline Address Book.
4. Notice the Default Offline Address Book. From the Actions pane, select New Offline Address Book to open the wizard. On the Introduction screen (shown in Figure 6.4), you are asked to provide the following information:
    - You are asked to provide a name.
    - You are asked to Browse and choose an Offline Address Book Generation Server, which is the mailbox server where OABs are generated.
    - There is a checkbox to Include the Default Global Address List.
    - You can select the checkbox Include the Following Address Lists and click Add to include additional lists.
5. After you answer the questions, select Next.
6. You are taken to the Distribution Points screen, where you can select the following:
    - Enable Web-Based Distribution—This is only for clients that run Outlook 2007. If you select it, you have to also choose the virtual directory it will be distributed from.
    - Enable Public Folder Distribution—For Outlook clients 2003 SP1 or earlier. This will use the Public Folder database to ensure the OAB is available to clients.

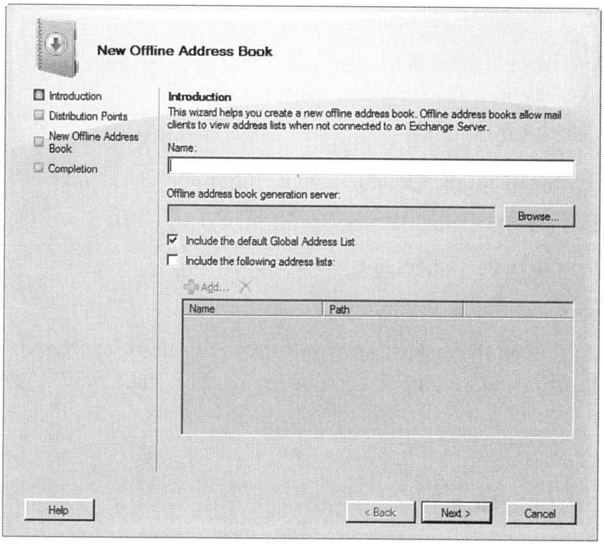

FIGURE 6.4
The creation of an Offline Address Book (OAB).

7. After you choose your distribution method, choose Next.
8. Review your Configuration Summary on the New Offline Address Book screen, and choose New.
9. When complete, click Finish.

Move the OAB Generation Server

To move the OAB generation server (which handles the creation and update process of the OAB before placing the files on a share) after the OAB has been created, perform the following steps:

1. Open the EMC.
2. From the Navigation Tree, expand the Organization Configuration work center.
3. Select Mailbox, and select Offline Address Book.
4. Select the OAB you want to move the generation server on.
5. From the Actions pane, select Move.
6. Click the Browse button to locate the other server you want to serve as the generation server, and click Move.
7. When complete, click Finish.

Change the Default OAB

Although it's not something you would consider doing often, you can alter the default OAB. To do this, after you have the new OAB created, perform the following steps:

1. Open the EMC.
2. From the Navigation Tree, expand the Organization Configuration work center.
3. Select Mailbox, and then select Offline Address Book.
4. Select the OAB you want to make the default.
5. From the Actions pane, select Set as Default.
6. You receive a warning message that asks, "Are you sure you want to set 'Name of OAB' as the default offline address book for all new mailbox databases?" Click Yes.

View and Modify OAB Properties

To access the properties of the OAB after it is created (or the default OAB), perform the following steps:

1. Open the EMC.
2. From the Navigation Tree, expand the Organization Configuration work center.
3. Select Mailbox, and then select Offline Address Book.
4. Select the OAB you want to access the properties of. From the Actions pane, choose Properties.
5. Notice there are three tabs—General, Address Lists, and Distribution:
   - General—Shows the name of the OAB and some other information, such as which server is the generation server, whether this OAB the default, and when it was last modified. It also shows the Update Schedule, which can be modified.
   - Address Lists—Here you can modify the selections you made initially when you created the OAB. You can include the default Global Address List or not. You can add or remove other address lists.
   - Distribution—This tab, shown in Figure 6.5, enables you to configure different types of distribution methods (web-based and Public Folder-based). You can select the clients that will be supported (if Outlook 2007, the web-based version is needed). You can select different Outlook clients pre-2007. You can configure web-based distribution by selecting the location of the OAB virtual directory, which is normally the default OAB directory with the IIS default site. You can enable Public Folder distribution as long as you have a Public Folder database.

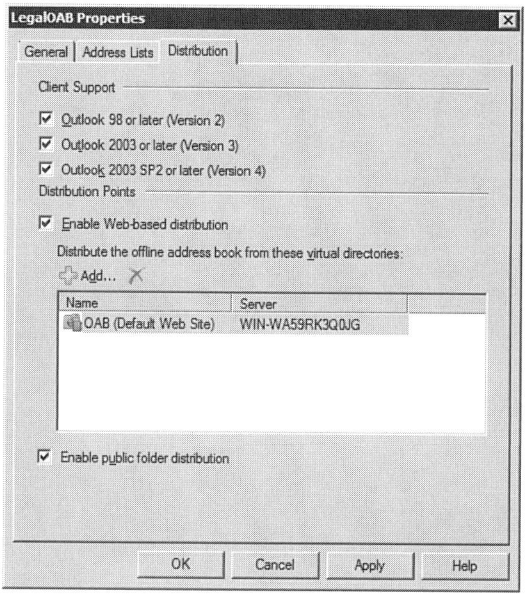

FIGURE 6.5
The Distribution tab of the OAB properties.

NOTE You can update the OAB at any time by selecting it and choosing the Update option from the Actions pane. You are asked, "Update causes the Offline Address Book to be regenerated, which can take several minutes. Are you sure you want to continue?" Click Yes and the update begins.

Require SSL for OAB Distribution

In the event you are working with all Outlook 2007 clients and using a virtual directory through your IIS server, you might feel that a Secure Socket Layer (SSL) connection is a necessary aspect to security.

To require SSL for your OAB virtual directory, perform the following:

1. Click Start, click Administrative Tools, and then click Internet Information Services (IIS) Manager.
2. You can see your server in the Navigation pane. You can expand Sites by clicking the plus sign.
3. You should see the Default Web Site option, which can be expanded by clicking the plus sign.
4. Locate the OAB folder, and in the Results pane, scroll down to the IIS category and choose SSL Settings.
5. Click the checkbox Require SSL and the secondary checkbox Require 128-bit SSL, as you can see in Figure 6.6.

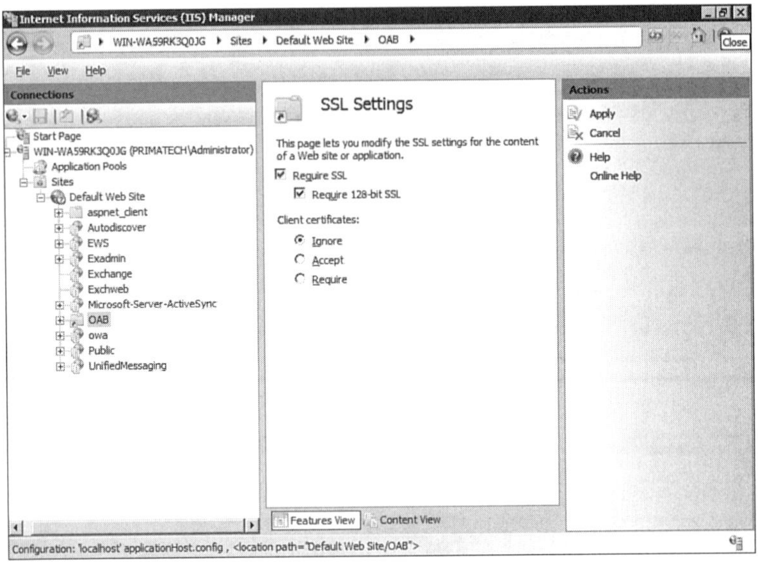

FIGURE 6.6
Configuring SSL requirements for the OAB virtual directory.

6. In the Actions pane, select Apply to apply the changes.

Assign OAB to Clients at the Database and Individual Mailbox Levels

Eventually you have to make a decision about which OABs should go to which persons. You can perform this on a database level or on an individual mailbox level.

To establish an OAB for an entire database, perform the following:

1. Open the EMC.
2. From the Navigation Tree, expand the Server Configuration work center.
3. Select Mailbox and the server you wish to make adjustments to the mailbox database on in the Results pane.
4. Select the mailbox database from the Work pane and go into the Properties of the mailbox database.
5. Select the Client Settings tab, and under the Offline address book settings, choose Browse.
6. Select the OAB you want all mailboxes to use within this mailbox database. When finished, click OK.
7. Then click OK to close the Properties.

> **PS NOTE** The cmdlet through the EMS used to configure the database to use a Public Folder database and offline address book is `Set-MailboxDatabase`. You use it in the following way: Set-MailboxDatabase -Identity <DatabaseIdParameter> -OfflineAddressBook <OfflineAddressBookIdParameter> -PublicFolderDatabase <DatabaseIdParameter>

To configure the OAB for an individual recipient, you should use the `Set-Mailbox` cmdlet from the EMS. You can configure multiple recipients by filtering and pipelining them into the `Set-Mailbox` cmdlet

```
Set-Mailbox -Identity <MailboxIDParameter> -OfflineAddressBook
➥ <OfflineAddressBookIdParameter>
```

Note that you cannot configure the Public Folder side from the recipient level. This must be done at the database level.

Use Managed Content Settings

> **Scenario/Problem:** Users require assistance in managing their content, particularly when it comes to permanently deleting items they no longer need. At times, they might also need additional folders they can access and use. How do we resolve the use of managed content settings for both default and custom-made folders? How do we create the policies needed for these settings and then apply those policies to our users?

Solution: Before we begin, it's important to learn the real-world application to managed content settings for your organization before you learn the steps involved in implementing it. Otherwise you might have a difficult time grasping the purpose of any of this. Let's review a few scenarios where this technology is going to help you do your job as an administrator better.

Grasp the Meaning of Managed Content Settings

The umbrella that this topic comes under is Messaging Records Management (MRM), which is another acronym relating to working with messages when they are at rest—that is, they are sitting somewhere, not flying around your network. They are in an Inbox, Deleted Items, a custom folder, but they are sitting and have been sitting, perhaps for some time.

So, what does a user have in his mailbox? He has default folders (Inbox, Sent Items, Deleted Items, and so on). He might have custom folders (you will soon learn how to create custom folders for all users through policy application). All those folders hold messages that might include emails, voicemails or faxes. Certainly these are included if you use the UM features in Exchange 2007. Will Journal, RSS, and Task Items be included? Perhaps, you might be surprised at the various items in a user's mailbox that are all at rest, taking up storage space, and are most likely never to be accessed again in the majority of cases.

Managed content settings help in the following ways:

- Establish rules to move content
- Establish rules to journal content
- Establish rules to purge content
- Use a mixture of the preceding to move, journal, and purge content

It sounds a bit overwhelming. However, consider a situation in which your users delete content, but it goes into their Deleted Items folder. Therefore, it is still in their mailboxes and still part of their storage spaces. You can create a policy that purges the data in their Deleted Items folder automatically after a period of time.

A buildup of voicemail in a user's Inbox can be handled by moving those items from the Inbox to a custom folder with the understanding that after 30, 60, or 90 days, they will be purged (giving your users the opportunity to move them elsewhere if they are important).

There are several uses for this technology to ensure that the data is protected while the storage is preserved. Let's consider the steps to creating a policy.

The Process of Managed Folders and Policy Creation and Application

To begin with, open your EMC, expand the Organization Configuration, and select Mailbox. Note the three remaining tabs that we haven't discussed in this chapter:

- Managed Default Folders
- Managed Custom Folders
- Managed Folder Mailbox Policies

Note that these tabs are empty with the exception of Managed Default Folders. That includes all the standard folders that a user would have.

Each instance of a folder has managed content settings attached. If you select the Inbox or the Deleted Items folder, in the Actions pane you see the option New Managed Content Settings. It is here that you can define a set of criteria that can be added later on to a policy.

You might find it odd that there is an option in the Actions pane called New Managed Default Folder. This is not going to create additional copies of the default folders (in other words, you cannot create two Inboxes for a user); it creates additional instances that can then have additional managed content settings.

Ultimately, you put a policy together and you place those custom folders and managed default folder instances together under a policy that you apply to a user. You can apply only one policy per user, so you might want to have different instances and managed content settings to create different policies for different users. It can easily become complicated if you let it.

You can create a custom folder without any additional settings simply to have a special folder, perhaps for users to use for certain items. You might also create a voicemail folder that users can create rules to put their voicemails in. Then again, you can create managed content settings that apply rules over those voicemails past a certain time-frame. It's up to you.

The process for creating managed content settings is as follows:

1. Create instances of default folders (or use the default instances), and create those custom folders you wish to use (if any).
2. Create managed content settings over those instances.
3. Create a policy (or policies) pulling together the instances that have settings applied already.
4. Apply a policy to a user.
5. Make sure the Managed Folder Assistant is running.

Let's break this down into the steps.

Create New Managed Default Folders

To begin with, determine which folder you want to create another instance of. You can use the folders that currently exist to establish managed content settings on, but it might be better to create instances to stay organized. To do this, follow these steps:

1. Open the EMC.
2. From the Navigation Tree, expand the Organization Configuration work center.
3. Select Mailbox and then select Managed Default Folders.
4. From the Actions pane, choose the New Managed Default Folder link to open the wizard.
5. Provide a name and then choose the Default Folder Type. Click the down arrow, and select a folder type.
6. You can enter a comment to be displayed when the folder is viewed in Outlook. You can also click the checkbox Do Not Allow Users to Minimize This Comment in Outlook.
7. When all the options are configured, click New.
8. When complete, click Finish.

Create New Managed Content Settings

Now that you have a default folder to apply settings to, you want to create managed content settings over that folder. To do this, perform the following:

1. Open the EMC.
2. From the Navigation Tree, expand the Organization Configuration work center.
3. Select Mailbox and then select Managed Default Folders.
4. Locate the instance of the default folder to which you want to apply settings. Right-click the folder, or from the Actions pane, select the New Managed Content Setting link to open the wizard.
5. On the Introduction screen shown in Figure 6.7, you are told that the settings allow you to control the lifespan of items of the specified message type. First, you have to provide a name for the managed content settings.

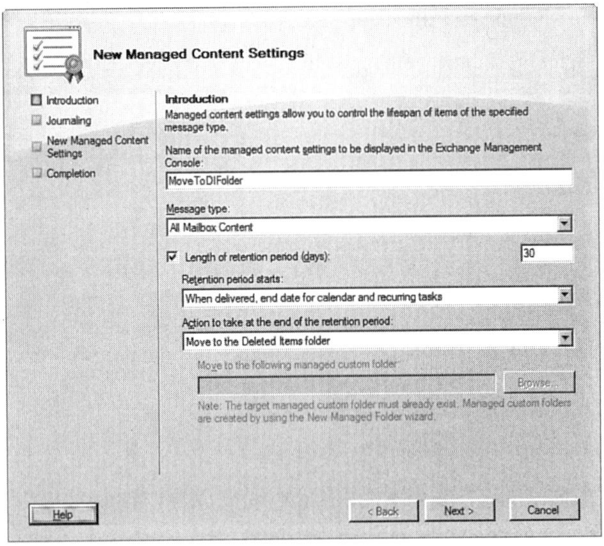

FIGURE 6.7
The New Managed Content Settings Introduction screen.

6. Select the down arrow to choose a message type. You can leave the default All Mailbox Content or select other types.
7. Select the checkbox Length of Retention Period (Days) and provide the number of days the items can reside within the folder before action is taken.
8. Under Retention Period Starts, you can select one of the following:
   - When Delivered, End Date for Calendar and Recurring Tasks
   - When Item Is Moved to the Folder

9. Then choose Action to take at the end of the retention period, which can be one of the following:
    - Move to the Deleted Items Folder
    - Move to a Managed Custom Folder
    - Delete and Allow Recovery
    - Permanently Delete
    - Mark as Past Retention Limit

10. If you chose Move to a Managed Custom Folder, you can select Browse and locate the folder. After all answers are provided, click Next.
11. On the Journaling screen, you can use journaling to automatically forward a copy of an item of the specified message type to another location. To do this, click Forward Copies To, and then choose an email address. Then in the Assign the Following Label to the Copy of the Message dialog, write your message. You can select the Outlook Message Format (.msg) or the Exchange MAPI Message Format (TNEF). When you finish, click Next.
12. Confirm the Configuration Summary, and then click New.
13. When complete, click Finish.
14. Notice that now, beneath your folder, you have the managed content settings that you can alter by going into the Properties.

Create a New Managed Custom Folder

If you want to create a new managed custom folder that can also be deployed through a policy or in harmony with content settings that you establish for a default folder, perform the following:

1. Open the EMC.
2. From the Navigation Tree, expand the Organization Configuration work center.
3. Select Mailbox and then select Managed Custom Folders.
4. From the Actions pane, choose the New Managed Custom Folder link to open the wizard.
5. You have one screen with information you need to fill out, as you can see in Figure 6.8. Input the information in the following fields:
    - Name
    - Display the Following Name When the Folder Is Viewed in Office Outlook
    - Checkbox: Storage Limit (KB) for This Folder and Its Subfolders
    - Display the Following Comment When the Folder Is Viewed in Outlook
    - Checkbox: Do Not Allow Users to Minimize This Comment in Outlook

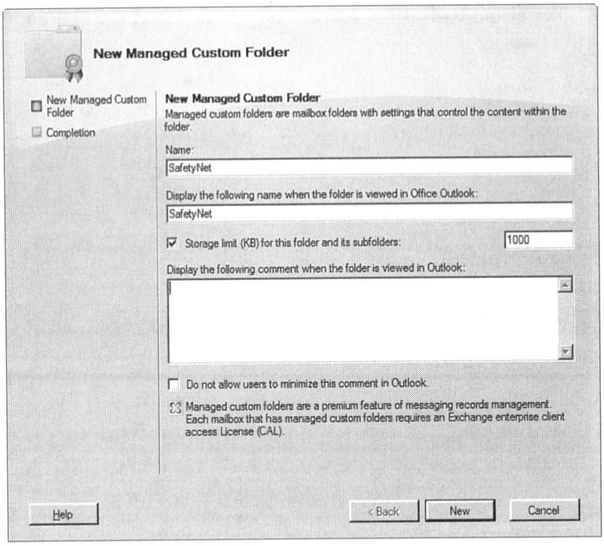

FIGURE 6.8
The New Managed Custom Folder screen.

6. After all information is entered, click New.
7. When complete, click Finish.

NOTE There is a note when you create a custom folder that says, "Managed custom folders are a premium feature of messaging records management. Each mailbox that has managed custom folders requires an Exchange enterprise client access License (CAL)."

At this point, you can simply add the custom folder to the mailbox policy and it will appear in those recipients' mailboxes, or you can use that folder in folder settings from your default folders. However, you can also select the custom folder and, from the Actions pane, create new managed content settings for that folder. It is completely up to you and the needs you have for your organization and your users.

Create a Managed Folder Mailbox Policy

After you have the default and custom folders you need and all of the managed content settings you require, it is time to create policies. Note that although you can create many policies, in the end you can apply only one policy per user. The goal is to ensure that the one policy includes everything you need.

To create a managed folder mailbox policy, perform the following:

1. Open the EMC.
2. From the Navigation Tree, expand the Organization Configuration work center.
3. Select Mailbox and then select Managed Folder Mailbox Policies.
4. From the Actions pane, choose the New Managed Folder Mailbox Policy link to open the wizard.
5. The actual policy creation process is simple. You provide a name and then click the Add button to specify the managed folders that you want to link to this policy. Click Add.
6. You are not shown the folder settings, only the folders themselves. So, you can choose only folder instances to apply through the policy. Choose those default and custom folders you want to apply and click OK.
7. After you make the choices for the policy, click New.
8. When complete, click Finish.

You can go into the properties of the policy to add or remove certain folders. You can always go back to the settings of certain folders to make changes to those settings, too.

Applying a Folder Policy to a Recipient

Many ways to apply a policy to a recipient exist. One way is during the creation of the mailbox account itself. During the Mailbox Settings configuration, you are asked if you want to apply a managed folder mailbox policy, and you can click Browse to choose the policy.

If you already created a recipient and want to make changes to the policy you selected or add a policy, you would enter the properties for the user and go to the Mailbox Settings tab. Select the Messaging Records Management option and enter the properties. Then you can select a folder policy for the recipient.

However, it might be easier to use the EMS to accomplish this task. You can use the `Set-Mailbox` cmdlet for a user:

```
Set-Mailbox  -ManagedFolderMailboxPolicy "name of policy here"
```

Now you can use this cmdlet with an individual mailbox. Imagine you had a mailbox for Joel User and the policy was called Executive Policy. You would type:

```
Set-Mailbox "JoelUser"  -ManagedFolderMailboxPolicy "Executive Policy"
```

However, if you want to really enforce in bulk, you would probably want to try and apply policies to larger groups, such as distribution groups.

You might first use the `Get-DistributionGroupMember` cmdlet, or the `Get-Mailbox` cmdlet if you know the parameters you are looking for, and then pipeline the results (using the | for the pipeline) with the `Set-Mailbox` cmdlet using the `–ManagedFolderMailboxPolicy` setting.

The Managed Folder Assistant

There is one more step in this. You have to actually configure the mailbox server(s) to schedule and run the managed folder assistant. If this assistant doesn't run, nothing happens. No custom folders are created and no policy settings are enforced.

To ensure the Managed Folder Assistant is running, perform the following:

1. Open the EMC.
2. From the Navigation Tree, select the Server Configuration work center.
3. From the Results pane, select the server you need to run the assistant on. Click Properties from the Actions pane.
4. Select the Messaging Records Management tab.
5. By default, the assistant is set to Never Run. You can select the down arrow to choose Use Custom Schedule and then configure a schedule for the assistant to run on. You don't want this to take up more time on your server than needed, so you might do well to select 15-minute increments a few times per day.

NOTE After you have everything in place, the best way to ensure it is all working is to log on as a user with the policy applied and see whether the settings take effect. Look for things like a new custom folder in your folder list. This is a guarantee that the settings work.

Configure Mailbox Properties and Settings

Scenario/Problem: For the most part, the options and dialog boxes that are part of the mailbox properties for a recipient are self-explanatory. However, three tabs (Mailbox Settings, Mail Flow Settings, and Mailbox Features) are more complicated and seem important. How do we configure a mailbox using these three tabs and their corresponding settings?

Solution: It's true, these tabs might involve a bit more knowledge to configure the mailbox settings properly. Let's consider them individually and see what settings they each contain and how they can benefit you.

Mailbox Settings Tab

Under Mailbox Settings, by default you have two options:

- Messaging Records Management
- Storage Quotas

If you select each, you are provided a description at the bottom of the tab. You can also select the Help button in any location to learn more about that set of options.

If you select Messaging Records Management and choose Properties, you are given the option we discussed earlier to provide a mailbox policy, as you can see in Figure 6.9.

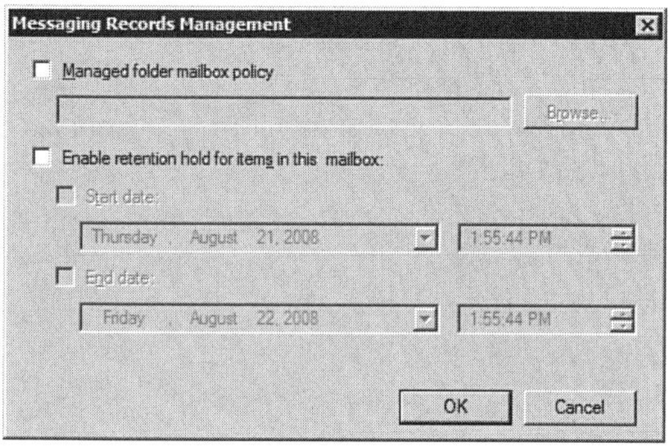

FIGURE 6.9
Messaging Records Management.

However, you can also select the Enable Retention Hold for Items in This Mailbox option and provide start and end dates. This allows a time where you suspect the expiration of items from the mailbox. The policy is still in force, but for that period of time it will not be applied.

You also have Storage Quotas, which has two portions that you are welcome to leave as the database defaults:

- Storage Quotas—Here you can configure an individual mailbox warning, prohibit send and prohibit send and receive quota.
- Deleted Item Retention—Here you can change the deleted item retention time and enable the option Do Not Permanently Delete Items Until You Back Up the Database.

Mail Flow Settings Tab

Under Mail Flow Settings, you have the following three options by default:

- Delivery Options
- Message Size Restrictions
- Message Delivery Restrictions

Starting with Delivery Options, as you can see in Figure 6.10, there are several interesting options such as:

- Send On Behalf—Gives permission to other recipients (who you select using the Add button) to send emails on behalf of your account. If a user has this capability, he can put your mailbox in the From field for email messages he sends. You might give this capability to a person's assistant.

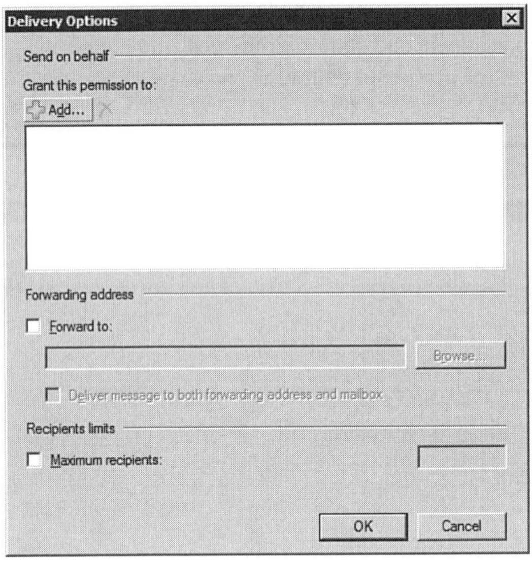

FIGURE 6.10
Delivery Options.

NOTE Another way to allow users or a group the capability to send messages as the owner of another mailbox is by using Manage Send As Permission. This is found by selecting the user and from the Actions pane choosing the Manage Send As Permission link to open the wizard. From the wizard, you can click the Add (or Remove) buttons to grant or deny users or groups the capability to send messages as that mailbox.

- Forwarding Address—This allows a person's mail to be forwarded to another address. Also, a checkbox enables mail to be delivered to both a forwarding address and the mailbox itself.
- Maximum Recipients—This setting places a limit on the maximum number of persons that the user can send an email message to at one time.

The next option is Message Size Restrictions. This enables you to determine a sending and receiving message size. To do this, you select the checkbox and indicate the restriction in KB.

The final option is Message Delivery Restrictions. By default, the settings, as shown in Figure 6.11, are set to accept messages from all senders and reject messages from no senders. However, you can alter this to Only Senders in the Following List, where you add persons to a list for either accepting and rejecting messages. You can also select the Require That All Senders Are Authenticated checkbox.

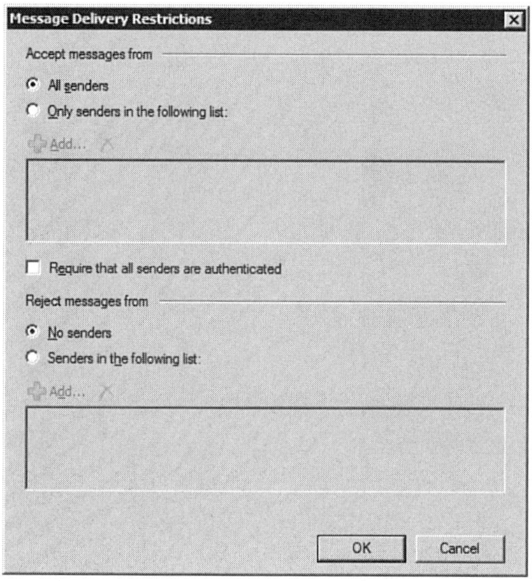

FIGURE 6.11
Message Delivery Restrictions.

Mailbox Features Tab

The Mailbox Features tab is a simple but important group of settings for your recipients. You'll notice in Figure 6.12 all the settings that you can enable or disable (most of which are enabled by default). These settings include the following:

- Outlook Web Access
- Exchange ActiveSync
- Unified Messaging
- MAPI
- POP3
- IMAP4

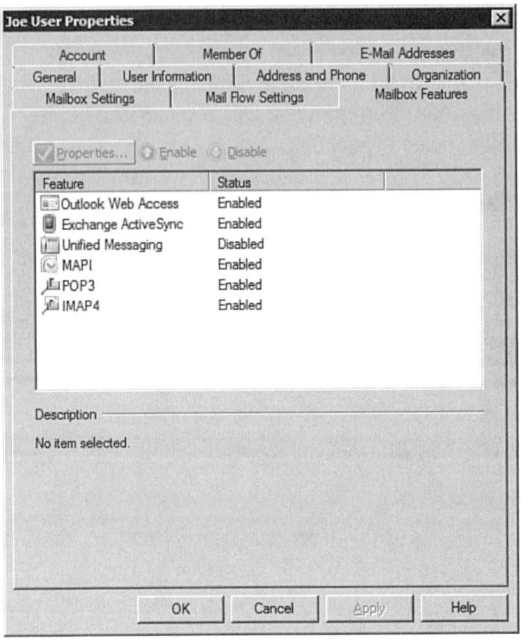

FIGURE 6.12
Mailbox features.

You can do more than select any one of these and choose Enable or Disable from the options. Some also have Properties. When you select an option, you see the Properties button light up and in some cases, such as with ActiveSync, you can choose a policy for the recipient. In other cases, such as MAPI or Outlook Web Access, there are no additional property configuration changes you can make.

CHAPTER 7

Configure the Client Access Server (CAS)

IN THIS CHAPTER

- Administer the CAS Role
- Manage OWA
- Manage Exchange ActiveSync
- Create and Apply ActiveSync Mailbox Policies
- Enable and Configure Outlook Anywhere
- Enable POP3 and IMAP4

Administer the CAS Role

Scenario/Problem: The CAS server role is equated with the Exchange 2000/2003 front-end server, but it works quite differently and seems to have more features involved to administrate. What does the CAS role do and how do you administer its many features?

Solution: It's true that the front-end servers of Exchange 2000/2003 are similar in nature to the CAS server role in that all non-MAPI connections are made through the CAS. However, more processing power was given to the CAS server than previously with front-end servers to offload some of the processing load placed upon the mailbox servers.

The CAS server is the first one you install if you are breaking up your server installations into roles. You need to ensure you have a CAS server in every site that has a mailbox server because the two work hand in hand with each other.

Administration can be performed through the Exchange Management Console (EMC) and the Exchange Management Shell (EMS), as you will soon see. However, because of the extensive use of Internet Information Server (IIS), you might find yourself using the IIS Manager to handle certain aspects of CAS as well, especially when working with SSL certificates for more secure connections.

The primary features of the Client Access Server include the following:

- Outlook Web Access (OWA)—Provides your users with the browser-based connection to their mailboxes. If configured to allow incoming connections from the outside, users can check their email from home using OWA.

NOTE One of the problems for your users using pre-Outlook 2007 software is that some of the mailbox features provided by Exchange (such as the new Out of Office changes) are not available to them. However, one of the benefits of the CAS server is that they can enable those features through an OWA connection because the CAS server provides the latest flavor of OWA, and therefore, it provides the latest features, too.

- Exchange ActiveSync (EAS)—Provides access to users with mobile devices. This includes all devices that have the ActiveSync protocol (this means BlackBerrys and the earlier iPhones will not work). You need to confirm that your devices can make the Exchange ActiveSync connection. With

Exchange 2007 SP1, some stronger policy settings are in place, so if you haven't purchased the mobile devices for your users just yet, you might want the latest version of Mobile. ActiveSync policy settings are controlled at the Organizational Configuration work center level.

- Outlook Anywhere—Previously called RPC over HTTP in Exchange 2003, this enables users to use Outlook from a home or laptop connection outside the company, but with the level of security you would expect if you were sitting at your desk. This is done without a VPN tunnel. Outlook Anywhere instead encapsulates the RPC packets inside of HTTP packets, which can go over the Internet to your Exchange server, which then peels off the HTTP packet. (Note: Only Outlook 2003 and Outlook 2007 are supported for these types of connections.)
- POP3 and IMAP4—These protocols are still heavily used to work with your Outlook Express clients, Mozilla Thunderbird clients, and Windows Mail clients. With these protocols, not many features are supported, but they do provide the basics and sometimes that is all you need.
- Autodiscover Service—This provides users with Outlook 2007 the capability to locate and connect automatically with the Exchange server that houses their mailbox.
- Availability Service—This used to be called free/busy data, and it is essentially for Outlook 2007 clients or those using OWA on an Exchange 2007 system. The availability service retrieves live free/busy information for mailboxes from Public Folders, views attendee working hours, and shows meeting time suggestions. This used to be part of the Public Folder structure, but now the CAS server handles these loose ends.

IIS Integration

IIS is an integral part to the CAS role. This is easy to see if you simply open the IIS Manager from within Administrative Tools and note that the default website includes many of the features we have discussed through virtual folders, as you can see in Figure 7.1.

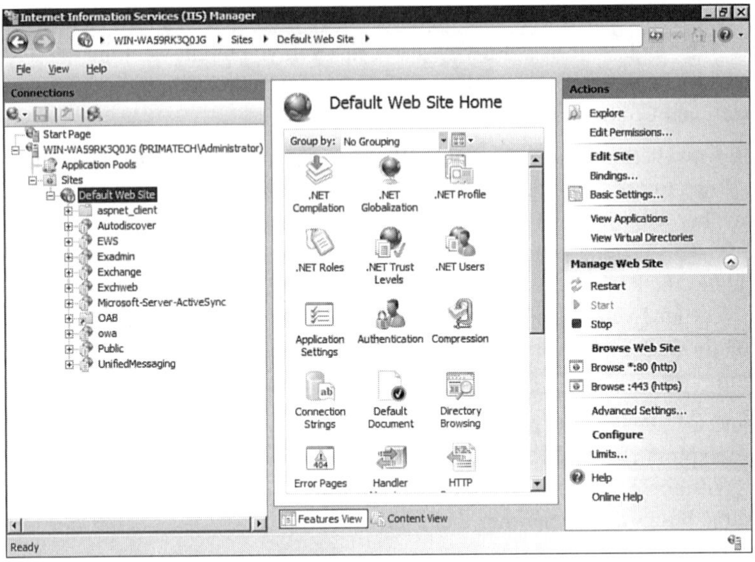

FIGURE 7.1

The virtual folders created upon Exchange installation within IIS.

Table 7.1 provides a list of virtual folders and their purpose:

TABLE 7.1 **IIS Virtual Folders for Exchange 2007**

Virtual Folder	Purpose
Autodiscover	Handles auto-provisioning for clients
EWS	Exchange Web Services
Exchweb	For OWA clients that connect to legacy mailboxes (Exchange 2000/2003)
Exchange	For OWA clients that connect to legacy mailboxes (Exchange 2000/2003)
Microsoft-Server-ActiveSync	Handles mobile connections from supported devices
OAB	Provides Outlook 2007 Offline Address Book distribution
OWA	For OWA connections to Exchange 2007
Public	For OWA access to Public Folders
UnifiedMessaging	For access to some UM information

Of course, knowing what the CAS server does is half the battle. The next part is managing it all.

Manage OWA

Scenario/Problem: Although OWA is installed by default with the CAS role, there is quite a bit we can do to manage this aspect of Exchange mailbox access. What options do we have and what settings can we configure?

Solution: For the most part, you can manage OWA through the EMC (or EMS) and the IIS Manager. You can configure many different settings to provide a customized solution or a more secure solution for your OWA experience. Often the challenge is to know those solutions exist and then where to find them.

Configuring the OWA Properties in the EMC

To begin with, if you want to locate the settings within the EMC, perform the following:

1. Open the EMC.
2. From the Navigation Tree, expand the Server Configuration work center and click Client Access.
3. From the Work pane, select the Outlook Web Access tab.
4. Notice the OWA (Default Web Site) option. Select it and choose Properties.

This takes you to a dialog with six different tabs. Let's consider these.

General

The General tab provides information: the server name, website, OWA Exchange version, and last date modified. In addition, however, are two configurable options for the internal and external URL to access the OWA site.

Keep in mind that you might want to use an HTTPS connection for the external URL because you should use SSL for security purposes.

NOTE It's hard to say if these settings are more than informational. Essentially, you can put whatever you like in here, but it is the IIS settings and DNS settings that come together to provide your URL. However, just in case, you might want to fill out this information. The Help file is not much help in either case.

Authentication

The Authentication tab, shown in Figure 7.2, provides the capability to define standard authentication methods for your OWA connection or forms-based authentication.

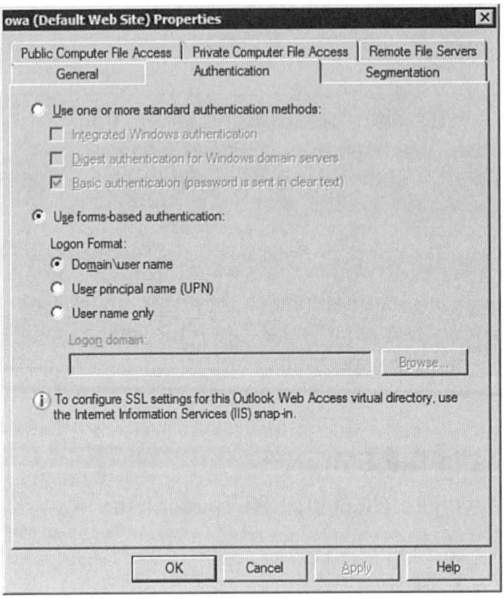

FIGURE 7.2
The Authentication tab from OWA Properties.

If you select a standard authentication method, you can choose:

- Integrated Windows Authentication—Requires that the user has a valid account and password on a Windows Server. Users are not asked for their account information, but the negotiation is handled between the server and client, which should be a member of the same domain (or be part of a trusted domain).
- Digest Authentication for Window Domain Servers—Transmits passwords over the network as a hash value. This provides greater security.
- Basic Authentication (Password Is Sent in Clear Text)—Before sending the credentials, they are encoded and sent to the server. SSL is recommended to provide encryption of the process.

The default option is to use forms-based authentication, which avoids popup windows but provides a web-based form, as shown in Figure 7.3.

You can make changes to the type of information requested from the forms-based logon by selecting one of the following:

- Domain\user name—This is the default arrangement and requires a user to put his domain and username in the logon. So a user named `JDillon` in the `PrimaTech` domain would type **`PrimaTech\JDillon`**.
- User Principal Name (UPN)—This is usually the same structure as the email address. So, a person would type something like **`jdillon@primatech.com`** at the logon prompt.

- User Name Only—Doesn't require the domain name be included in the logon process. You can select the Browse button to choose the Logon domain from which users should come.

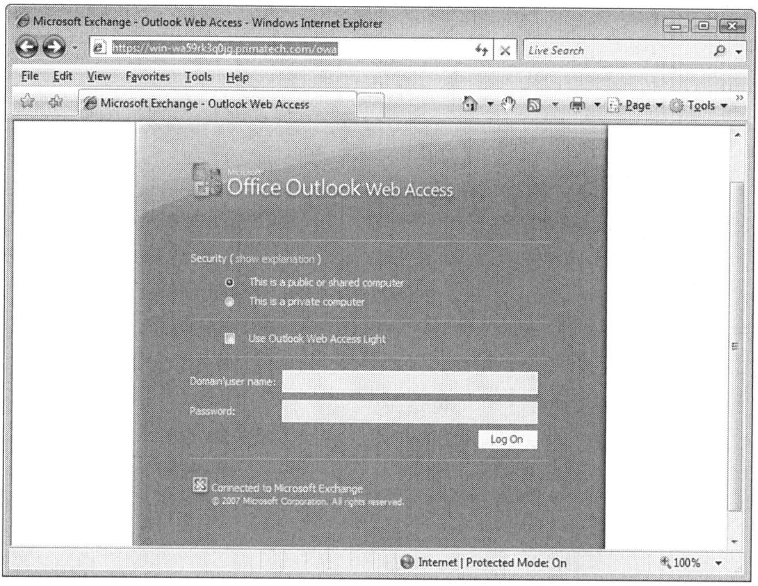

FIGURE 7.3
The OWA forms-based login interface.

Segmentation

The Segmentation tab is a great way to quickly see all the features included with OWA. It's also a great way to enable or disable features for OWA. If you establish these settings on all users, you can still use the `Set-CASMailbox` cmdlet to provide different settings for individual users if you like.

By default, all these settings are enabled. The features that you enable or disable here apply to all users who access their mailbox through the virtual folder OWA off the server you are configuring the settings on. So, you can have different OWA connection points that have different segmentation settings if you like. The settings you can enable or disable include the following:

- Exchange ActiveSync Integration
- All Address Lists
- Calendar
- Contacts
- Journal
- Junk E-Mail Filtering
- Reminders and Notifications
- Notes

- Premium Client
- Search Folders
- E-mail Signature
- Spelling Checker
- Tasks
- Theme Selection
- Unified Messaging Integration
- Change Password
- Rules
- Public Folders
- S/MIME
- Recover Deleted Items

Public and Private Computer File Access

As you saw in Figure 7.3, you have the option to choose if you access the OWA from a public or private computer. Depending on which you choose, there are settings you can configure. The settings on these two tabs are the same. As you can see from Figure 7.4, they relate to file access and WebReady Document Viewing.

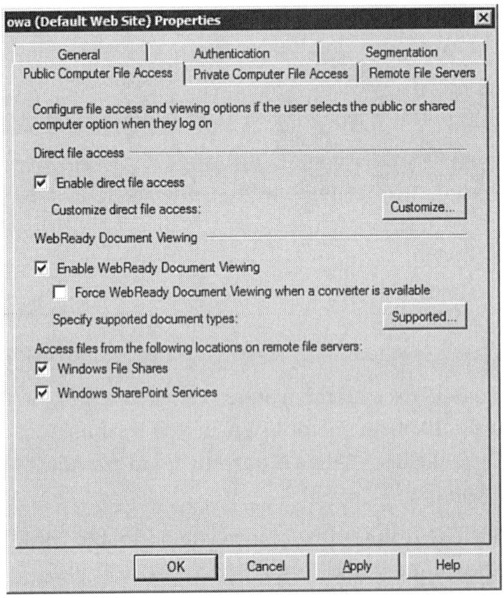

FIGURE 7.4
Public Folder Computer File Access settings.

To begin with, we have the Enable Direct File Access checkbox. Along with it is the Customize option, which enables you to make some changes in how direct file access works.

NOTE What is direct file access? This feature provides users with the capability to have access to read files that are in email attachments or on SharePoint libraries and shared files that are connected with OWA.

With configuration options, you can define both file extensions (such as .bmp) as well as MIME types (such as image/bmp). To customize the process of handling attachments, you can choose the following options:

- Always Allow—Click the Allow button to select which file types can always be accessed without saving to disk. The options provided here will override all other settings. If you say a file type is allowed but it is blocked in the Always Block settings, it will be allowed.
- Always Block—Click the Block button to select which file types can never be accessed. The options provided here will override the Force Save options.
- Force Save—Click the Force Save button to select which file types must be saved to disk before being opened.
- Unknown Files—Select the drop-down arrow to choose what should be done if a file is unknown. You can Allow, Force Save (the default), or Block.

Another group of settings is the WebReady Document Viewing checkbox. This allows known document types (Word, Excel, and so on) to be displayed within the client without the application installed on the local machine. This is truly an incredible tool for those who travel and find themselves in Internet cafes all the time; now they can view documents without having to worry if the location has that application on the system.

In addition, now the user doesn't have to worry about saving the document locally to open it (which can be a problem technically or from a security perspective) and can read the document from the OWA browser.

By default, the option Enable WebReady Document Viewing is enabled. You can choose to enable the other setting Force WebReady Document Viewing when a converter is available. This setting overrides the direct file access settings for a document.

Selecting the Supported button brings up a dialog where you can see all supported document types and determine whether there are some you wish to add and others you wish to remove.

NOTE WebReady Document Viewing has a limit of 5MB for files that it will display in HTML. It also has some limitations on displays of certain advanced Office 2007 charts and other application features. There is a way to override the 5MB limit, however. You can enter the registry and go to the `HKEY_Local_Machine\System\CurrentControlSet\Services\MSExchange OWA` and create a new key called `WebReadyDocumentViewing` and create a DWORD setting called `MaxDocumentInputSize`. You can then place the limit in KB and restart the World Wide Web Publishing Service. Don't make the setting too high, because you can cause the CAS server to suffer performance loss.

The final two checkboxes on these tabs are under the heading Access Files From the Following Locations on Remote File Servers: with the options Windows File Shares and Windows SharePoint Services.

Remote File Servers

The Remote File Servers tab works in harmony with the direct file access settings because you are configuring the servers that you want to allow access to for clients. You can specify servers that are specifically allowed or blocked access. If there are unknown servers, you can specify if they are blocked or allowed, too. You can enter the domain suffix for sites whose FQDN names are treated as internal by selecting the Configure button.

The basic rule is that only internal SharePoint Service servers and file share servers can be accessed with remote file access. Internal servers can be accessed by their host names or FQDNs. OWA uses a simple method to figure out whether a server is internal. If the URL provided had dots in it, it is considered external and not accessible (unless the domain suffix has been added to the list of sites you can configure for the domain suffix). If there are no dots, it is considered internal.

PS NOTE There are two primary sets of cmdlets to administering OWA. The first is the server side to the configuration options, which is the `OWAVirtualDirectory` cmdlet (using various verbs such as `Set`, `New`, `Remove`, `Get`, and so on). Although that cmdlet is geared toward the server configuration side, the user configuration side for OWA is handled through the `Set-CASMailbox` cmdlet.

Using the IIS Manager to Simplify the URL for OWA

It is common for administrators to want to alter the process for users to log in to the OWA site. One way to do this is to use the IIS Manager to alter the way the site is accessed. Keep in mind however that IIS is different between Server 2003 and Server 2008. In 2003, it is IIS 6.0. In 2008, it is IIS 7.0 (which is different to work with).

If you want to simplify the URL through Server 2003 IIS 6.0, perform the following steps:

1. Select Start, Administrative Tools, and then select IIS Manager.
2. In the Navigation Tree, expand the server, Sites, and Default Web Site.
3. Right-click Default Web Site and choose Properties.
4. Select the Home Directory tab.
5. Make sure the radio button A Redirection to a URL is selected.
6. In the Redirect To field, type in the directory (for example, `https://www.primatech.com/owa`).
7. Then in the The Client Will Be Sent To field, select the option A Directory Below URL Entered.
8. Then complete the configuration to the correct OWA folder from the Application settings.

Doing the same thing in Server 2008 under IIS 7.0 is not as straightforward. To redirect, perform the following:

1. Select Start, Administrative Tools, Internet Information Services (IIS) Manager.
2. Make sure you have Default Web Site selected.
3. On the Features view of the Default Web Site, double-click Error Pages.
4. In the Actions pane, click Edit Feature Settings, and under Error Responses, select Custom Error Pages. Then click OK.
5. In the Actions pane, click Add and configure the following:
   - Status code: 403.4
   - Click Respond with a 302 redirect and provide the absolute URL: https://owa.yourcompany.com/owa.
6. Next, double-click the HTTP Redirect icon.
7. Select the option Redirect Requests to This Destination: (shown in Figure 7.5), and type the absolute OWA URL: **`https://www.primatech.com/owa`**.

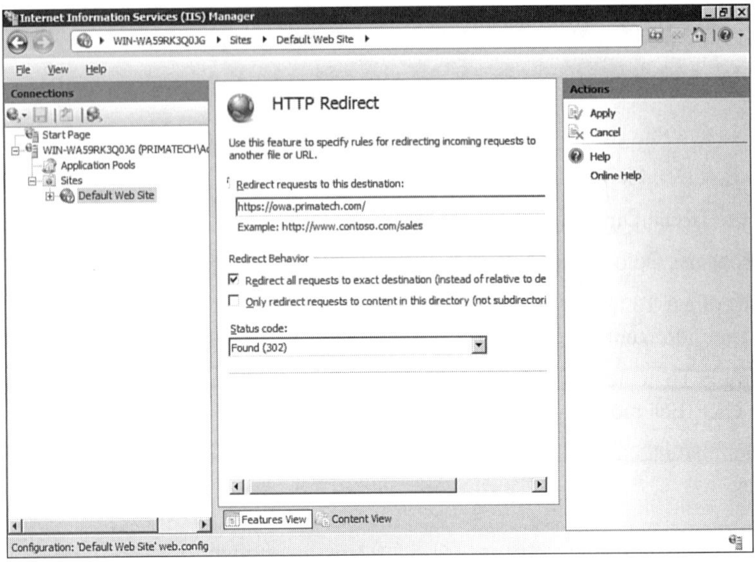

FIGURE 7.5
Configuring the HTTP Redirect.

8. Under the Redirect Behavior section, select the option Only Redirect Requests to Content in This Directory (Not Subdirectories).
9. From the Status Code drop-down menu, select Found (302).
10. Click Apply to save the settings.
11. Then, you can run the `IISRESET /noforce` command in `CMD` for the settings to take effect.

> **NOTE** If you do not see the HTTP Redirect icon, you might not have that service installed. Return to your Server Manager and check to make sure this service is selected with the other options you selected when you installed IIS.

Configure SSL and Certificates

When you install the CAS role, a self-signed SSL certificate is created using the NetBIOS name of the server. This allows you the capability to use SSL within your internal network. (Note: SSL is enabled by default on your OWA connections.) That certificate, however, is not qualified to be used for external connections.

The client attempts to connect, and the server presents the self-signed certificate with no third-party validation. The client waits for the user to explicitly trust that the connection is okay. Although it works, users are prompted with certificate warnings, the browser address bar glows red (indicating something isn't right), and there might be problems with mobile clients connecting. In addition, it doesn't look professional.

You need a third-party certificate. In the past, this would be a simple process. You would contact any agency that offers them and then you are off and running.

The difficulty here is that two services require the certificate: OWA and the Autodiscover service. So, you might begin to question whether you need two certificates or whether you should have separate IP addresses.

You can employ many different solutions, and it is your choice in the end. Here are some of the solutions to the SSL dilemma:

- Subject alternative certificates—Not supported by all certificate authorities, this solution enables you to use one certificate, one website, and one public IP address. If you want to use mail.yourcompany.com, autodiscover.yourcompany.com, and a group of other names, you can do that. After you have your list of names, you can create a certificate request using the `New-ExchangeCertificate` cmdlet.
- Two single-name certificates—Here you would purchase one for Autodiscover and one for OWA. You would need two websites: public IPs and pay the cost for two certificates. However, it still might be cheaper than a multi-named certificate depending on prices.
- Single-name certificate with HTTP redirection—In this case, you require two websites and two public IP addresses. When the redirection occurs, the users will be asked if they trust the redirected URL (which defeats the purpose somewhat).
- Unified Communications Certificate—One solution is to find a certificate authority that will provide you with a Unified Communications Certificate (also called a Subject Alternative Name Certificate [SAN]) with multiple names in one certificate. So, you can request autodiscover.yourcompany.com, mail.yourcompany.com, and other names you need.

Other creative solutions involve complex configuration at times or simply leaving the self-signed certificate (which isn't a valid option for long).

After you have your certificate, what do you do next?

You use the Exchange Management Shell to import the certificate using the following command:

```
Import-ExchangeCertificate -path "path to the certification file"
```

Next, you need to enable it by typing

```
Enable-exchangecertificate
```

If you wanted to enable it for a variety of services, you can use the `-services` parameter with the IIS, POP3, IMAP, SMTP, or Unified Messaging (UM) services included.

You are next asked for a thumbprint, which should have been displayed when you imported the certificate. If you don't see it, you can type **`Get-ExchangeCertificate`** and locate the thumbprint.

That installs your certificate and enables it. You should be set, especially for the next topic, ActiveSync, because ActiveSync does not work if you are trying to use a certificate that is not trusted by the device.

Manage Exchange ActiveSync

Scenario/Problem: With the increase in mobile devices and companies such as BlackBerry offering the technology to push mail to their devices, there is an obvious need for Microsoft to increase its ActiveSync capabilities within Exchange 2007 SP1, and it did this. For starters, what configuration options do you have on the server?

Solution: To locate the properties you can configure for your ActiveSync services, perform the following:

1. Open the EMC.
2. From the Navigation Tree, expand the Server Configuration work center and click Client Access.
3. From the Work pane, select the Exchange ActiveSync tab.
4. Notice the Microsoft-Server-ActiveSync option. Select it and choose Properties.

You are presented with three tabs: General, Authentication, and Remote File Servers. The configuration for each of these is relatively simple:

- General—From here you can see the server and site name, whether SSL is enabled (which it should be by default) and the last date of modification. You also have an Internal and External URL that is informational regarding the location of the ActiveSync virtual directory on the CAS server.
- Authentication—Here you select the authentication method or methods that the virtual directory will accept. You can enable basic authentication by selecting the checkbox, although if you use this form of authentication, you should use SSL to ensure encryption of the data between the mobile device and the server. You can also use client certificate authentication. If you make changes here, they automatically update the IIS metabase.
- Remote File Servers—Recall that with OWA, clients can access files and file servers. The same is true with ActiveSync clients. You can configure the servers you wish to block or allow from within in the same manner as you did for OWA. In addition, you can configure domain suffixes that are treated as internal.

The most powerful aspect of ActiveSync is the capability to control devices through policies.

Create and Apply ActiveSync Mailbox Policies

Scenario/Problem: Your company has quite a number of different mobile devices being used. How do you control the different devices and to what degree can you control them? Also, what do you do if a device is lost or stolen?

Solution: With the use of more mobile devices, some obviously will work more smoothly with ActiveSync, such as those that are created by Microsoft and use the ActiveSync protocol implemented on the device. For example, devices that have an underlying operating system as Mobile 6 or later are going to be more manageable than earlier Mobile devices or other devices from other vendors.

What about BlackBerry devices? Those require their own BlackBerry servers that connect with Exchange 2007, pull the mail from Exchange, and push it down to clients. What about the iPhone? The first version of iPhones had no way of connecting with Exchange. You could use the web interface to perform an OWA connection, but the screen was small and hard to work with. With the more recent releases of the iPhone, there is support for EAS.

Exchange ActiveSync allows for control over mobile devices using policies. You create the policies in the EMC and apply the policy to users.

NOTE If you have an Exchange 2007 RTM system and an Exchange 2007 SP1 system, you will be amazed at how different the ActiveSync policy settings are. This is one area that has been improved upon greatly in terms of more settings and more powerful control options.

To view the default ActiveSync policy (which is applied to all users with mobile connectivity by default) as well as create a new policy, perform the following:

1. Open the EMC.
2. From the Navigation Tree, expand the Organization Configuration work center and click Client Access.
3. Note that there is only one tab here, the Exchange ActiveSync Mailbox Policies tab. Within the tab is a Default policy. You can double-click the policy to open it.
4. If you want to create a new policy, you can choose New Exchange ActiveSync Mailbox Policy from the Actions pane to open the wizard.
5. From within the wizard, you can configure the following items, as shown in Figure 7.6.

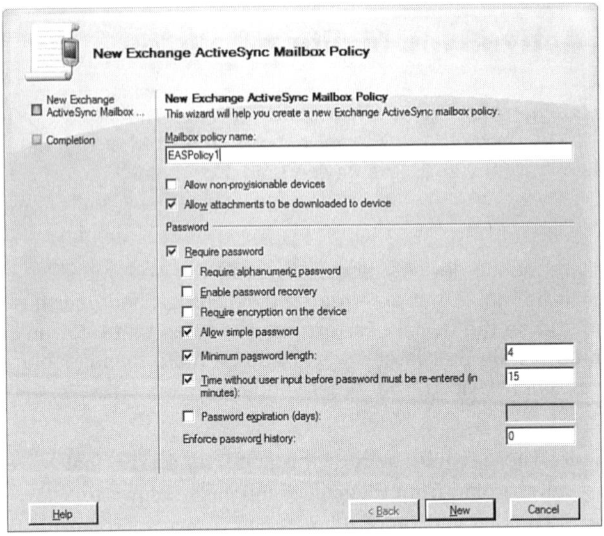

FIGURE 7.6
Creating a new EAS policy.

- Mailbox Policy Name—Provides a unique policy name.
- Allow Non-provisionable Devices—Selecting this checkbox enables older devices that do not have the EAS support for policies to still connect to their mailboxes in Exchange 2007.
- Allow Attachments To Be Downloaded to Device—Selected by default, this allows the device to download attachments from emails.
- Require Password—Deselected by default, but if checked, you are presented with a collection of options, including the following:
  - Require Alphanumeric Password
  - Enable Password Recovery
  - Require Encryption on the Device
  - Allow Simple Password
  - Minimum Password Length (default: 4)
  - Time Without User Input Before Password Must be Re-entered (In Minutes) (default: 15)
  - Password Expiration (Days)
  - Enforce Password History (default: 0)

6. When you finish making your selections, click New to create the policy.
7. When complete, click Finish.

> **NOTE** If you want to take a policy you've created and set it as the default, you can right-click the policy and choose Set as Default or select the policy and choose Set as Default from the Actions pane.

Creating the policy is only part of the configuration process. To ensure the policy is designed the way you prefer, you have to select the policy and choose Properties from the Actions pane. Note that many options are available to configure, including the following five tabs: General, Password, Sync Settings, Device, and Advanced. Let's consider these one step at a time.

The General Tab of the ActiveSync Policy

The General tab shows you the name of the policy. It indicates whether it is the default policy and when it was last modified. The setting to allow nonprovisionable devices is available for you to change the setting from when you first created the policy. Next we have the Refresh Interval (Hours) checkbox, which establishes the number of times a device updates the policy from the server (in hours). Two checkboxes relate to file access through SharePoint or a file server. You can select or deselect the Windows File Shares or Windows SharePoint Services checkboxes.

The Password Tab of the ActiveSync Policy

When creating the policy, you noted that there were several settings that make up the password side to the policy. Well, only on the Password tab can you find some of the additional settings available.

For example, under Require Alphanumeric Password is another setting: Minimum Number of Complex Characters (default is set to 3).

Another extra setting is Require Encryption on the Storage Card, which enforces encryption on the storage card. Note that because this is not a supported option on all mobile devices, make sure the device allows for this before enabling this as a requirement.

The Sync Settings Tab of the ActiveSync Policy

This tab has a group of synchronization settings we can configure, including the following:

- Include Past Calendar Items—Here you can determine a date range of calendar items to sync with devices. The default is All, but you can select the drop-down and choose All, Two Weeks, One Month, Three Months, and Six Months.
- Include Past Email Items—Similar to the calendar items, you can determine a date range of email to sync with devices. You can choose All (the default), One Day, Three Days, One Week, Two Weeks, and One Month.
- Limit Message Size To (KB)—Establishes a maximum download size for messages to the mobile device. Select the checkbox and configure a maximum message size in KB.

- Allow Synchronization When Roaming—Enabling this can be a bit expensive because when the device is roaming, charges tend to be higher. However, if you do enable it, the device will sync even when in roaming mode.
- Allow HTML Formatted Email—Whether you have this option selected or not, email that has been formatted as HTML will still be delivered. It is converted to plain text first. However, you can select this checkbox to allow HTML formatted email.
- Allow Attachments To Be Downloaded to This Device—A simple one-click checkbox to enable/disable if users with this policy can download attachments from within their email. Note that you were able to configure this setting when you first created the policy. However, you weren't provided the next option.
- Maximum Attachment Size (KB)—From within the policy, you can configure the maximum file size you want to allow to be downloaded to the device. If you leave this blank, users are allowed downloads of all sizes.

The Device Tab of the ActiveSync Policy

The options on the Device tab are specifically SP1 advancements (as are many of the settings we've discussed thus far). Obviously with newer mobile devices having items like cameras, it was decided that administrators should be able to control the use of those devices. Note in Figure 7.7 that you can turn the following devices on/off with the click of a checkbox:

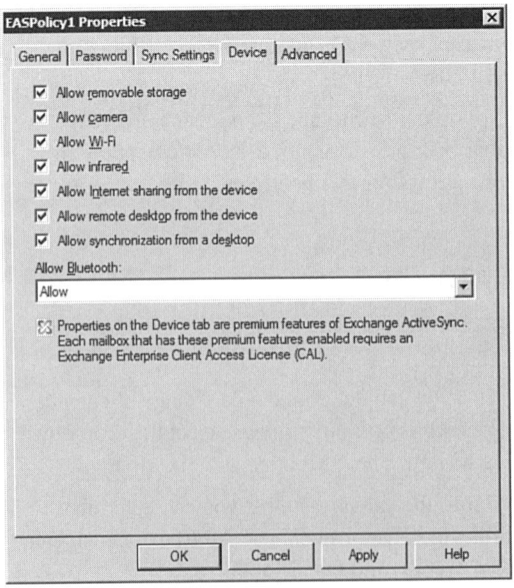

FIGURE 7.7
The Device tab of the EAS policy.

- Allow Removable Storage
- Allow Camera
- Allow Wi-Fi
- Allow Infrared
- Allow Internet Sharing From the Device
- Allow Remote Desktop From the Device
- Allow Synchronization From a Desktop
- Allow Bluetooth: Select the down arrow and choose: Disable, Handsfree Only, or Allow

NOTE The settings on the Device tab and the Advanced tab we discuss in the next section are called premium features. There is an Exchange note directly on the tab at the bottom that says, "Properties on the Advanced tab are premium features of Exchange ActiveSync. Each mailbox that has these premium features enabled requires and Exchange Enterprise Client Access License (CAL)." Before purchasing this extended CAL, make sure your mobile devices can support the policy application of these settings. If not, there is no point to spending the extra money if the devices will not be able to be controlled through the policy settings.

The Advanced Tab of the ActiveSync Policy

The Advanced tab (shown in Figure 7.8) includes the remaining premium features that do not involve devices but applications. For example, you have the following settings:

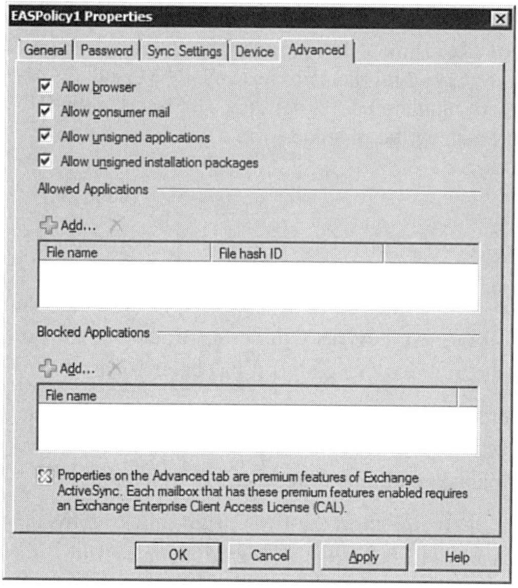

FIGURE 7.8

The Advanced tab of the EAS policy.

- Allow Browser
- Allow Consumer Mail
- Allow Unsigned Applications
- Allow Unsigned Installation Packages

You can also configure allowed and blocked applications by clicking the Add button and selecting the applications that apply.

Assign an ActiveSync Policy to Users

After you have the policies you need for your ActiveSync mobile devices, you need to apply those policies to users. To accomplish this for an individual user, perform the following steps:

1. Open the EMC.
2. From the Navigation Tree, expand the Recipient Configuration work center.
3. From the Results pane, select the user you want to apply the policy toward. Then from the Actions pane, select Properties.
4. Select the Mailbox Features tab.
5. Select the Exchange ActiveSync feature and click the Properties button.
6. You are presented with the option to leave the default EAS policy or select Browse and choose a new policy. After you select the policy, click OK, and the new policy is applied to that user.

> PS **NOTE** The cmdlet through the EMS to assign the policy is `Set-CASMailbox`. You would type in the following: **`Set-CASMailbox 'UserName' -ActiveSyncMailboxPolicy (Get-ActiveSyncMailboxPolicy "Policy Name")`**. If you want to apply the policy to multiple users, perhaps within a distribution group, you can stack the commands using the pipeline (|) to allow for a greater application of policies.

Manage a Mobile Device

You might think that you can give your users a mobile device, set up a policy, and you are done. Not quite. Passwords will be forgotten, devices will be lost or stolen, and so on. There are several ways to manage the mobile device after it has been released.

Users can manage their own devices through the OWA settings. (You can disable this, but you might want to leave it alone because you might want users to handle their own problems. This creates less stress for you as an administrator.)

You can manage the device by locating the recipient in the EMC, right-clicking the user, and choosing Manage Mobile Device, which opens the wizard. (This setting appears only if the user has a mobile device associated with that person. When users initially synchronize their mobile devices with their mailboxes using Exchange ActiveSync, Exchange 2007 creates a partnership with that device. After this partnership has been established, the option to manage mobile devices will appear.) As an administrator, this is the quickest way to wipe a device or recover a password.

You can also use the Exchange Management Shell to manage mobile devices.

For OWA Users: Wipe a Device or Recover a Password

The most important aspect of mobile management is the capability to clear a device of all data (wipe its memory) in the event it is lost or stolen. Who knows what data is on that device? With ActiveSync, it doesn't matter. The moment it's turned on and checks in, the data is cleared out.

For users, Outlook Web Access provides the capability to wipe all data from a device and display the recovery password. To accomplish this, they need to perform the following:

1. Log onto Outlook Web Access.
2. Select the Options link in the upper right-hand corner.
3. From the Navigation pane of options, scroll down until you find Mobile Devices and select that link.
4. Notice you can see your device, the last sync time, and the status. There are also links for Wipe All Data from Device and Display Recovery Password, as you can see in Figure 7.9.

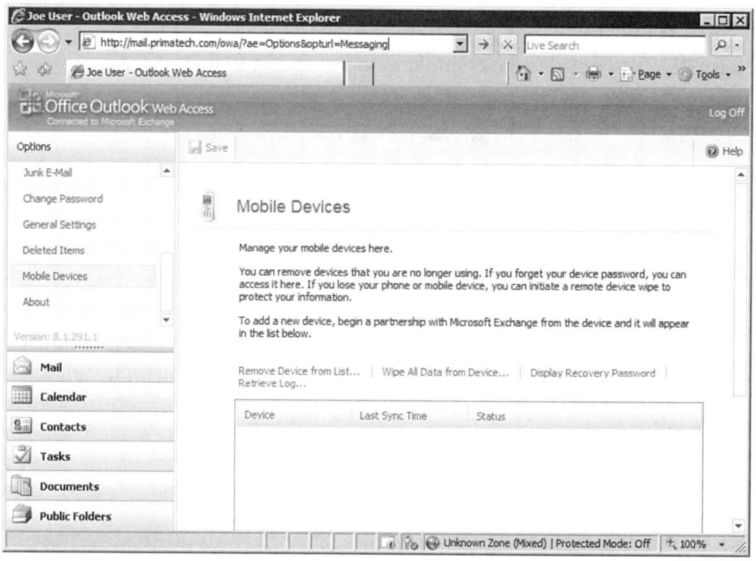

FIGURE 7.9
Remote wipe and password recovery of your mobile device through OWA.

After you clear a device, in SP1 there is now a link for cancelling the request. If you decide to cancel (let's say you find your phone), you should do it quickly because after that phone connects and the device begins the process of wiping, there is no cancel process.

Another new SP1 feature is that after the remote process has completed, users receive an email to let them know it has completed.

Enable and Configure Outlook Anywhere

Scenario/Problem: In Exchange 2003, there was a feature called RPC over HTTP. Now that has been reinvented as Outlook Anywhere. What do you need to do to enable it on your CAS server? And how do you configure your users to use Outlook Anywhere from their home systems?

Solution: To begin with, you have to remember that SSL is an important aspect of Outlook Anywhere, so ensure that you have a valid SSL certificate from a trusted CA in place. We discussed this earlier in the chapter.

There are two steps to the process of enabling Outlook Anywhere. The first is to install the RPC over HTTP Windows Networking Component. The second is to enable Outlook Anywhere on the CAS server.

Depending on the version of Windows Server (2003 or 2008), there are different steps to enable RPC over HTTP. Let's look at both, then look into enabling Outlook Anywhere and finally, we consider the client side to the configuration process.

Install RPC over HTTP on Windows Server 2003

To install RPC over HTTP on Windows Server 2003, perform the following:

1. Select Start, Control Panel, and enter Add or Remove Programs.
2. Select Add/Remove Windows Components.
3. Select Networking Services and click Details.
4. From the Networking Services page, under Subcomponents of Networking Services, click the checkbox for RPC over HTTP Proxy. Then click OK, click Next, and finally, click Finish.

Install RPC over HTTP on Windows Server 2008

To install RPC over HTTP on Windows Server 2008, perform the following:

1. Select Start, Administrative Tools, Server Manager.
2. In the Navigation pane, select Features. You will be able to see the features currently installed.

3. Select the Add Features link.
4. From the Add Features Wizard, locate the RPC over HTTP Proxy and select the checkbox.
5. You might be notified that your selection is part of role services that must be installed for your Web Server (IIS). If this is the case, select the button Add Required Role Services. Then click Next.
6. You are shown a Web Server (IIS) introduction page. Click Next.
7. Role Services will be shown. Click Next.
8. You are shown the feature you are installing and the role services under the Confirmation screen. Click Install.
9. After the Results screen shows the installation is successful, click the Close button.

Enable Outlook Anywhere

To enable Outlook Anywhere on your CAS server, perform the following steps:

1. Open the EMC.
2. From the Navigation Tree, expand the Server Configuration work center and select Client Access.
3. From the Actions pane, select Enable Outlook Anywhere to open the wizard, shown in Figure 7.10.
4. Type in the external host name, which is what users will type into their Outlook client; it has to match the SSL certificate name.
5. Next you have to select a Client authentication method of either Basic or NTLM. Basic sends credentials in clear text. NTLM encrypts the credentials before sending them. NTLM also notes whether you are using a domain system and uses those credentials, so you will not have to continually put in the credentials (which is what you have to do if you choose Basic).
6. The checkbox Allow Secure Channel (SSL) Offloading is necessary only if you plan to use a separate server, such as an ISA 2006 server, to handle the SSL encryption and decryption.
7. After you configure your options, select Next.
8. When complete, select Finish.

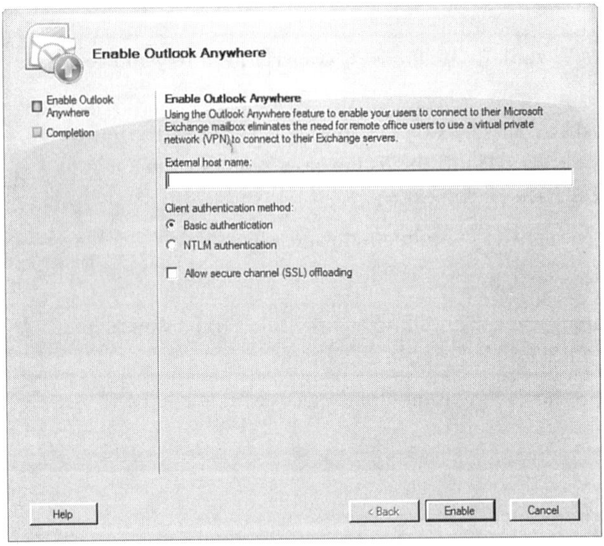

FIGURE 7.10
The Enable Outlook Anywhere Wizard.

NOTE It might take a while for the Outlook Anywhere services to become available for your clients to connect to. Some have reported waits of up to 15 minutes.

Configure Clients to Use Outlook Anywhere

With the process of enabling Outlook Anywhere, all users with mailboxes can now use the connection unless you change that within their settings.

Only Outlook 2003 and Outlook 2007 clients can perform Outlook Anywhere connections. The concept is the same, although the steps can be different. We are going to walk through the steps for Outlook 2007.

To begin, you want to create a new profile. You can do this in Windows Vista by performing the following steps:

1. Select Start, Control Panel, Mail.
2. From the General tab, click Add.
3. Provide a name for the profile (perhaps **`OutlookAnywhere`**).
4. You are taken to the Auto Account Setup. Click the checkbox at the bottom that says Manually Configure Server Settings or Additional Server Types. Then click Next.
5. From the Choose Email Service tab, click Microsoft Exchange, and then click Next.

6. From the Microsoft Exchange Settings tab, you can input your Exchange server name (FQDN or NetBIOS) and the username. You can check the name with the Check Name button. Click More Settings.
7. Select the Connection tab.
8. At the bottom, notice the heading Outlook Anywhere. Select the checkbox Connect to Microsoft Exchange Using HTTP, and then select Exchange Proxy Settings.
9. Note from the Exchange Proxy Settings dialog (shown in Figure 7.11) that you can configure the URL for the connection to the proxy server for Exchange. You want to configure the use of SSL and the proxy servers that have the principal name in their certificate. You have two checkboxes regarding how to connect in a fast and slow network situation (using HTTP first and then TCP/IP). Finally, you can select your authentication settings to use Basic or NTLM, which depends on how you configured your Outlook Anywhere settings earlier.

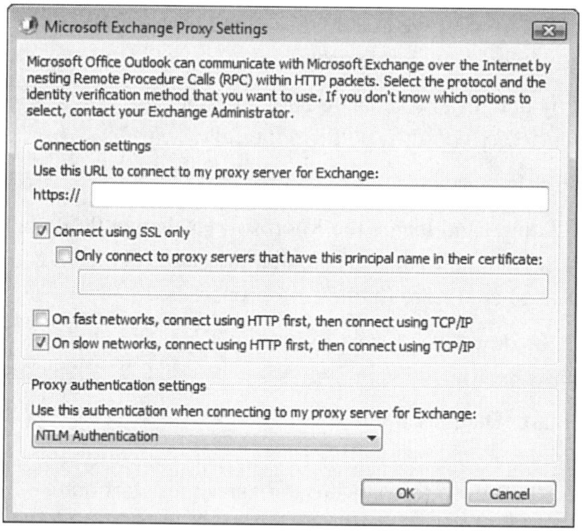

FIGURE 7.11
Configuring Exchange proxy settings.

10. Complete making configuration adjustments, and click Next.
11. When you see the Congratulations screen, click Finish.

From within the Mail settings, you can choose to prompt for a profile to be used when you open Outlook. Or, you can choose Always Use This Profile and select the one you want.

NOTE To confirm the connection status, hold the Ctrl key down and right-click the Outlook icon in your system tray. Select Connection Status. You should be able to see HTTPS connections that are established and going through the CAS server we've configured it to use for Mail.

Enable POP3 and IMAP4

Scenario/Problem: With Exchange 2007, RTM, POP and IMAP were not configurable through the EMC. You had to configure them using the `Set-PopSettings` and `Set-ImapSettings` cmdlets. Now, however, they are. How do we configure POP and IMAP access to our Exchange servers?

Solution: Many Exchange admins would attempt to dissuade you from the use of POP or IMAP as connection methods to an Exchange server, regardless of the millions of clients that use only those protocols to connect to servers. The reason is simple: you aren't able to use the full potential of your server when using applications that rely on POP or IMAP. However, sometimes you just need to compose, read, and reply to email.

It's not always our decision anyway as to what we enable. If a client wants POP or IMAP connectivity to an Exchange server, how do we provide it?

Both POP and IMAP are disabled by default in Exchange 2007. So, the first step to using either option is to start the service. To do this, perform the following:

1. Select Start, Administrative Tools, Services.
2. From the Services tool, scroll down and locate the Microsoft Exchange POP3 or Microsoft Exchange IMAP4 service and you will see that the status is blank. Double-click the one you want to configure to open the properties.
3. From the General tab, select the down arrow next to Startup Type, and choose Automatic.
4. Under Service status, click Start. Then click OK.

PS NOTE The cmdlet through the EMS used to configure the service to start automatically and start is

```
Set-service msExchangePOP3 -startuptype automatic  (or
msExchangeIMAP4)
Start-service -service msExchangePOP3   (or msExchangeIMAP4)
```

The configuration settings for POP and IMAP are practically identical. There are minor distinctions between the two protocols; for example, POP uses 110 (for TLS and unencrypted sessions) and 995 (for SSL connections), whereas IMAP uses ports 143 and 993, respectively. To configure POP and IMAP settings through the EMC, perform the following:

1. Open the EMC.
2. From the Navigation Tree, expand the Server Configuration work center and select Client Access.

3. From the Work pane, select the POP3 and IMAP4 tab. You will see the two protocols.
4. Select the protocol you wish to configure, and select Properties. You will see five tabs (each one has a set of tabs where the format is identical, so we will cover only one here).
    - General—Provides modification information and lets you know whether the service is ready.
    - Binding—Provides ports that are bound for TLS or unencrypted sessions as well as SSL connections. The ports are shown for both IPv4 and IPv6. You can add, edit, or remove any of these settings.
    - Authentication—Enables you to specify the type of authentication you want users to use. Options include the following:
        - Plain Text Logon (Basic Authentication)—No TLS connection is required for the client to authenticate to the server.
        - Plain Text Authentication Logon (Integrated Windows Authentication)—No TLS connection is required for the client to authenticate to the server.
        - Secure Logon—A TLS connection is required for the client to authenticate to the server.
        - X.509 Certificate Name (for a TLS Session)
    - Connection—Includes time-out settings, connection limits and proxy target port.
    - Retrieval Settings—Here you can configure the following:
        - Message MIME format—This setting can actually be changed through the recipient directly from the Message Features options. Options include Text, HTML, Enriched Text, Best Body Format (the default), and others.
        - Message Sort Order—Only for POP settings, this enables you to choose Ascending or Descending.
        - Calendar Retrieval—You can choose iCalendar, Intranet URL, Internet URL, or Custom, and then provide the URL of the Outlook Web Access server.

CHAPTER 8

Administrate Transport Settings

IN THIS CHAPTER

- Work with Accepted Domains
- Implement Email Address Policies
- Work with Remote Domains
- Set Transport Rules
- Configure Journaling
- Manage Connectors (Send and Receive)
- Establish EdgeSync Subscriptions
- Enable Antispam Configuration

Work with Accepted Domains

Scenario/Problem: The capabilities of Exchange Server go beyond simply sending and receiving email within a single domain, but also include the capability to serve as an accepted domain that can send and receive emails for additional domain namespaces. There are also concepts such as authoritative domains and internal/external relay domains that require both design and configuration know-how. How do these different concepts work and how can you configure them on your transport servers?

Solution: To begin, what is the difference among all these different domain types? How do they provide you great flexibility when configuring your organization? The following are domain types:

- Accepted domains—If an Exchange organization is configured to send and receive email for a particular SMTP namespace, it considers that an accepted domain. This doesn't necessarily mean that mailboxes are hosted within the organization for that namespace. It could simply mean that email is relayed through your organization.
- Authoritative domains—These are accepted domains that officially host mailboxes for a domain namespace. An Exchange organization can have more than one authoritative domain. For example, if your company has two different products and therefore two different namespaces, you can have persons send email to users at either one, but your Exchange server will be able to determine, by namespace, where that mail should go. When you first install Exchange, you are given one authoritative, accepted domain configured on your Hub Transport server. You are not provided an automatic accepted domain on your Edge Transport server, however.
- Relay domains—When a person sends an email that is by namespace designed to come to your Exchange servers, if the email is not for an internal mailbox (in other words, if the email was not sent to the authoritative domain), it checks to see whether there is a relay domain it should send the email toward. There are both external and internal ways to configure these relay domains. On the external side, you configure your Edge Transport server to relay over to the other domain's Edge Transport server (if it has one; if not, it can be the other domain's Hub Transport). On the internal side, you allow the message to come through the Edge Transport server and then the Hub Transport server will relay it over to the other domain's Hub Transport server.

NOTE Because an Edge Transport server is a recommended role whereas a Hub Transport server is mandatory, we perform most actions from the viewpoint of the Hub Transport role. Performing the tasks on the Edge Transport is identical, with the exception of having additional elements in the Exchange Management Console to be visually concerned with.

Confirm the Domain Type

To quickly see (or alter) the type of domain you have configured on your transport server, perform the following:

1. Open the Exchange Management Console (EMC).
2. From the Navigation Tree, expand the Organization Configuration work center and click Hub Transport.
3. From the Results pane, select the Accepted Domains tab.
4. Select a domain (in most cases, you see only the first one created when you install the server).
5. From the Actions pane, choose Properties.
6. From the General tab (shown in Figure 8.1), you can see whether the domain is an accepted domain. You can also choose one of the following options:

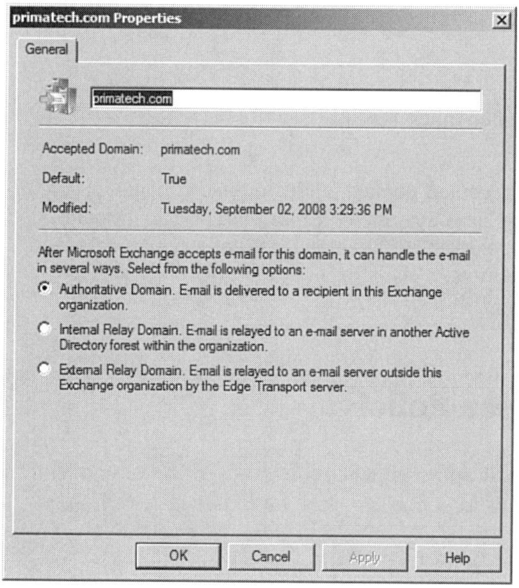

FIGURE 8.1
The General tab for your accepted domains.

- Authoritative Domain—Email is delivered to a recipient in this Exchange organization.
- Internal Relay Domain—Email is relayed to an email server in another Active Directory forest within the organization.
- External Relay Domain—Email is relayed to an email server outside this Exchange organization by the Edge Transport server.

7. After you complete your check or make a change, click OK to return to the console.

Create a New Accepted Domain

Remember, an accepted domain is one that allows inbound email routing. If you need to create additional accepted domains, perform the following:

1. Open the EMC.
2. From the Navigation Tree, expand the Organization Configuration work center and click Hub Transport. (To create an accepted domain on an Edge Transport server, within the console tree, from that computer, select Edge Transport, and then within the Work pane, click the Accepted Domains tab.)
3. From the Actions pane, select the New Accepted Domain link to open the wizard.
4. Provide a display name for the accepted domain.
5. Provide the accepted domain SMTP namespace.
6. Select the type of accepted domain you wish to create: Authoritative, Internal Relay, or External Relay.
7. Click New.
8. When the domain has been created, click Finish.

NOTE Keep in mind that after the accepted domain is created and configured, you still have to ensure that the Domain Name System (DNS) for public email includes a mail exchange resource record (MX) for the SMTP namespace that you just included and that it points to the server IP address.

Implement Email Address Policies

Scenario/Problem: What are email address policies and how can you configure them to generate different primary and secondary email addresses for different recipients?

Solution: Every user, resource (room, equipment, and so on), contact, or group that is mail-enabled receives a mailbox and an email address. That email address is generated because of an email address policy. By default, when you install Exchange, a simple, all-encompassing policy is created that applies a primary SMTP address to the objects you mail-enable. This default policy takes the recipient's alias and places it before the @ sign and then appends the default accepted domain at the end.

One of the changes you can make within your organization, for example, is that you can alter how the email address is configured. Rather than using the alias, you can always go with firstname.lastname@domainname.com. You can also configure additional email addresses for a single recipient.

Alter the Default Email Policy

The default policy is automatically applied to all recipient types. You cannot alter that fact. If, however, you need to make a change that will affect all recipient types, you can open and edit the default policy. For example, if you wanted to alter the manner in which email addresses are configured, you can do so at the organizational level through the policy itself.

To alter the default email policy, perform the following:

1. Open the EMC.
2. From the Navigation Tree, expand the Organization Configuration work center and click Hub Transport.
3. Select the E-mail Address Policies tab.
4. Select Default Policy. From the Actions pane, select Edit to open the wizard.
5. The Introduction screen shows all recipients types and is grayed out so you cannot alter this aspect of the policy. Click Next.
6. The Conditions screen displays, and again, this cannot be altered. Click Next.
7. The Email Addresses screen displays. Here, you can see the default SMTP address scheme. Click Add to include other SMTP addresses. Click Edit to make changes to the email configuration, as you can see in Figure 8.2. As you can see, you can alter the configuration and the accepted domain for the email address. Click OK when you are finished making changes. Then click Next.

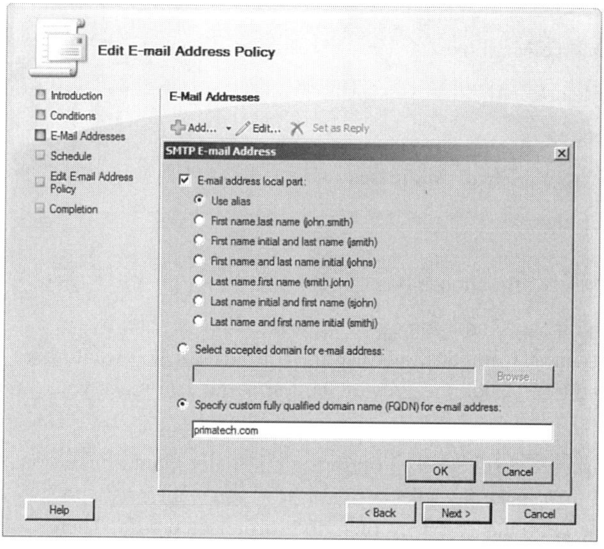

FIGURE 8.2
Altering your SMTP email address structure.

8. On the Schedule screen, you can determine whether you want this policy to go into effect immediately or at a specific time. Then click Next.
9. Review the Configuration Summary, and if changes are needed, go Back. If not, click Edit.
10. When the edit is complete, click Finish.

Create a New Email Policy

You can create additional policies and then order the priority level of those policies so that the default policy is ignored over another policy you design. These created policies can be directed toward specific recipient types and conditions can be placed upon them, so that you can really control the application of the policy.

To create a new email policy, perform the following:

1. Open the EMC.
2. From the Navigation Tree, expand the Organization Configuration work center, and click Hub Transport.
3. Select the E-mail Address Policies tab.
4. From the Actions pane, select New E-mail Address Policy to open the wizard.
5. On the Introduction screen, you need to provide a name. Then choose the recipient types you need included. You can leave the default option All Recipient Types or you can select The Following Specific Types and choose one or more of the following:
    - Users with Exchange Mailboxes
    - Users with External Email Addresses
    - Resource Mailboxes
    - Contacts with External Email Addresses
    - Mail-Enabled Groups
6. After you make your selections, choose Next.
7. The Conditions screen displays, and you can establish a filter of sorts by Department, State, Province, Company, or Custom Attributes. If you want to see the results of your conditions, click the Preview button. After you make your selections, click Next.
8. The Email Addresses screen displays. The options are initially blank. First, you have to click Add and then make the selections for how you want emails to display and the accepted domain you want them to be connected with. Then click Next.
9. On the Schedule screen, you can determine whether you want this policy to go into effect immediately or at a specific time. Then click Next.

10. Review the Configuration Summary, and if changes are needed, click Back. If not, click New.
11. When the new policy is created, click Finish.

NOTE The moment you create a new policy, it is given a priority level of 1. That is higher than the default policy level, which is lowest. You cannot alter the priority level of the default policy; however, as you add more policies, you can right-click a policy (or select the policy and look in the Actions pane) and choose a different priority level to assist you in organizing your policies.

Work with Remote Domains

Scenario/Problem: Your Exchange organization has a default remote domain configuration in place. This establishes a modicum of control over all message transfer between your organization and all other domains. How can you alter the default remote domain entry and create additional remote domain entries to provide more control?

Solution: You have the capability to make changes to the default remote domain settings or to create additional remote domain settings that are specific to a domain toward which you wish to control certain access.

For example, you can control the out-of-office message types delivered to a domain. You can also control the types of messages sent to that domain.

Alter the Default Remote Domain Settings

To alter the default remote domain settings, perform the following:

1. Open the EMC.
2. From the Navigation Tree, expand the Organization Configuration work center and click Hub Transport.
3. Select the Remote Domains tab.
4. From the Results pane, select the default policy. From the Actions pane, select Properties.
5. You can see the domain name is *.

NOTE Note that the default domain is for *, which translates to all domains that the Exchange organization doesn't have as an accepted domain (authoritative, internal relay, external relay) or as an explicit remote domain.

6. From the General tab, you can select the out-of-office message types delivered to this remote domain. They include the following:
    - Allow None
    - Allow External Out-of-Office Messages Only (default setting)
    - Allow External Out-of-Office Messages, and Out-of-Office Messages Set by Outlook 2003 or Earlier Clients or Sent by Exchange Server 2003 or Earlier Servers
    - Allow Internal Out-of-Office Messages, and Out-of-Office Messages Set by Outlook 2003 or Earlier Clients or Sent by Exchange Server 2003 or Earlier Servers

7. Next, you can select the Format of Original Message Sent as Attachment to Journal Report tab, as shown in Figure 8.3. From here you can select the following:
    - Message Format Options (checkboxes)
        - Allow Automatic Replies
        - Allow Automatic Forward
        - Allow Delivery Reports (default)
        - Allow Non-delivery Reports (default)
        - Display Sender's Name on Messages (default)
        - Use Message Text Line Wrap at Column (indicate column number)
    - Exchange Rich-Text Format: (radio buttons)
        - Always Use
        - Never Use
        - Determined by Individual User Settings (default)
    - Character Sets
        - MIME Character Set (default: Western European [ISO])
        - Non-MIME Character Set (default: Western European [ISO])

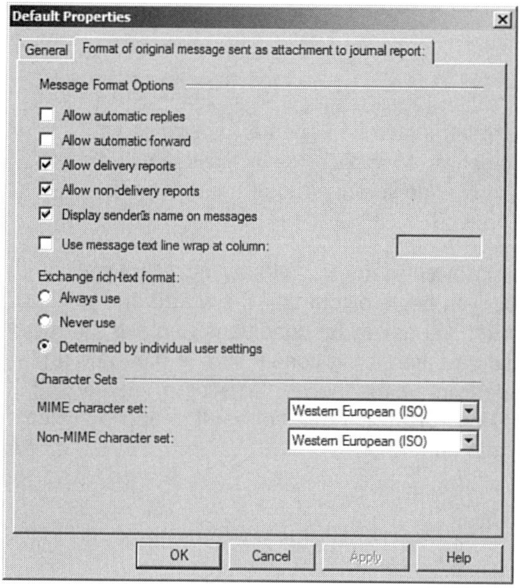

FIGURE 8.3
The various message format options for a remote domain.

Create a New Remote Domain

Perform the following to create a new remote domain:

1. Open the EMC.
2. From the Navigation Tree, expand the Organization Configuration work center, and click Hub Transport.
3. Select the Remote Domains tab, and from the Actions pane, select New Remote Domain to open the wizard.
4. On the New Remote Domain screen, enter the name of the remote domain and the domain name itself. You can also select a checkbox to include all subdomains.
5. Then click New. When complete, click Finish.

After the creation of the explicit remote domain, you can enter the Properties and configure the out-of-office settings and message format options the same way we did previously.

Set Transport Rules

Scenario/Problem: With all email within your Exchange organization going through the Hub Transport servers, there should be benefits you see and can use. One of these benefits is the capability to apply rules to messages in transit. What kind of rules can you apply and how do you use those transport rules?

Solution: There are no default rules in place to control messaging within your organization. To establish these rules, you begin by starting the wizard and working through three main portions of the rule. You have your conditions to make the rule go into effect, the actions that should be taken if the condition(s) is met, and any exceptions that might disqualify a rule from being applied. Creating a rule doesn't automatically mean it is enabled. You can disable a rule so that it is applied when you determine it is time to turn the rule on.

Design a Transport Rule

You might imagine a few different reasons to create transport rules. For example, let's say you have to append a legal disclaimer to all messages that leave your organization and go to outside persons. You might tell your users to ensure the message is included at the bottom of their emails, but that would be putting a great deal of trust on the part of your people with something that can easily be forgotten. Rather, you can use a transport rule to ensure it is done automatically.

Another possible rule is one that prevents individuals from different departments from communicating with each other in the event they are not legally allowed to do so. This might seem a bit odd, but in larger companies where legal obligations are in place, one side of the company cannot discuss things with another side. Rather than leave it up to employees to follow the rules on this, you can establish a transport rule to ensure it happens.

You can use transport rules to filter confidential information, to prevent known virus extensions from running rampant through your organization, to track or archive messages that are sent to or received from specific individuals, to redirect inbound and outbound messages for inspection before delivery, and much more.

You can create hundreds of different rules. It's simply impossible to review all the different methods of combining conditions, actions, and exceptions. We review the options for each.

Conditions

- From people
- From a member of distribution list
- From user inside or outside the organization
- Sent to people

- Sent to a member of distribution list
- Sent to user inside or outside organization
- Between members of distribution list and distribution list
- When any of the recipients in the To field are people
- When any of the recipients in the To field is a member of distribution list
- When any of the recipients in the Cc field are people
- When any of the recipients in the Cc field is a member of distribution list
- When any of the recipients in the To or Cc field are people
- When any of the recipients in the To or Cc field is a member of distribution list
- Marked with classification
- When the Subject field contains specific words
- When the Subject field or body of the message contains specific words
- When a message header contains specific words
- When the From address contains specific words
- When the Subject field contains text pattern
- When the Subject field or the body of the message contains text pattern
- When the message header contains text pattern
- When the From address contains text pattern
- When any attachment file name contains text patterns
- When a spam confidence level (SCL) rating is greater than or equal to limit
- When the size of any attachment is greater than or equal to limit
- Mark with importance

Actions

- Log an event with message
- Prepped the subject with string
- Apply message classification
- Append disclaimer text using font, size, color with separator and fallback to action if unable to apply
- Set the spam confidence level to value
- Set header with value
- Remove header
- Add a recipient in the To field addresses
- Copy the message to addresses
- Blind carbon copy (Bcc) the message to addresses

- Redirect the message to addresses
- Send bounce message to sender with enhanced status code
- Silently drop the message

Exceptions

- Except when the message is from people
- Except when the message is from members of distribution list
- Except when the message is from users inside or outside the organization
- Except when the message is sent to people
- Except when the message is sent to a member of distribution list
- Except when the message is sent to users inside or outside the organization
- Except when the message is sent between members of distribution list and distribution list
- Except when any of the recipients in the To field are people
- Except when any of the recipients in the To field is a member of distribution list
- Except when any of the recipients in the Cc field are people
- Except when any of the recipients in the Cc field is a member of distribution list
- Except when any of the recipients in the To field or Cc field are people
- Except when any of the recipients in the To field or Cc field is a member of distribution list
- Except when the message is marked as classification
- Except when the text specific words appear in the subject
- Except when the text specific words appear in the subject or body of the message
- Except when the text specific words appear in a message header
- Except when the From address contains specific words
- Except when the text pattern appears in the subject
- Except when the text pattern appears in the subject or body of the message
- Except when the text pattern appears in the header
- Except when the From address contains text patterns
- Except when the text pattern appears in any attachment file name
- Except when the spam confidence level (SCL) is greater than or equal to limit
- Except when the size of any attachment is greater than or equal to limit

Create a Transport Rule

On a Hub Transport server, there is a Transport Rules agent, whereas on an Edge Transport server, there is an Edge Rules agent. They are similar in concept but different in usage. If you use an Edge Transport server, you want to ensure rules you might apply on your Hub Transport servers ordinarily are also included on the Edge Transport for further protection. For example, in the event a virus is detected and you know the extension you are looking to drop, you would place the rule on both the Hub and Edge Transport servers to ensure it is dropped internally and from external messages as well. Prior to the update of your antivirus software, you might create a quick transport rule that drops messages with that extension, but you need to create the rule on both the Hub and Edge transport sides.

Rules created for the Hub Transport servers are established at the organizational level and will apply throughout your organization. Those created on an Edge Transport server apply only on that server. The rules are not shared and so must be individually established on each Edge Transport server.

> **NOTE** The instructions to follow and corresponding screenshots are from an Edge Transport server. The only distinction you would make on the Hub Transport side is that you would select the Organization Configuration work center and click Hub Transport and then the Transport Rules tab. On the Edge Transport server, you have less in the Navigation pane to be concerned with but the wizard is the same. You might notice that the Edge Transport server doesn't allow for as many options to configure, and that is because it has a limited scope of application, whereas the Hub Transport server offers all the options previously mentioned.

To create a transport rule on the Edge Transport server, perform the following:

1. Open the EMC.
2. From the Navigation Tree, select Edge Transport.
3. Select the Transport Rules tab, and from the Actions pane, select the New Transport Rule link to open the wizard.
4. On the Introduction screen, you are asked for a name for the rule and a comment where you can explain the purpose of the rule you are creating. You can also select/deselect a checkbox for the rule to be automatically enabled or disabled after it is created. Enter the information and click Next.
5. The Conditions screen, shown in Figure 8.4, enables you to choose one or more conditions you want met before action is taken on a message. In Step 1, you select the condition, and in Step 2, you alter the condition by selecting an underlined value and indicating your personal need. If you want to have emails from a group moved into a certain folder, you can select the option in the first part and indicate the exact group in the second. After you have your condition(s) established, click Next.

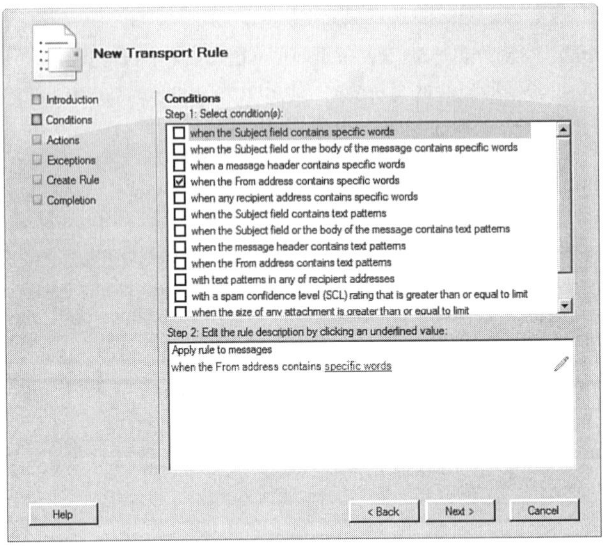

FIGURE 8.4
The Conditions screen for the transport rule.

6. The Actions screen enables you to select an action or actions to perform in the event the condition is met. After the action(s) is determined, click Next.
7. The Exceptions screen is not mandatory. Here you can select a variety of exceptions to this transport rule if you need them. Configure your exceptions and choose Next.
8. After the three aspects of the rule are in place, the Create Rule screen allows you to review the Configuration Summary for the rule. If something is amiss, click Back. If everything is fine, click New.
9. After the rule has been created, click Finish.

After the rule is in place, you can select the rule at any time and from the Actions pane choose to disable the rule, remove the rule, or edit the rule.

Configure Journaling

Scenario/Problem: There are government regulations in place that affect the world of email (such as the Sarbanes-Oxley Act and SEC Rule 17A-4). In harmony with that, there is a tool provided within Exchange to assist you in making sure you have a copy of email going through your organization, called journaling. How do you use this technology to protect yourself?

Solution: One of the ways we have already discussed in Chapter 4, "Manage Storage and Databases," is the capability to journal messages going to and from a mailbox database. This requires setting up a journaling mailbox and sending all duplicates of the message to that mailbox. The journaling mailbox is a simple SMTP address, which means it can be another Exchange mailbox within your organization, it can be a SharePoint location, or some other solution you have in place for archiving.

A journaled message is wrapped in a "journaling envelope." The journaled message contains information regarding the sender, the recipient, the subject, and other information regarding that message that should be retained for informative or legal purposes.

However, because all mail goes through the Hub Transport role, we can configure journal rules that give us a great deal of control over duplicating our incoming and outgoing mail.

NOTE Exchange has two different journaling options—Standard and Premium. As we examined in Chapter 4, with Standard, you can journal a mailbox database (also called per-mailbox database journaling). Premium requires an Enterprise CAL and allows you to use the rules from the Hub Transport role to focus on a specific mailbox or group (also called per-recipient journaling).

To configure a journal rule, perform the following:

1. Open the EMC.
2. From the Navigation Tree, expand the Organization Configuration work center, and click Hub Transport.
3. Select the Journaling tab.
4. From the Actions pane, select New Journal Rule to open the wizard.
5. The New Journal Rule Wizard opens, as shown in Figure 8.5. Here you are asked to provide the following information:
    - Rule Name—Choose a name that will make it easy to remember the purpose of the rule.
    - Send Journal Reports to Email Address—Select Browse and choose the mailbox that will receive reports regarding the journaling process. This mailbox receives the "journaling envelopes" with all the additional information that is wrapped within.
    - Scope—You can choose one of the following:
        - Global—All Messages
        - Internal—Internal Messages Only
        - External—Messages with an External Sender or Recipient

- Journal Messages for Recipient—Here you can select Browse and choose an individual mailbox or distribution group if you need to journal a specific person or group email. Note that if you leave this blank, it focuses on the entire organization by default.
- Enable Rule—This checkbox is selected by default but you can deselect it to enable the rule at a later time.

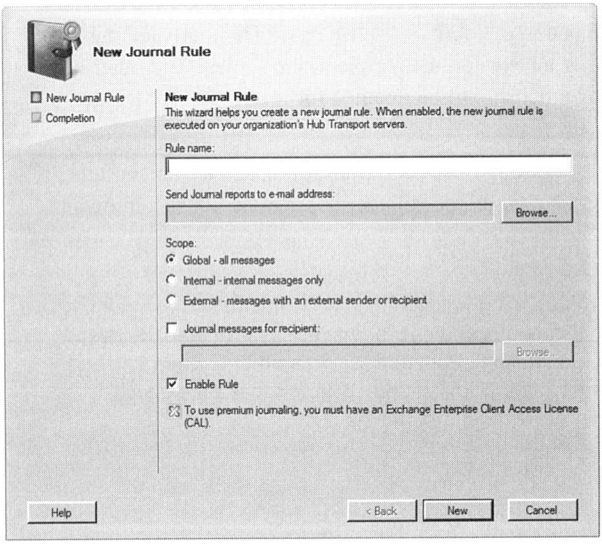

FIGURE 8.5
Creating a new Journal rule.

6. After the settings are configured, click New.
7. After the rule has been created, click Finish.

Manage Connectors (Send and Receive)

Scenario/Problem: After Exchange is installed, you still need to configure how mail will be sent and received. This is done through Send and Receive connectors that seem to be in different locations in your console. How do you configure the connectors and where do you go to do so?

Solution: Although two default Receive connectors are automatically created on each Hub Transport server when you install Exchange, the Send connectors are not. Send connectors are needed to send messages from your organization either to your Edge Transport server or directly to the Internet.

NOTE If an Edge Subscription is made with an Edge Transport server, a Send connector with an address space of "*" is configured automatically on the Hub Transport so that the Hub will send outgoing messages to the Edge Transport, which will send it to the Internet.

The Send connectors are configured at the Organization level, whereas the Receive connectors are configured on the Server level within the Navigation pane of your EMC. When you create these connectors, they are stored within the Active Directory.

Hub Transport servers can communicate between each other automatically because of implicit connectors that exist based upon the AD site topology. So, the primary focus of your Send and Receive connectors is to structure what happens when an email needs to come into your organization from an external source (either the Internet or an Edge Transport server) or when email needs to be sent out of your organization. When an email goes through a Hub Transport server and it sees that the SMTP address is not for any of the domains within the organization, it will route the message to a Send connector source server or servers (you can configure multiple source servers).

NOTE One of the interesting aspects of the default Receive connectors is that although they exist, they are not configured to allow you to receive email from anonymous users. Persons who attempt to send you email will most likely receive the message NDR with the error "530 5.7.1 Client was not authenticated." You must alter the configuration of the Receive connector to allow anonymous users.

To create a Send connector, perform the following:

1. Open the EMC.
2. From the Navigation Tree, expand the Organization Configuration work center, and click Hub Transport.
3. Select the Send Connectors tab.
4. From the Actions pane, select New Send Connector to open the wizard.
5. On the Introduction screen, you have to provide a name for the connector and choose its intended use: Custom, Internal, Internet, or Partner. In the event you are configuring a Hub Transport without an Edge Transport, you might call it Internet and choose Internet for the intended use. Then click Next.
6. On the Address Space tab, you need to configure the SMTP address space. In the event you are configuring all mail to be sent through this connector, you can use a "*". Then click Next.
7. Under Network Settings, you can use DNS MX records or smart hosts. Configure your options and choose Next.

8. On the Source Server screen, you can associate the connector with one or more Hub Transport servers or with Edge Subscriptions. When complete, click Next.
9. You are shown a Configuration Summary. When satisfied with your options, click New.
10. After the connector is created, click Finish.

After the Send connector is created, you can go into the properties of the connector and make changes to any of the settings.

To create a Receive connector, perform the following:

1. Open the EMC.
2. From the Navigation Tree, expand the Server Configuration work center and click Hub Transport.
3. Select the Receive Connectors tab.
4. From the Actions pane, select New Receive Connector to open the wizard.
5. On the Introduction screen, you have to provide a name for the connector and choose its intended use: Custom, Internal, Internet, Client, or Partner. For example, you might call it From Internet and choose Internet for the intended use. Then click Next.
6. You are now faced with Local or Remote Internet Settings. Note that depending on the type of intended purpose you selected for your connector, you might be presented with local or remote Internet settings to configure (or both). This includes configuration of IP addresses for receiving mail and the ports to look for. After configuration, choose Next.
7. Review your options on the Configuration Summary and choose New.
8. When complete, click Finish.

Having mail come into your organization through a Receive connector allows you a modicum of control over the security involved and authentication allowed for that mail. After you have the Receive connector created, you can return to the Properties of the connector and make adjustments. Two tabs available to you that were not part of the creation process are the Authentication tab and the Permission Groups tab.

Under the Authentication tab, shown in Figure 8.6, you can specify which security mechanisms are available for incoming connections, including the following:

- Transport Layer Security (TLS)
- Enable Domain Security (Mutual Auth TLS)
- Basic Authentication
- Offer Basic Authentication Only After Starting TLS
- Exchange Server Authentication
- Integrated Windows Authentication
- Externally Secured (for example, with IPsec)

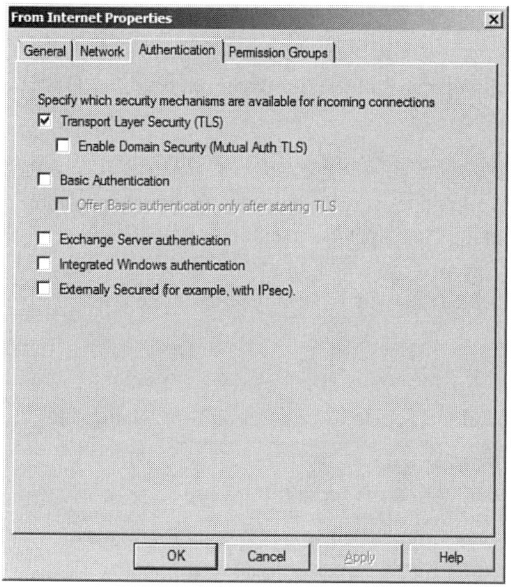

FIGURE 8.6
The Authentication tab for Receive connector properties.

Permission Groups options include the following:

- Anonymous Users
- Exchange Users
- Exchange Servers
- Legacy Exchange Servers
- Partners

Establish EdgeSync Subscriptions

Scenario/Problem: Exchange servers, from a working perspective, should not be directly connected to the Internet. There is important information involved in addition to a connection to Active Directory, which should be protected. You might protect your servers by establishing firewalls and other hardware-based solutions; however, another form of protection to consider is that of the Edge Transport server. After you have the server up and running, how do you link it to your back-end, internal Exchange organization?

Solution: EdgeSync Subscriptions allow you to connect your Edge Transport and Hub Transport servers together. To create an EdgeSync Subscription, you have to begin the process on the Edge Transport server. Perform the following:

1. Open the Exchange Management Shell (EMS).
2. Type **`New-EdgeSubscription -FireName "c:\EdgeSubscriptionInfo.xml"`** and press Enter. (Note that you can call the file whatever you like. This is just an easy-to-remember example.)
3. You will be asked to confirm the process. Type **`Y`** and press Enter.
4. Now, take the file that was created and move it (with a thumb drive or through some other valid means) over to the Hub Transport server.

On the Hub Transport server, perform the following to complete the EdgeSync Subscription process:

1. Open the EMC.
2. From the Navigation Tree, expand the Server Configuration work center and click Hub Transport.
3. Select the Edge Subscriptions tab.
4. From the Actions pane, select New Edge Subscription to open the wizard.
5. On the New Edge Subscription screen, shown in Figure 8.7, Provide the Active Directory Site toward which you want this subscription to apply. You also have to Browse to the location of the .xml file that was created from the Edge Transport server. After you have the options selected, click New.

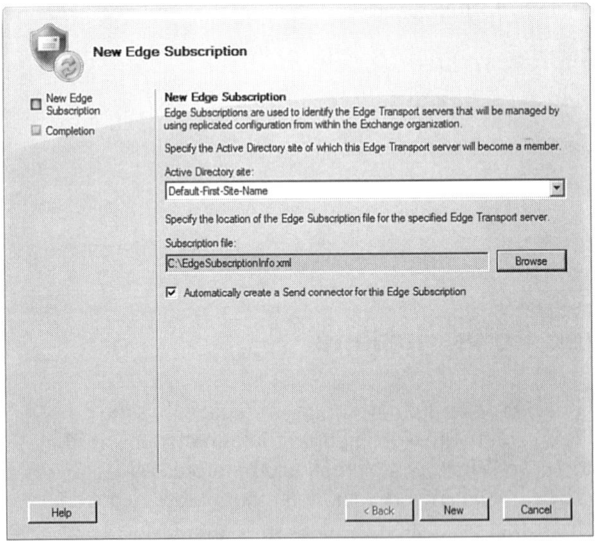

FIGURE 8.7
Establishing the Edge Subscription on the Hub Transport server.

6. After the EdgeSync Subscription is complete, click Finish.

PS NOTE You can use the `Test-EdgeSynchronization` cmdlet in the EMS to confirm that Active Directory and ADAM are synchronized, as well as to confirm the synchronization status of a single recipient.

Enable Antispam Configuration

Scenario/Problem: Both the Edge Transport and Hub Transport servers have the capability to protect your organization from spam. However, the Hub Transport server doesn't seem to have the features turned on. How do you get my antispam working on the Hub Transport Server and how do you configure the settings?

Solution: The recommendation is to work with your antispam settings on your Edge Transport server. However, in the event you do not have an Edge Transport server, you can enable these same features on your Hub Transport server. To do this, perform the following:

1. Open the EMS.
2. If you installed Exchange to the default directory, change your directory location within the shell to **`C:\program files\Microsoft\Exchange Server\Scripts`**.
3. Then type **`./install-AntiSpamAgents.ps1`**.
4. Next, restart your Transport Service.
5. Return to the EMC, and under the Organization work center and Hub Transport settings, look for the Anti-Spam tab (which didn't exist before).

To locate the tools on the Edge Transport server, open the EMC, select Edge Transport, and then look for them on the Anti-Spam tab.

The Nine Antispam Features

As you can see in Figure 8.8, you can configure nine different antispam features. Each one has its own ability to protect (some might be used more than others). This is not to say you shouldn't consider additional antispam or antivirus products. Many solutions can assist in the battle against spam.

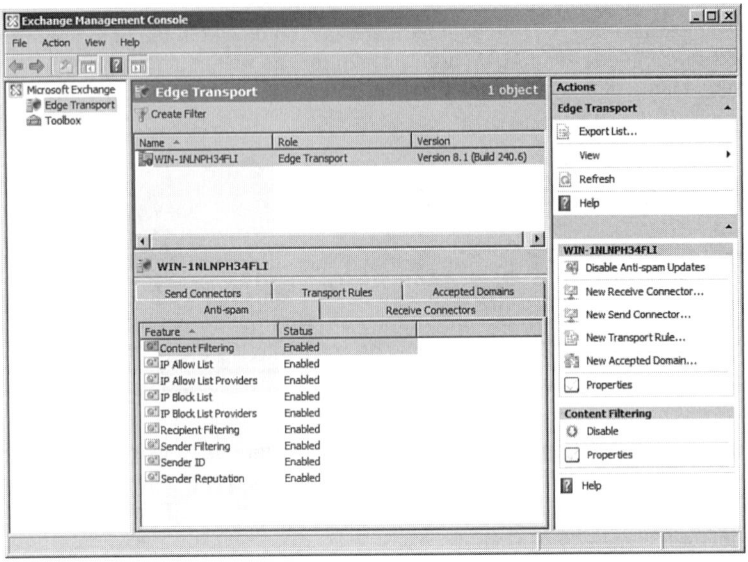

FIGURE 8.8
The nine antispam features.

To work with the antispam features, double-click any of them from within the list. The key then is to know how to configure the settings. Let's review each of the options and how they work.

- Content Filtering—Filters junk email by using a probability-based algorithm that can learn what is and what isn't spam. Use the Content Filtering feature to filter junk email based on the content of the message. You can set the filtering threshold actions, how content is analyzed, recipient exceptions, and specific words and phrases for the Content Filtering feature to act upon. You can configure custom words and exceptions. You can also determine Spam Confidence Level (SCL) rating thresholds, as shown in Figure 8.9.

NOTE Messages with an SCL of 9 are more likely to be spam, whereas those of 0 are likely not to be spam. Depending on the types of issues found with an email, the SCL rating will rise. You can configure the SCL response to delete the message if it reaches a threshold, or to quarantine it or reject the message. If you quarantine it, you have to provide a quarantine mailbox for the server to use.

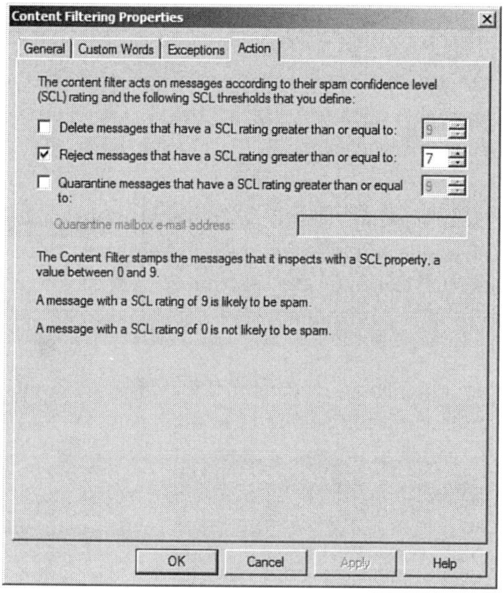

FIGURE 8.9
Spam Confidence Level (SCL) ratings.

- IP Allow List—Specifies IP addresses that you are always allowed to connect to and transmit email messages to this server. Accept connections from individual IP addresses or from ranges of IP addresses.
- IP Allow List Providers—Maintains lists of sender domains that can be relied on not to send junk email. Use this feature to determine which IP Allow List provider to use.
- IP Block List—Similar to its Allow List counterpart, you specify IP addresses that you are blocking from connecting to and transmitting email messages to and from.
- IP Block List Providers—Maintains lists of sender domains that cannot be relied on and that must be blocked from connecting to and transmitting email messages to and from. These block list providers can be invaluable in that they maintain up-to-date lists that you can connect to and utilize.
- Recipient Filtering—A simple feature where you can specify a list of email recipients from which the server will not accept messages. You can block individuals or domains. There is also a checkbox option on the Blocked Recipient tab that enables you to, with one click, block messages sent to recipients not listed in the Global Address List.

- Sender Filtering—Specifies a list of email senders that you want to block completely. You can block individuals, domains, or whole domain hierarchies. You can also specify how Exchange Transport servers respond when a blocked sender or domain transmits a message. The Sender Filter feature also lets you block messages that do not specify who sent a message. This means no messages with blank senders.
- Sender ID—Intended to combat email spoofing and to provide enhanced protection against phishing schemes. Use Sender ID to examine a senders purported responsible address (PRA). If the check fails, you can determine whether you want to reject or delete the message, or send it along with a stamped message of Sender ID results.
- Sender Reputation—Collects information about recent email messages received, and if a sender appears to be the source of junk email, the address is added to a list. There is some flexibility as to the length of time a sender can be blocked, and you can also enable/disable open proxy testing.

Antispam Updates

To update the Edge Transport servers' antispam agents, you can disable and then re-enable the updates from the Actions pane. This presents you with the Enable Anti-Spam Updates Wizard, shown in Figure 8.10.

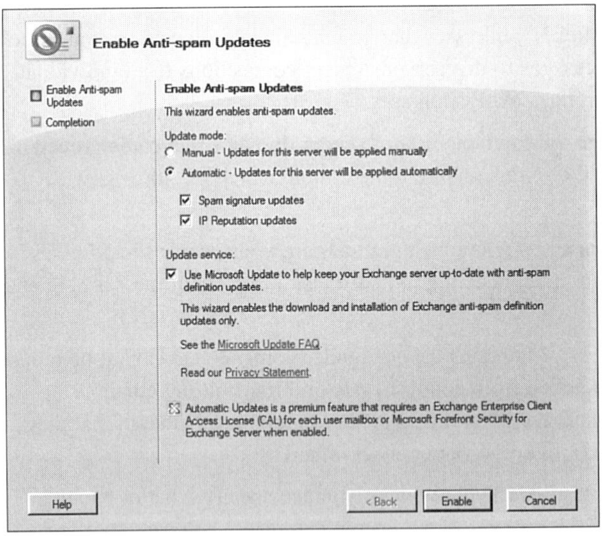

FIGURE 8.10
Antispam updates.

You can configure the updates to occur manually or automatically. You can allow/deny spam signature updates and IP reputation updates. You can also configure the update service to use the Microsoft Update process to keep definitions up to date.

CHAPTER 9

Design and Deploy Disaster Recovery Settings

IN THIS CHAPTER

- Design for Disaster
- Recover Deleted Items and Mailboxes
- Backup and Recover Data (Server 2003 and 2008)
- Implement Database Portability
- Work with Recovery Storage Groups
- Use Dial-Tone Restores
- Recover a Non-Mailbox Role

Design for Disaster

Scenario/Problem: Prior to deployment, an Exchange administrator should already have a plan to recover in the event of a disaster. What does this mean? What does Exchange 2007 offer in terms of recovery solutions?

Solution: You can hope for the best, as long as you plan for the worst. In the world of Exchange 2007, what is the worst? Certainly, in modern times we have seen situations in which an entire site (with all our servers and onsite backup data) is lost in a moment. A business can be permanently ruined by the loss of its data and equally so through the loss of its mailbox databases.

What does an Exchange administrator need to know to design a solution? To begin with, it's good to remember that five server roles (with clustered services perhaps, or high availability solutions in place) need to be prepared for in terms of restoring your environment. It's also important to consider the solutions that Exchange 2007 offers, such as dial-tone restores and recovery storage groups. You might want to keep in mind third-party solutions that can offer you features that Microsoft hasn't provided in terms of disaster recovery.

However, you cannot fight what you cannot see. You need to see the various situations that can come your way. What if someone simply deletes mail messages? This might not be a disaster but is a situation that might require you to reach for your backup tapes. What if a mailbox is deleted? What if a database or storage group is corrupted? What if the server was literally picked up and thrown out of a window? (It can happen, and you need to be prepared!) External services can fail (Active Directory [AD], Domain Name Service [DNS], and so forth).

What solutions are in place to assist you?

Disaster Recovery Solutions

Keep in mind that fault-tolerant disk solutions and high-availability solutions (which are discussed in Chapter 10, "Design and Deploy High Availability for Exchange 2007") are not what we are referring to when discussing disaster recovery.

Here are the solutions we are referring to:

- Deleted item and deleted mailbox retention
- Backup and recovery solutions
- VSS backups
- Recovery storage groups
- Database relocation solutions
- Dial-tone recovery
- Non-mailbox server restoration

Disaster Readiness

Although the majority of this book has focused on the step-by-step, "how-to" aspect of Exchange, preparing for disaster requires a brief step into the what-if world. It's true, you hope to never face a major disaster that forces you to recover your Exchange environment, and you might spend a great deal of time focusing on the common problems (failed disk, server crash, and so forth), but in the event you face fire, flood, and so on, you need to think about the following:

- Have a documented disaster recovery plan for as many different scenarios (mailbox to entire site) for all of your servers, roles, and certificates (if you are using Secure Socket Layers [SSL], which you most likely will be) you can think of. Ensure that document is in multiple locations so you can access it off-site if needed. Perhaps keep a copy with your off-site backup solution.
- Have a daily, weekly, and monthly backup plan in place. Whether you back up to tape, disk and then to tape, to a mirrored location, or to an Internet site, you must have an off-site location for your backup.
- Document the configuration of each of your servers. Ensure you have the entire structure on paper for yourself, or the next person who handles the servers. This includes information such as your mailbox policies, ActiveSync policies, UM configuration settings, and so forth. Document as much as possible.
- Restoration drills. It all comes down to if you can fix it if a disaster strikes. The only way to know is to run drills that put the planning to the test. Ensure your people know where the documentation server software, service pack software, Exchange software, hardware replacement solutions, and so on are located.

Recover Deleted Items and Mailboxes

Scenario/Problem: Users typically delete items permanently and need to have them restored. In addition, sometimes you delete a mailbox, assuming a user is not returning, and when they do you have to restore that mailbox. What is an easy solution for handling these matters?

Solution: Although not true disasters, these are items that usually come under the disaster recovery discussion because there is a point of no return where an item or a mailbox has to be restored from a backup. A backup/restore is definitely within the category of recovery.

To mitigate the amount of frustration that an administrator deals with over deleted items and deleted mailboxes, we have to configure Deleted Item Retention and Deleted Mailbox Retention, as discussed in Chapter 4, "Manage Storage and Databases." The default on items is 14 days, and on mailboxes, it is 30 days.

In the event that you do need to restore a deleted message or mailbox, how would you go about doing it?

Deleted Item Recovery

To recover a deleted item or assist a user in recovering his own deleted items, perform the following:

1. Open Outlook 2007.
2. Select the Deleted Items folder.
3. Select Tools, and then click Recover Deleted Items.
4. Locate the message you want to restore. Select the message and click Recover Selected Items.

When you restore the item, you will not see it back in your Inbox. It will restore back to your Deleted Items folder. If it is important, you might want to move it to another folder.

> **NOTE** If the message that needs to be restored has been permanently deleted beyond the 14-day mark, you have to first make a decision. Is the individual requesting the restoration worth the time and effort it might take to locate and restore the message? If she is, you might ask her directly, "Is the message you are looking for something that is irreplaceable and absolutely necessary to have restored?" If the answer is yes to both questions, consider some of the other backup restoration solutions.

Deleted Mailbox Recovery

When you delete a mailbox, you essentially disconnect it from the user's AD user account. If you delete the AD account, the mailbox is disconnected automatically from the deleted account. That disconnected mailbox is placed in the Disconnected Mailbox section under the Recipient Configuration work center. You can reconnect that mailbox (as long as you do so prior to the 30-day deleted mailbox retention time expiring).

To connect a mailbox with a new account or with an existing AD user account, perform the following:

1. Open the Exchange Management Console (EMC).
2. From the Navigation Tree, expand the Recipient Configuration work center and click Disconnected Mailbox.
3. Locate and select the mailbox you wish to connect.
4. From the Actions pane, select Connect to open the wizard.

5. Initially, you are taken to the Introduction screen, where you are asked to choose the mailbox type: User, Room, Equipment, or Linked. Make your choice and select Next.
6. Next, you are presented with the Mailbox Settings screen, shown in Figure 9.1. Here you can choose the following:
    - Matching User—Select the Browse button to locate a user object in AD that should match the mailbox.
    - Existing User—If you select this option, you can click Browse to locate a list of users that do not currently have connected mailboxes associated with them.
    - Alias—Supply an alias name.
    - Managed Folder Mailbox Policy—Select Browse to select a policy.
    - Exchange ActiveSync Mailbox Policy—Select Browse to select a policy.
7. After your options have been selected, click Next.
8. After the wizard completes, select Finish.

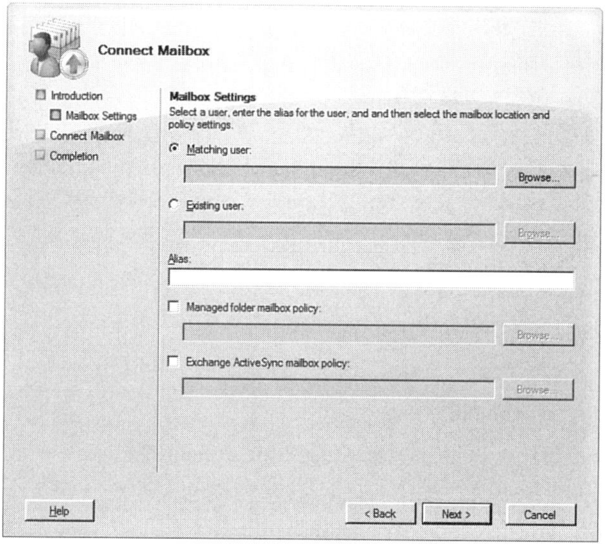

FIGURE 9.1
The Connect Mailbox Wizard's Mailbox Settings screen.

Backup and Recover Data (Server 2003 and 2008)

Scenario/Problem: Knowing you need a daily, weekly, and monthly backup of your Exchange environment should encourage you to look at third-party solutions that might provide more than the basics. However, if the basics are all you are interested in, Microsoft provides a backup solution within your Windows Server 2003 that is prepared to handle Exchange when you install Exchange 2007. Server 2008 actually doesn't provide that capability. Let's consider how to back up and restore data using the provided tools.

Solution: NTBackup is a tool that has been included with Windows Server since NT 4.0. However, this product is discontinued after Server 2003 and now with Server 2008, we have Windows Server Backup. This cannot be used to obtain backups of Exchange. Let's first look at Server 2003 and performing backups with the NTBackup utility, and then discuss options for Server 2008.

NOTE If you obtain Small Business Server 2008, which includes Exchange 2007, you actually can obtain backups of your Exchange server with the Windows Server Backup tool.

Backup and Recovery with Server 2003

NTBackup performs a streaming backup (not a Volume Shadow [VSS] backup, which we discuss shortly). It can back up only the local system that Exchange is running on (as opposed to backing up remote Exchange servers). It can back up to a network share, though. So, if you have multiple Exchange servers, you can back them up to a network share and then use software that can back up the shared location.

Using NTBackup to Back Up Your Data

To use NTBackup to back up your data on Server 2003, perform the following:

1. Select Start, Run, and type **`ntbackup.exe`**.
2. There is a Wizard Mode that you can use, but it isn't for Exchange admins. Select the Advanced Mode link.
3. You are on the Welcome tab. Select the Backup tab.
4. Click the plus sign to expand the information beneath the Microsoft Exchange Server option.
5. If you expand the settings, you see the Server, Information Store, and then the various storage groups, as you can see in Figure 9.2.

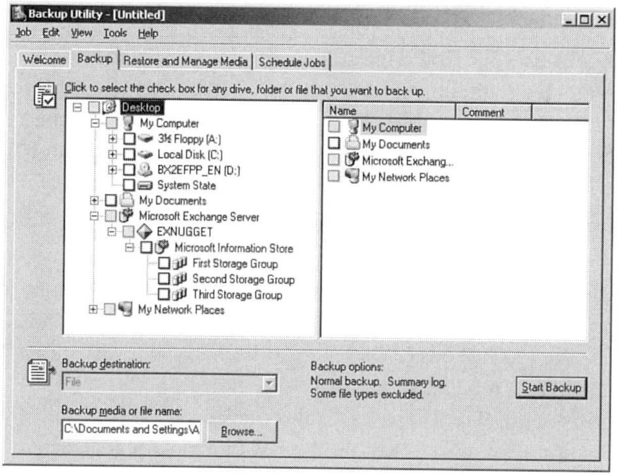

FIGURE 9.2
Working with NTBackup.

6. Select individual storage groups or all of them.
7. In the Backup media or file name, type the path.
8. Select the Tools menu option and click Options. Confirm that the backup is Normal.
9. Click Start Backup.
10. Before the job begins, you are shown the Backup Job Information. You can change the backup description, or determine how you want the backup to perform when it comes to the media already having backups. You can choose Append This Backup to the Media or Replace the Data On the Media With This Backup. You can establish a label for media that is overwritten by the backup.
11. Choose Advanced and verify the data of the backup.
12. Click Start Backup.
13. When the backup completes, you can view the detailed report or click Close.

Typical Backup Types

When performing the backup with NTBackup, we checked to see that the backup was normal. There are different backup types we might decide to use. Some backup solutions might work with a reduced backup window (where you have a short amount of time to back up the data and lots of data to back up). Other solutions might work when you have a need to restore quickly.

Backup types include the following:

- Full—A full backup backs up your Exchange storage groups and databases and all transaction logs associated with the databases. It then purges the transaction logs from the database. If possible, you should always run full backups because they provide the fastest restore from a failure. If you perform full backups and the server needs to be restored, simply restore the latest full backup. For many, this isn't a possibility and so it is recommended that you at least perform one full backup a week.
- Incremental—These back up the changes that are made to a database and back up the transaction logs and purges them. The incremental backup backs up only the changes made since the last full or last incremental backup. So, every day the incremental backup takes a relatively short period of time to perform and remains somewhat consistent in that. However, as the week progresses, if the server requires a restoration, you need to restore the last full backup and each incremental backup since that time. So, it is a shorter backup process but a longer restoration.
- Differential—These back up the changes made to the database since the last full backup. The transaction logs are not purged using this type of backup, and throughout the week, the backup takes a little longer each day. However, in the event of a restoration, you need only to restore the last full backup and the last differential backup. So, you have a shorter restoration period if you use differential backups.

How do you structure your backup schedule? That depends upon many things, and you have to consider your own environment. Can you perform nightly full backups? Or do you perform a full backup on Sunday night and incremental or differential backups throughout the week?

When do you perform your backups? Have you considered alternative solutions to your backup media type? Are you using tape? Would it be faster if you backed up to disk and then performed a backup of your backup (which you can perform any time because users are not directly accessing it) to tape that you can take off-site?

Have you considered a third-party solution that uses improved methods over NTBackup, such as VSS (which we discuss later in this chapter)?

Using NTBackup to Restore Your Data

You might need to use that backup to restore a database. There are times when the entire server might have crashed or the disk itself has crashed, or perhaps you have simply had a corruption of the database. In the latter, the simplest of scenarios, your Exchange server is still up and running and the disks seem to be functioning, but you need to restore the database. To restore a database from your backup, perform the following:

1. Open the EMC.
2. From the Navigation Tree, expand the Server Configuration work center and click Mailbox.

3. Select Mailbox Server from the Results pane.
4. Select the storage group with the database you want to restore.
5. Select the database, and from the Actions pane, click Properties.
6. From the General tab, select the option This Database Can Be Overwritten by a Restore. Click OK.
7. From the EMC, select Dismount Database from the Actions pane for that database.
8. Although the database is dismounted, open your NTBackup application (Start, Run, NTBackup.exe).
9. Select the Restore and Manage Media tab.
10. Locate the storage group with the database you want to restore, as you can see in Figure 9.3.

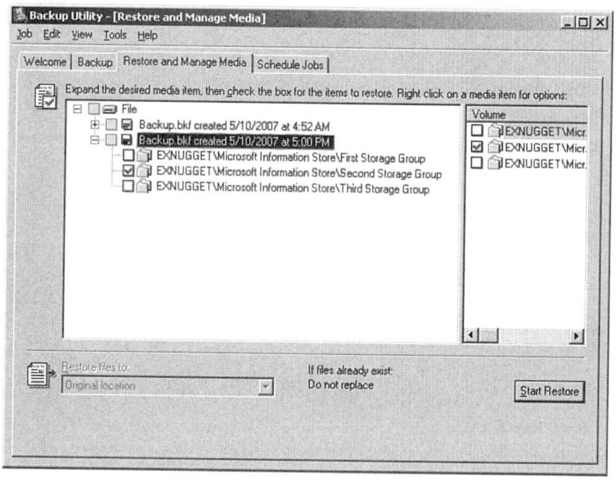

FIGURE 9.3
Performing the restoration process.

11. Click Start Restore.
12. You are presented with the Restoring Database Store dialog. You can restore to another server, but in this case, you are restoring to the same server, so you can leave the server you have or click Browse to locate the other server.
13. You can provide a temporary location for log and patch files.
14. To get your database up and running quickly, select the Last Restore Set (Log File Replay Will Start After This Restore Completes) and then also check Mount Database After Restore, which will become available after you click the former.
15. When you are ready, click OK.
16. You can watch the restore progress, and when complete, you can view the detailed report or click Close.

The Server 2003 backup application works for these local streaming online backups. However, they don't provide VSS copies and they aren't included in Server 2008

Backup and Recovery with Server 2008

Logically, if Server 2008 doesn't support a streaming online backup of Exchange databases, you have to pursue a third-party solution. The support is still in place internally for streaming backups (although remote streaming backup support has been removed on Server 2008). What you are looking for in a backup solution is one that supports both streaming and VSS solutions.

You might look into a third-party solution that can perform the streaming backup (or VSS backup), but remember that you cannot make a remote streaming backup regardless of the solution you employ because a remote backup with Exchange 2007 SP1 and Server 2008 is not supported.

Microsoft offers a solution called Microsoft System Center Data Protection Manager (DPM) 2007, shown in Figure 9.4. The Microsoft System Center product line is designed to assist administrators with managing their server infrastructures. Data protection is a key aspect of administrative management and so the DPM is designed to assist with Exchange, SQL, SharePoint Services, and even file shares from 2003/2008 Windows servers.

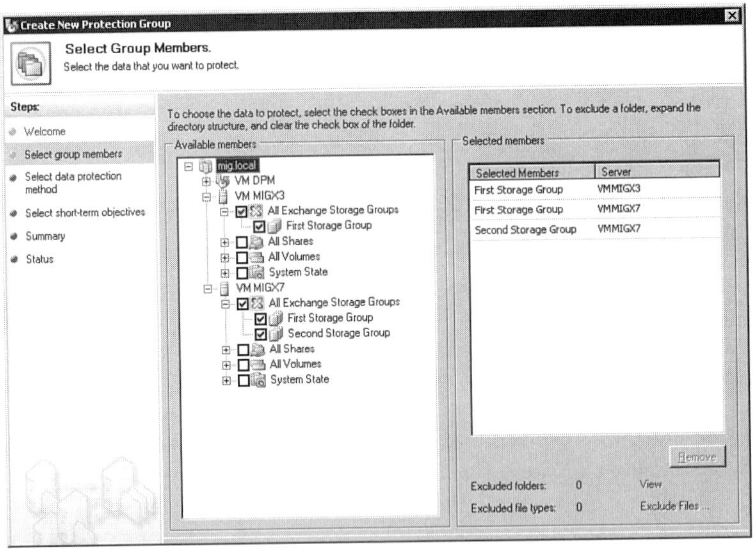

FIGURE 9.4
Using DPM to perform an Exchange 2007 backup.

> **NOTE** Both Server 2003 and 2008 have VSS capabilities. With Server 2003, the NTBackup program cannot perform VSS backups, so you require a third-party solution to take advantage of this solution. Server 2008 Windows Server Backup does include this feature; however, as already mentioned, not for Exchange. In both cases, you can install Data Protection Manager. This provides VSS support for your Server 2003 system and provides VSS and standard backup support for both Server 2003 and Server 2008.

We can say much regarding the capabilities of DPM. A few items that stand out are that it has the capability to perform more than a storage group or database backup and restoration. You can also restore an individual mailbox or Public Folder, which is a time saver and eliminates an administrative headache. Keep in mind though that third-party solutions offer that capability too, and DPM, although not a third-party solution, is still an external solution. It's a solution that doesn't come with the operating system, costs you money, and requires time to learn, similar to a third-party backup solution. It simply comes from Microsoft and that might appeal to you in that it should function well with other Microsoft products, in this case Exchange 2007 with all of its features.

One of the features supported by DPM is the high availability options and creating copies of your data from the passive nodes of your clusters. You have the capability to go from disk to disk and then to tape for your offline solution.

Finally, DPM uses VSS shadow copies (a feature not supported by NTBackup) to create quick block-level difference backups.

What are Volume Shadow Copies?

Volume Snapshot Service, or Volume Shadow Copies (typically expressed as VSS) is a feature that we might be more familiar with functionally than technologically. The reason we say this is because it isn't a new concept; in fact, we have had aspects of VSS in our Windows operating system since Windows XP SP1. Server 2003, 2008, and Vista all have aspects of VSS implemented. If you have used the System Restore or Previous Versions features, you have used a form of VSS.

However, the question is: What is VSS?

Simply put, your system takes a point-in-time snapshot of your data. It first looks at what you have from the first snapshot and then, rather than performing complete backups going forward, looks for changes to data and only backs up the changes.

Here is the overall process of an Exchange backup using VSS:

1. The VSS requester (your backup software, which is going to have to be a third-party solution for Exchange with either Server 2003 or 2008) is told to begin the VSS backup or create the shadow copy.
2. The VSS writer (the Exchange database information store) freezes the databases to ensure you have no new writes to the databases. Note that for this reason, with continuous replication solutions and clusters, it is recommended you use the passive copy of the database because you have less of a chance that the procedure will fail due to writes coming in.

3. The VSS provider (the hardware and software that create the snapshot) creates the snapshot.
4. The VSS writer is told when the copy is complete and will allow writes to the database again.
5. The VSS requester (your backup software) lets you know the copy was complete.

There are varieties of ways the technology is advancing on all fronts (software and hardware) to improve the way these copies work. However, overall they are faster and take up less disk space then a traditional backup would.

Implement Database Portability

Scenario/Problem: If you need to restore a database, can you restore it to another server? What is database portability and how can you use it? Do you have to use a backup/recovery solution?

Solution: You can restore any mailbox database to any server within the same organization. This is a new aspect to database recovery, which only allowed a database to be restored to a recovery storage group or a server with the same name as the original server or from another server within the same administrative group.

How does it work? You might have a situation where a database is up and running just fine on a server and you simply want to move the database, or you need to perform an upgrade maintenance on the server and decide to move the database to another server. This can be handled without using backup/recovery software.

If you have a system crash and you don't want to wait until the server is up and running again to restore your backup of the database, you can restore it to another server in your organization. In that case, you need backup/recovery software.

Let's review both.

Relocate a Database

To relocate a database, we dismount the database we want to move and then, on the relocation server, we configure the storage group and database for the move.

NOTE Before you begin this procedure you will want to make sure your database is in a Clean Shutdown state. You can type **ESEUTIL /R <Enn>** to commit uncommitted log files and ensure a clean starting point. Note: **Enn** is the log prefix for the storage group you are performing the clean shutdown on. If you are unsure what that is, you can type **Get-StorageGroup ServerName\StorageGroupName ¦ fl LogFilePrefix** in the EMS.

To relocate a database, perform the following steps:

1. Open the EMC.
2. From the Navigation Tree, expand the Server Configuration work center and click Mailbox.
3. Locate the server from the Results pane and select it.
4. From the Work pane, select the Storage Group and the Database you want to move.
5. From the Actions pane, select Dismount Database.

PS NOTE A much easier and faster way to dismount a database is with the EMS by typing **dismount-database "ServerName\StorageGroupName\DatabaseName"**.

6. Now, select the server where you want to move the database.
7. Create a new storage group that has the same name as the source storage group.
8. Create a new database with the same name as the source database. (Note: Do not mount the database.)
9. Select the new database and then Properties from the Actions pane.
10. On the General tab, select the option This Database Can Be Overwritten by a Restore.
11. Move over all the database files (.edb, log, and catalog files) to the new database folder location.
12. Now you can mount the database through the EMC. Although through the EMS, you simply type **mount-database DatabaseName**.
13. You need to modify the mailbox configuration to know that the accounts point to a new server. To move these in the EMS, type the following:

```
Get-Mailbox -Database <SourceDatabase> ¦where {$_.ObjectClass
-NotMatch
 '(SystemAttendantMailbox¦ExOleDbSystemMailbox)'}¦ Move-Mailbox
-ConfigurationOnly -
TargetDatabase <TargetDatabase>
```

Modifying the user account settings through the `Move-Mailbox` cmdlet should work for your Outlook 2007 and OWA clients, who will be redirected through the Autodiscover service.

Restore a Database to a New Server

Keep in mind that this requires backup/recovery software (either NTBackup in Server 2003 or some other third-party solution, or a third-party solution in Server 2008).

If you need to perform a restoration from backup to a new server, perform the following:

1. Open the EMC.
2. From the Navigation Tree, expand the Server Configuration work center and click Mailbox.
3. Select the server where you want to restore the database to from the Results pane.
4. From the Work pane, create a new storage group with the same name as the source (original) storage group.
5. Next, create a new database with the same name as the source (original) database. Do not mount the new database.
6. Select the new database and from the Actions pane, select Properties.
7. On the General tab, select the option This Database Can Be Overwritten by a Restore.
8. At this point, on the physical server where you are attempting to restore the database, click Start, Run, and then type **ntbackup.exe**.
9. Choose Advanced Mode.
10. Select the Restore and Manage Media tab.
11. Select the Storage Group or database you want to restore.
12. Click Start Restore.
13. The Restoring Database Store dialog displays, as shown in Figure 9.5.

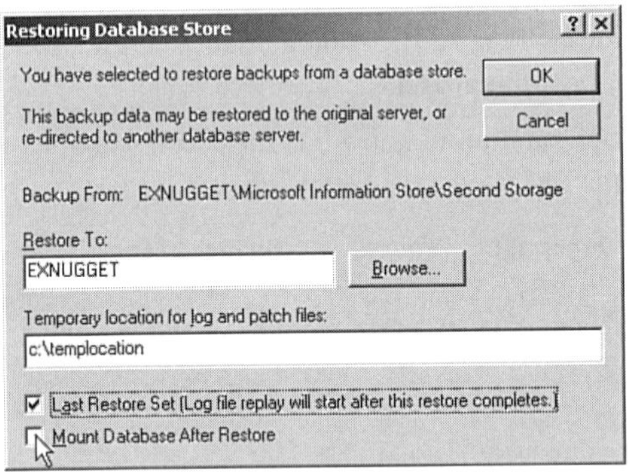

FIGURE 9.5
Restoring a database to a different server.

14. Make sure the Restore To field has the target server's name. If it doesn't, you can type it or click Browse to locate the server.
15. Type a path for the temporary location for log and patch files.

16. Select the checkbox Last Restore Set (Log File Replay Will Start After This Restore Completes). You can also select the Mount Database After Restore checkbox if you like, or you can mount afterward.
17. Select OK.

Work with Recovery Storage Groups

Scenario/Problem: If you need to restore items such as a database or mailbox, is it possible to restore directly to the same server and just move things over?

Solution: This scenario is describing the use of a Recovery Storage Group (RSG), which has been available since Exchange 2003. You can use an existing server and create a recovery storage group, to which you can then restore your databases. The backup application is not aware of the difference and so it performs the restoration without issue.

You can use an RSG in different ways. You can use it as a same server dial-tone recovery or alternate server dial-tone recovery (which we discuss in the next section). You can also use it to recover a mailbox that cannot be brought back from the deleted mailbox retention time. You can recover specific information and messages if need be (although a third-party solution might perform these features better).

Keep in mind that RSGs are not your best solution if you are trying to recover Public Folders (because they aren't supported; only mailbox databases are) or if you need to restore an entire server.

To create an RSG, perform the following steps:

1. Open the EMC.
2. From the Navigation Tree, expand the Toolbox work center.
3. From the options, open the Database Recovery Management tool.
4. Select the Go to Welcome Screen link.
5. The tool checks for updates for the Microsoft Exchange Troubleshooting Assistant. You can cancel the check by clicking the Cancel link.
6. You are asked for some information regarding the Exchange server name and domain controller name. Click Next.
7. The Troubleshooting Assistant provides a long list of options, as you can see in Figure 9.6. Locate the option under Manage Recovery Storage Group to create a recovery storage group.

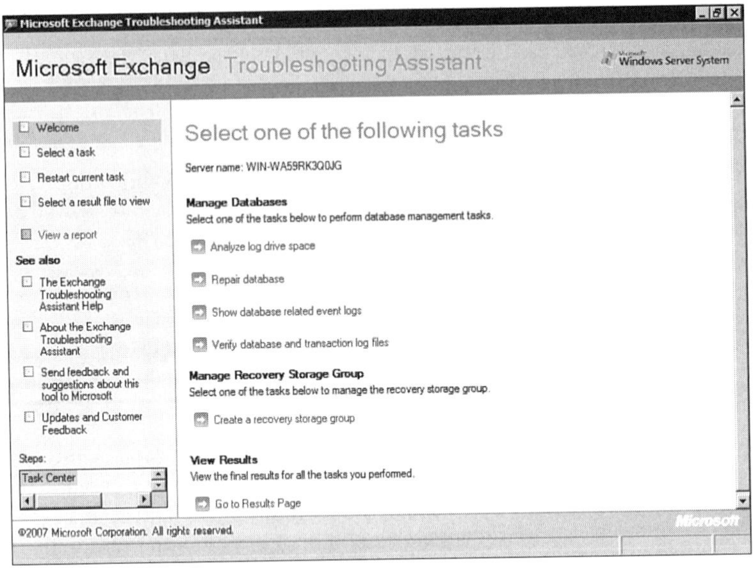

FIGURE 9.6
Creating a recovery storage group.

8. When asked to select the storage group to link with the RSG, locate the storage group and click Next.
9. On the Create the Recovery Storage Group screen, perform the following:
   - Provide a name for the RSG.
   - Confirm the location of the original Transaction log folder and the Recovery log path.
   - Confirm the location of the original System folder and checkpoint file folder and the Recovery path.
   - Confirm the location of the original Database folders and the file names and the Recovery database path.
10. Then select Create the Recovery Storage Group.
11. You receive a message indicating the success or failure of the creation of the RSG, and you can confirm that the new folders and files exist.

> PS **NOTE** You can verify the creation of the RSG through the EMS by typing **`Get-MailboxDatabase`**.

After you have the RSG in place, perform a restoration of the data you have backed up for that storage group the same way you usually would. You can choose to mount the restored database during the restoration process. However, if you do not, you will need to go back to the task center and select the Mount or Dismount databases in the RSG and mount the recovery group database. After it is restored and mounted, return to the Database Recovery Management Tool; however, this time perform the following:

1. Select Merge or Copy Mailbox Contents.
2. From the Select a Mounted Database in the Recovery Storage Group screen, select the Gather Merge Information link.
3. From the Select Merge Options screen, you can move forward with restoring the whole mailbox by selecting Perform Pre-merge Tasks. However, if you want to filter items that you want to restore (for example, a specific range of dates or a specific subject), you can select Show Advanced Options, shown in Figure 9.7.

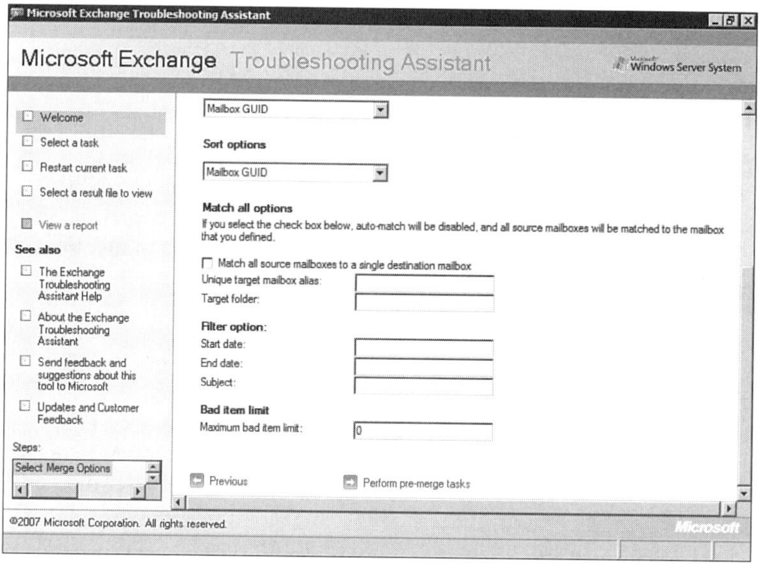

FIGURE 9.7
Advanced options for the restoration process.

4. After you select your options, choose Perform Pre-merge Tasks.
5. You are shown the results of your request.
6. You see mailboxes you can select if you want to merge or copy data. Select Perform Merge Actions.
7. Confirm the results, and click Go Back to Task Center.
8. Dismount the databases in the RSG and remove the RSG.

The reason you delete the RSG is because you can have only one at a time. You might want to clear the RSG now in preparation for a future time. After deleting it, however, you want to make sure you clean up the recovery files from their locations manually.

To remove the RSG, perform the following:

1. From the Database Recovery Management task center, select Mount or Dismount Database in the Recovery Storage Group.
2. Select the database you want to dismount. Click Dismount Selected Database.
3. After you dismount, you will receive the report that it was dismounted.
4. Select Go Back to Task Center.
5. Now select Remove the Recovery Storage Group.
6. Confirm the database name. Then select the Remove the Recovery Storage Group link.
7. You should receive a message saying the RSG has been removed successfully.

Use Dial-Tone Restores

Scenario/Problem: If your server goes down and you need to restore email functionality without the concern of previous mailbox data, is there some way to restore email to your users without worrying about the mailbox data until a later time? How would that be performed?

Solution: Because the mailbox itself is part of Active Directory and the actual mailbox data is within the Exchange databases, it is possible to restore an Exchange server quickly to the point of users having the capability to send and receive email again. This provides time for the actual database restoration to occur. This is called a dial-tone restore (also called the recover now, restore later method).

Some of the stress of this method comes from merging the two sets of data (the old recovered data with the new email sent back and forth in the dial-tone recovery database).

Keep in mind that there are several reasons to perform a dial-tone restore. One is that you have a failed server, and you need to use an alternate server for the restoration of email services. Another is that you simply have a failed or corrupt database that is just going to take too long to restore and your users need email now (so you might use the same server). You have to make some decisions regarding leaving the data on the recovery server or moving it back when the crisis is under control.

Perform a Dial-Tone Recovery on the Same Server

To mimic the failed database, you can dismount the database and locate the database file and delete it (or move it to another location). In Step 2, you create a new database, which does not require mailbox movements because this is the same server and storage group you are recreating. This gives you the time to recover the data to the RSG while your users have up-and-running mailboxes.

To achieve dial-tone recovery, perform the following:

1. If you have any log files from the failed database, you might want to move them to another location. They might be useful.
2. Open the EMC.
3. Attempt to mount the database and you receive the message shown in Figure 9.8 regarding the creation of an empty database. Click Yes to continue.

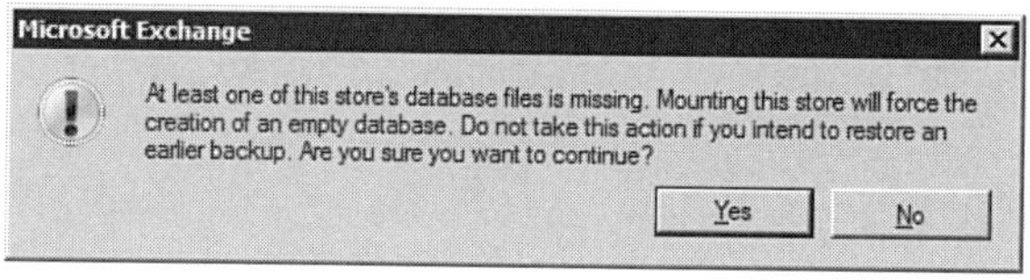

FIGURE 9.8
Warning message of an empty database.

4. From the Navigation Tree, expand the Toolbox work center.
5. From the options, open the Database Recovery Management tool.
6. Create a recovery group for the failed database.
7. Restore the backup you have of the failed database, but do not mount the database if you have any log files from the failed database. Place those in the proper location before mounting.
8. Mount the database from the task center.
9. From the task center, select the Swap Databases for Dial-Tone scenario.
10. Make sure the database is correct.
11. Select Gather Swap Information.
12. Select Perform Swap Action after confirming the information is accurate.
13. After the procedure is complete, the configurations for the original and recovery databases are swapped and remounted.

Swapping databases provides users the original mailboxes they had, but moves over the dial-tone database. The two should be merged to ensure no data is lost.

To do this, go back to the task center and use the Merge or Copy Mailbox Contents settings (just as you would with a normal recovery group) and merge that content over to the recovered and swapped database.

When you are done, remove the RSG.

Perform a Dial-Tone Recovery on a Different Server

The steps for a "new server" dial-tone recovery are almost identical to that of a "same server" dial-tone recovery. Here are some changes and additions:

- You have to create a new storage group and database with the names of the original on the new server.
- You need to use the `Move-Mailbox -ConfigurationOnly` command to point the user's mailboxes to the new database. In doing this, you are moving the configuration information, but the data will be restored with the restoration process. The official command is:

```
Get-Mailbox -Database <Mailbox Server Name\Storage Group
Name\database name> ¦
➥ Move-Mailbox -ConfigurationOnly -TargetDatabase <Mailbox Server
Name\Storage group
Name\Dial Tone database
name>
```

- If you plan to restore your backup to the new server, the steps are the same as previously explained. If you plan to restore your backup to the failed server, you need to use the same EMS command to move the mailboxes back when you are done.

NOTE Users might be somewhat surprised when they have no email. However, they might be even more surprised if they have email but no access to all their messages. You will want to alert them with a message about what is happening. Some people receive a message that gives them the capability to see their old data if they have Outlook 2007 in cached mode. However, if they choose to use old data, they cannot send and receive. They will be presented with the option to use a temporary mailbox, and this is the option they need to select to send and receive messages.

Recover a Non-Mailbox Role

Scenario/Problem: There are other server types to be concerned about, such as the Client Access server, the Hub and Edge Transport servers, and the Unified Messaging servers. How do we prepare for a disaster involving these important servers?

Solution: A variety of ways to restore servers exist; however, Exchange makes the procedure much easier with many of the server roles because the primary configuration data is stored in AD.

So, imagine a server has crashed with one of the four roles internal to your network (MB, CAS, HT, or UM). You can restore the roles themselves (let's not worry about MB at this point; we've covered quite a bit already regarding the restoration of the databases) by running the `setup /m:RecoverServer` command.

Perhaps you've purchased a whole new server and want that server role back up and running, or let's say you have another server that is running a different role and you want to put the role back on that server. You can do this thanks to the AD connection.

To start with, you need to reset the computer account within AD. Then the new server can join up without a conflict with the older configuration data. To do this, perform the following:

1. Select Start, Administrative Tools, and then Active Directory Users and Computers.
2. Locate the computer object for the failed server.
3. Right-click the server and choose Reset Account.

With the new server, you need to configure the same number of disk drives as the original and assign the disks with the same drive letters. After you have everything in place, install Windows Server and make sure the name is the same as the failed server and join the domain.

When you go to install Exchange, type **`setup.com /m:recoverserver`**, which will ask AD to restore the roles and settings that are stored to this server.

Keep in mind that customized settings and files on the server (depending on the type of server it was, such as UM, CAS, and so on) might require manual restoration.

Server Restore Points to Remember

Each server role still has pieces you might want to be aware of and ensure the recovery of in the event of a problem. For example:

- Client Access Server—Has IIS services running that require you to back up and restore the IIS metabase data. Microsoft offers direction to back up the data and a script to restore it at: http://technet.microsoft.com/en-us/library/bb124359(EXCHG.80).aspx.
- Unified Messaging—Some of the audio recordings that are associated with the UM server may be located in AD (such as the recorded name). If the UM server was the prompt publishing point for a dial plan, those files might be missing. If it wasn't the publishing point, those files might be intact.
- Hub Transport Server—You might want to alter the procedure with these. Instead type **`setup.com /m:RecoverServer /DoNotStartTransport`**. The reasoning is that you do not want to have the server come to life and begin sending messages here and there. Ensure the configuration is correct before you start up the transport service.

Edge Transport Recovery

The data is not held in AD logically, so these require a bit of manual intervention to recover. You need to export the configuration of the server. Microsoft provides a script to do this.

To use the script, perform the following:

1. On the Edge Transport server, open the EMS.
2. Navigate to the scripts folder, which is usually located where you installed Exchange. The standard location you are looking for is C:\Program Files\Microsoft\Exchange Server\Scripts.
3. Type **`./ExportEdgeConfig.ps1 -cloneConfigData: "DriveLetter:\EdgeBackupFile.xml"`** and then press Enter.
4. After you see the confirmation message, you can locate and move that file to another server for backup.
5. If you need to restore an Edge Transport server that has crashed—whether with a new server or new disk—install Server and all the service packs and hotfixes.
6. Install Exchange normally as an Edge Transport server. Use the same server name.
7. Run the ImportEdgeConfig.ps1 script. This creates an answer file based upon the .xml file you created earlier. You might need to edit the answer file to ensure you have the proper data, log paths, Send connector information, and so forth.
8. Run the ImportEdgeConfig.ps1 script again, but this time it will restore the server using the answer file you adjusted and bring your server back to its original configuration.
9. After you finish, run the EdgeSync process between a Hub Transport server and your newly restored Edge Transport server to restore communications between the two.

CHAPTER 10

Design and Deploy High Availability for Exchange 2007

IN THIS CHAPTER

- Choose a High Availability Solution
- Enable Local Continuous Replication
- Configure Cluster Continuous Replication
- Implement Standby Continuous Replication
- Utilize Single Copy Clusters
- Design CAS High Availability
- Design Hub Transport High Availability
- Design Edge Transport and Unified Messaging High Availability

Choose a High Availability Solution

Scenario/Problem: Exchange 2007 RTM offered three solutions for high availability. Exchange 2007 SP1 offers four solutions. First off, what is high availability? Second, how do the solutions within Exchange differ and which one should you choose?

Solution: The concept of high availability is nothing new. For many years, network administrators, realizing the possibility that a system can fail on any number of levels, have attempted to mitigate that failure by providing redundancy of system features (such as multiple disks, power supplies, and so on) and, in the most extreme of cases, disaster recovery methods. The goal is to make your systems fault tolerant, and failing in that, to make your systems quickly recoverable in a disaster-like circumstance.

High availability comes into play as a term in the Exchange world in absolute measurements of uptime that you strive for or offer to others when implementing a strategy. Uptime is more than the time the system is literally running; it implies access by a user. If a user cannot access the system (in this case, send or retrieve email), it doesn't matter if it is running. It is not available.

Although there are third-party solutions by a variety of vendors that are worth investigating, Microsoft offers four different solutions: Local Continuous Replication (LCR), Cluster Continuous Replication (CCR), Standby Continuous Replication (SCR) and Single Copy Clusters (SCC). Different techniques are used; for example, clustering might be required. Notice, however, that in three of the solutions, the term *continuous replication* is used. This involves the use of a technology that is called log shipping and replay. This section explains how that works.

Recall from Chapter 1. "Introduction to Exchange 2007 SP1," that we reviewed storage architecture and the use of storage groups, databases, and transaction logs. With continuous replication, your database is copied once. Then all log files that are created are shipped to the secondary copy and replayed into the duplicate database. In the event of a failure (be it disk or system, depending on the form of continuous replication high availability you've chosen), the secondary copy is ready to step in and take over.

Each flavor of high availability is a little different. Let's look at each one.

NOTE You might recall with Exchange 2003 that the transaction logs were 5MB in size, but they have been reduced to 1MB. One of the reasons for this change is that smaller logs can be transported faster and leave less data lost if there is a problem before a log can be shipped over and replayed.

Local Continuous Replication

Often called the poor man's cluster, LCR enables you to simply place another disk in a server and have the data mirror over using continuous replication (with transaction log shipping and the replay technology we discussed earlier), as shown in Figure 10.1.

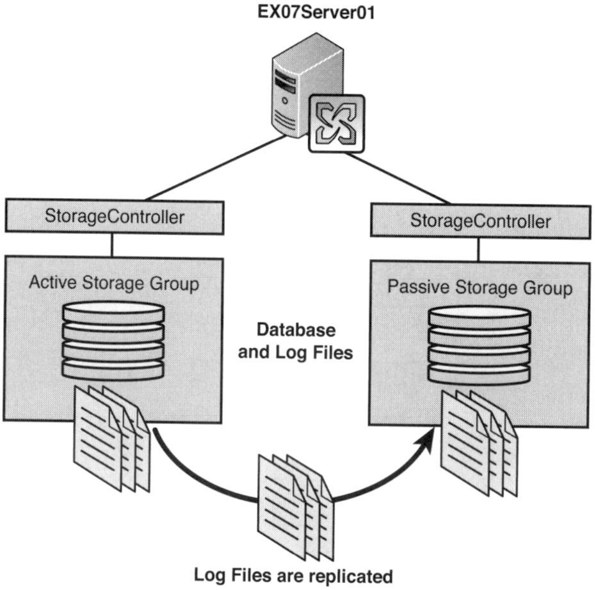

FIGURE 10.1
Local Continuous Replication in theory.

The positive side is that this is the cheapest solution you can implement, requiring only an additional drive (or drives), and you can perform volume shadow copies off the passive side of the data if you like. With SP1 there is also a transport dumpster solution on the HT server that allows you to recover mail that might otherwise be considered lost when the disk fails.

The negative side is that you aren't running cluster services, which means you have to manually switch from one disk to the other if a failure occurs. The time between when the first disk fails over to when you manually switch to the second disk is unavailable time for the server. The other negative is that there are issues that can take place with the system itself (such as power supply, motherboard, and network connection) that can hinder the availability of an LCR solution.

Cluster Continuous Replication

CCR works with the same technology in that it copies the transaction logs and replays them, but it uses cluster services from within your servers to provide an automatic failover solution. This provides more than automation; it also allows for a server and disk redundancy (whereas you saw that LCR only provides disk redundancy) as you can see in Figure 10.2. You also have the same ability to perform a volume shadow copy off the passive copy of the data.

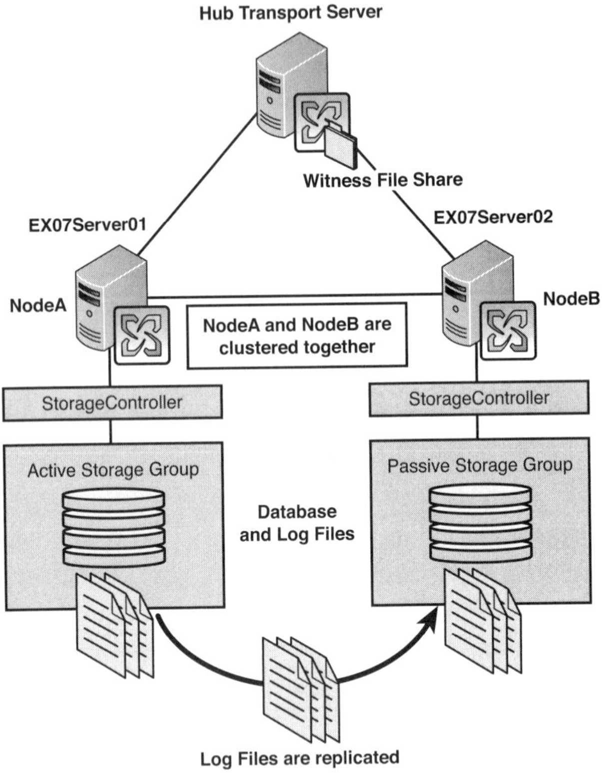

FIGURE 10.2
Cluster Continuous Replication in theory.

In addition, there are features in place to ensure that even data that might not be synchronized between the active and passive sides to the cluster can be retrieved from the Hub Transport servers transport dumpster, which retains email passing through the server for a period of time.

On the negative side, implementing CCR requires a knowledge of clustering services as well as the additional hardware and software necessary to implement it properly.

NOTE You need the Enterprise edition of Windows Server to use cluster services.

Standby Continuous Replication

SCR is a solution that was introduced with SP1, so it brings a fresh look at continuous replication, where the concept is the same as LCR, log shipping, and replay. However, rather than going from disk to disk, it is from server to server. This doesn't require cluster services, but it does provide the server and disk redundancy that you get from CCR, as you can see in Figure 10.3.

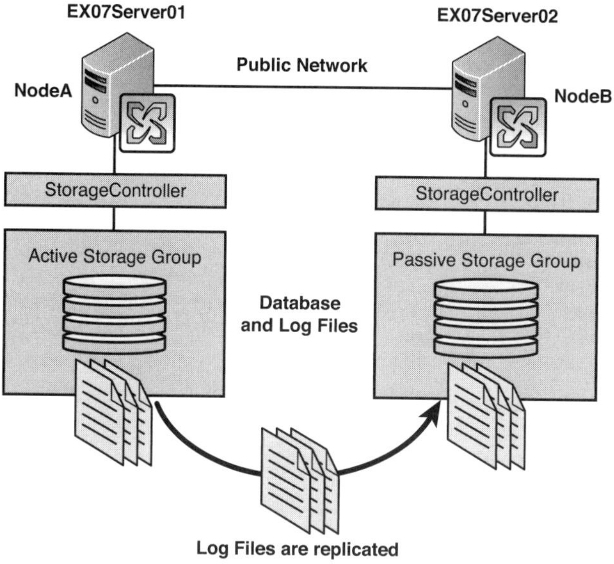

FIGURE 10.3
Standby Continuous Replication in theory.

Where the technology can become a bit intriguing is if used in conjunction with other solutions. For example, you can use SCR to replicate a storage group from a CCR or SCC cluster over to a remote location if you like. Another positive feature is the built-in delay for replay activity (which is wonderful if you want to prepare your organization for database corruption scenarios where the delay could prevent the corruption from making its way to the SCR copy).

From a negative angle, you need additional hardware with software costs and you can manage SCR only from the Exchange Management Shell (EMS). The lack of cluster services means the automation process is out of the picture, so you have to manually failover from the active to the passive database, which explains why you might use SCR in conjunction with another form of cluster high availability for that automatic rollover in case of failure.

Single Copy Clusters

For those who remember the Exchange 2003 high availability options with shared storage, you will see that this is familiar. With SCC, you cluster two servers together where they have the same shared storage between them, as you can see in Figure 10.4. The positive side here is that you have automatic failover in the event of a server failure. The negative side is that the data has no high availability solution in place for your SAN (although, most likely your SAN is already prepared with some form of RAID solution in place).

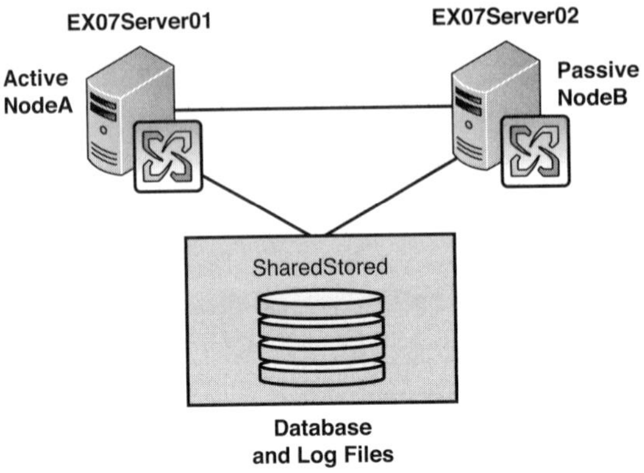

FIGURE 10.4
Single Copy Clusters in theory.

Choose a High Availability Option

The choices depend on a few simple factors. One is the size of your organization. If you have a small environment with a single Exchange server, it would hardly seem necessary for you to purchase a secondary server, upgrade everything to Enterprise Edition Windows Server software, cluster the two systems, and work out a CCR implementation. You might do well with LCR or perhaps, depending on your environment, with SCR.

- If you have a remnant from the SAN/NAS days of shared storage that you want to keep using, you might consider SCC.
- If you have a need to ensure automatic failover and you do not have shared storage, CCR is a logical solution for you.
- If you need to provide multiple levels of redundancy, you might consider a CCR deployment with a SCR failover from one CCR cluster to another.

Cost, need, organizational size, and level of complexity are all factors to consider. However, the percentage of availability you wish to provide also comes into play. If you are working with a small business, there are times when the server doesn't have to be online. For example, maybe everyone leaves for the weekend and you can perform maintenance during those periods. However, if you are setting up a hosted Exchange environment for a huge datacenter, not only is 100% availability a must, but you might decide to look into a third-party solution to help provide it for you.

In the meantime, let's take a step back and begin working on how you would set up each of these solutions.

Enable Local Continuous Replication

Scenario/Problem: You have decided to take your Exchange server and enable LCR on one of your storage groups. What do you need to do next?

Solution: Remember, to implement LCR you can only have one database per storage group. You want to make sure you certainly have sufficient disk space for your LCR copy. You can implement LCR in one of two ways—either during the creation of the storage group or afterward.

Enable LCR on an Existing Storage Group

If the storage group already exists, perform the following steps:

1. Open the Exchange Management Console (EMC).
2. From the Navigation Tree, expand the Server Configuration work center and click Mailbox.
3. From the Results pane, choose the server that has the storage group on which you want to enable LCR.
4. Select the storage group on which you want to enable LCR. (Note: If you select a storage group with more than one database, you will not even see the option to enable LCR.)
5. From the Actions pane, select Enable Local Continuous Replication to open the wizard.
6. On the Introduction screen, confirm the storage group name and database name, and click Next.
7. On the Set Paths screen, you are shown the default paths, but these are generally to a local disk. You might allow this for testing purposes, but it defeats the purpose of LCR. You want to relocate those to a separate disk. Click the Browse buttons to relocate those paths to a new disk. Then click Next.
8. You are shown the passive location of the database file (shown in Figure 10.5). Click Browse to alter this location as well. Then click Next.

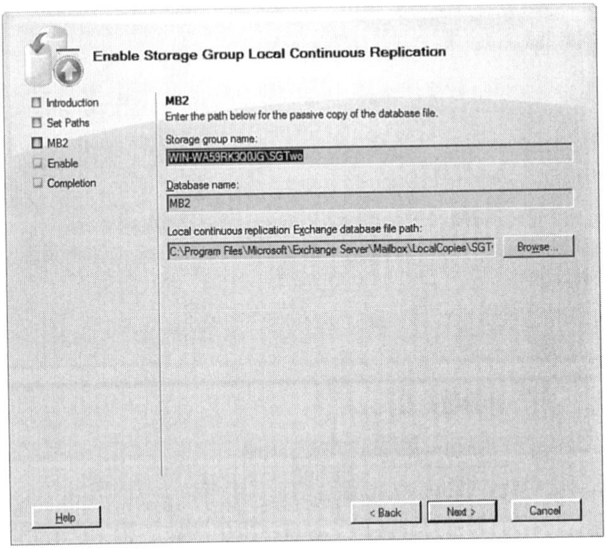

FIGURE 10.5
The Enable Storage Group Local Continuous Replication dialog.

9. You are shown a configuration summary of both actions: making a copy of the database and making copies of the log and system files. Keep in mind that the database is copied once. The way it is kept up to date is through transaction logging and replaying into the database on the passive side. After you confirm your settings, click Enable.
10. When complete, click Finish.

What happens next is a process called seeding, where your database is created in the passive disk and this is the creation of the starting point for your LCR version. After LCR is complete, you should notice a change in the icon next to your storage group. Some new options in the Actions pane for your storage group are to disable or suspend the LCR.

NOTE An easy way to confirm the functionality of LCR is to open the folder that holds the active location of your transaction log files. Then open the location of the passive copy of the logs. Through your Outlook client or Outlook Web Access, send a few messages through to mailboxes within that database. You should see the transaction logs grow on the active side and then shortly afterward you should see the passive copy increase, too. This provides a visual confirmation that LCR is working just fine.

PS NOTE The cmdlets through the Exchange Management Shell used to enable LCR on an existing storage group include two separate commands:

```
Enable-DatabaseCopy -Identity <Server>\<StorageGroup>\<Database> -
CopyEDBFilePath:<FullPathIncludingDatabaseFileName>
```

```
Enable-StorageGroupCopy -Identity <Server>\<StorageGroup> -
CopyLogFolderPath:<FullPath> -CopySystemFolderPath:<FullPath>
```

Enable LCR for a New Storage Group and Database

You recall when we created storage groups in Chapter 4, "Manage Storage and Databases," that we didn't address the checkbox for creating LCR. We need to revisit the process:

1. Open the EMC.
2. From the Navigation Tree, expand the Server Configuration work center and click Mailbox.
3. From the Results pane, choose the server where you want to create the Storage Group.
4. From the Actions pane, choose New Storage Group to open the wizard.
5. Using the Browse buttons, you can determine the location of the log and system files.
6. Select the checkbox Enable Local Continuous Replication For This Storage Group, and then use the Browse buttons to determine the location of the passive log and system files for replication.
7. When you are ready, click New and then Finish.

This completes the first part for creating a storage group that is LCR-enabled, but the next part is the database. When you create the database for the storage group, you need to browse for the location of the active database and for the location of the replicated database. When you are ready, click New and then Finish.

Verify LCR Is Functional

To see how your LCR performs, there is a tab in the properties of the storage group that shows you information regarding your LCR status. To view that information, perform the following:

1. Open the EMC.
2. From the Navigation Tree, expand the Server Configuration work center and click Mailbox.
3. From the Results pane, choose the server where you want to create the storage group.
4. From the Work pane, select the storage group for which you want to see the properties.

5. From the Actions pane, select Properties.
6. Select the Local Continuous Replication tab, shown in Figure 10.6.

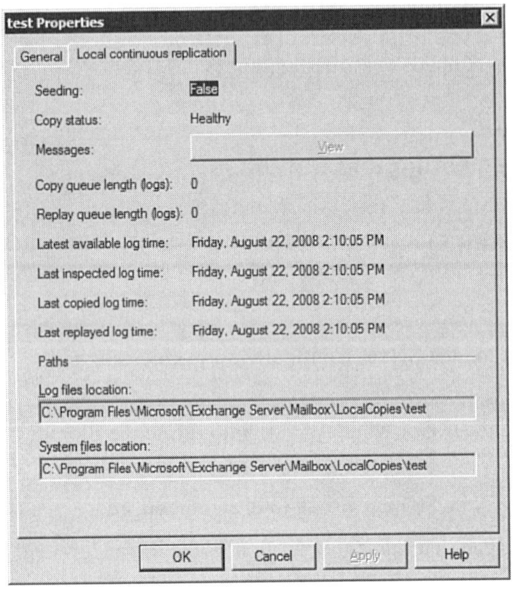

FIGURE 10.6
The Local Continuous Replication tab under the storage group properties.

7. Note the Copy Status is Healthy. If there is a problem, you might see Broken, Disabled, or Failed.
8. Assuming everything is healthy, you can click OK to close the dialog.

NOTE In the event you do notice a problem with your LCR replication, you can check to make sure the paths are all correct and accessible. If you find a problem, fix it and then suspend and restart LCR on the storage group. You might have a problem with a missing transaction log, which sometimes causes LCR to halt. Try the `Update-StorageGroupCopy` cmdlet to reseed your LCR. However, if you need to find other problems, the following TechNet article will assist you: http://technet.microsoft.com/en-us/library/aa996038.aspx.

Recover from Disk Failure

Unfortunately, there are times when your active disk might fail. With LCR you have to manually intervene, but you can recover your working environment quickly depending on how fast you are notified and how rapidly you can respond to the failed disk.

The process requires three actions:

- Dismount the database.
- Alter the pointer for the database to point at the passive copy. Note: If the disk itself is not harmed but the database has become corrupt, you don't have the change the pointers; simply move the database over to the production location and remount. If the disk went bad, you need to alter the pointers.
- Remount the database.

To perform these actions, do the following:

1. Open the EMC.
2. From the Navigation Tree, expand the Server Configuration work center and click Mailbox.
3. From the Results pane, choose the server where the disk has failed.
4. From the Work pane, select the database, and choose Dismount from the Actions pane.
5. You can activate the copy that has been moved to the production location or activate the copy that is in the passive location depending on whether the disk died or the database simply corrupted. In either case, you will use the `Restore-StorageGroupCopy` cmdlet.
    - If you want to activate the copy that has been moved to the production storage group, so the paths are unchanged, type **`Restore-StorageGroupCopy -Identity:<Server>\<StorageGroupName>`**
    - If you want to activate the copy that is on the passive disk, so you will have the indicate the alteration of the production path, type **`Restore-StorageGroupCopy -Identity:<Server>\<StorageGroupName> -ReplaceLocations:$true`**
6. Select the database and choose to mount it from the Actions pane.

Keep in mind that LCR is no longer functioning on the storage group because you just disabled it by switching to your passive copy. You have to put in a new disk or simply configure LCR again to use the locations on different disks that you have prepared in your system.

Configure Cluster Continuous Replication

Scenario/Problem: You have decided to use CCR between two Exchange mailbox servers. What do you need to do next?

Solution: CCR uses the same continuous replication technology that we see in LCR; however, it performs the failover automatically. It does this through cluster services that we have to install and configure. Then we need to install the active and passive mailbox roles. Essentially, this is the process involved with CCR:

- First, begin with two systems with either Server 2003 or 2008 installed on them. You must use the Enterprise Edition because cluster services work only on that edition of Server. Ensure that neither has Exchange 2007 Server installed. We are installing only the Mailbox roles (active and passive) on these machines. The systems will need to have a public and private network connection. The public connection is for users to send and retrieve email to each other through the servers. The private connection is for the two servers to be able to speak to one another through a heartbeat that lets the active and passive roles know the other is alive and well.
- When configuring the cluster, we will set up a two-node cluster. This might seem like a problem because with only two nodes, there is the chance for a problem called *split brain syndrome*. That is a situation where, for example, the passive system believes the active has gone down and decides to promote itself as the active system. However, let's say the active didn't go down—the cable connection is disconnected or something simple. Now you have two active servers at one time. That is a problem. To resolve this problem, many clusters use three or more servers. What was needed was a new form of quorum model, and the Exchange Team decided to use a Majority Node Set (MNS) quorum.
- A quorum is like a referee. The way the MNS quorum works is off a file share that you can set up anywhere. However, it is recommended you set it up on a Hub Transport server. The file share acts as a witness between the two servers because if their heartbeat seems to fail, they can connect to the file share and confirm that the other server really is down before the passive takes over as the active.
- One aspect of this entire procedure is called the *transport dumpster*, which is enabled on the Hub Transport servers when you install CCR. This helps ensure less mail is lost in the event of a failover. The way it works is that if the active node fails and the passive takes over, in the brief time span in which this occurs, data can be lost or in transit. The most recent mail might be in logs and might not have been shipped over and replayed in time. So, the Hub Transport servers maintain a queue of recently delivered mail in an area called the transport

dumpster. When the passive takes over, it checks the Hub Transport servers for any items that it doesn't have. Duplicates are weeded out, but anything the passive doesn't have will be added. Note: With SP1, this feature exists for use with LCR, as well.

Although LCR remains the same for both Server 2003 and Server 2008, there are some slight changes between the two for CCR. The reason is that cluster services receive a slight makeover (and a new name—Failover Clustering) in Server 2008. Let's look into configuring both of these, starting with Server 2003.

Configuring Cluster Services with Server 2003

Keep in mind that in some of these steps, you are considered capable of going forward and carrying out the instruction without a step-by-step aspect to it because it assumes basic networking knowledge. Other parts walk you through step by step because cluster services is not something every administrator has the chance to work with.

So to configure cluster services, perform the following:

1. You should create a separate account for the cluster services and make that account a member of the Exchange Server Administrators group or Exchange Organization Administrators group. The account should also be put in the local Administrators group for each node.
2. On a Hub Transport server in the same site as the clustered nodes, create a folder and give it any name you like (within reason, such as MNSCluster) and share that folder out on the network. Set the share permissions to Full Control for the cluster administrators account that you created.
3. Configure your network adapters. As mentioned previously, you should have a public and private connection. It's recommended, for the sake of organization, that you properly label these in your Network Connections so you know which one you are looking at quickly. You want to have static addresses for both the public and private networks. The private network needs to use a different IP addressing scheme and Microsoft recommends the addresses 10.10.10.x for both (you can go with 10.10.10.10 and 10.10.10.11 for the active and passive private connections). Check your binding order on the network adapters, too (on the Adapters and Bindings tab of the Advanced Settings for your connection) and put the Public connection to the top of the binding order.
4. Before proceeding, on both nodes of the cluster you want to download and install KB 921181. This is an update fix that you want to ensure is installed on these servers. It allows them, as clusters, to use the file share witness we created earlier and to configure the heartbeats feature. You should read the KB and then install the hotfix.

After your systems are ready, you can perform the following on the active node of the two-node cluster:

1. Select Start, Administrative Tools, and then Cluster Administrator to open the wizard (or from the command line, type **`cluster /create/wizard`**).
2. From the drop-down box, select Create New Cluster and then OK.
3. Read the first page of the wizard, and then click Next.
4. On the Cluster Name and Domain screen, the Domain is already filled in for you, but you have to provide a unique name for the cluster. You might try a name like E2K7Cluster or something similar; it is your choice. Then click Next.
5. You are asked to type in the name of the server that will be the first node of the cluster. You can name your servers something logical like Node1, Node2, or something similar. Then click Next.
6. The wizard will now analyze the configuration. When it completes, note any warnings and click Next.
7. You are asked for the IP address that the cluster management tools will use to connect up to the cluster. This is a public IP address, not a private one, and you want to ensure it is a unique address on the system. Then click Next.
8. You are asked for the Cluster Service Account at this point, and if you followed the instructions earlier, you should have an account prepared for handling your cluster services already in place. Fill in that information and click Next.
9. Here you are shown the Proposed Cluster Configuration, and here is where you need to choose the type of quorum. Select the Quorum option, shown in Figure 10.7. Then select the down arrow, choose Majority Node Set, and click OK.

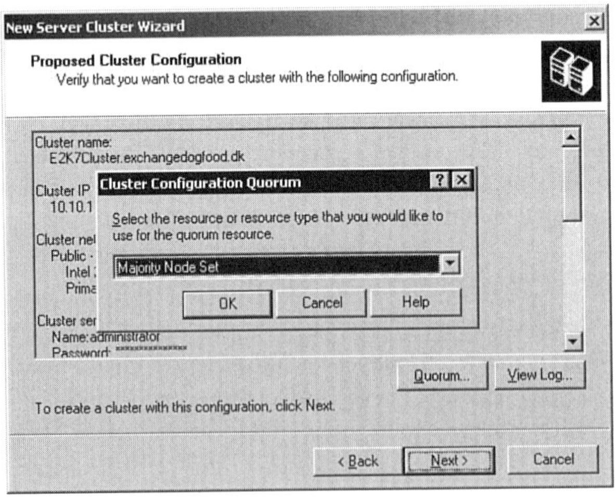

FIGURE 10.7
Choosing the Majority Node Set quorum for your cluster configuration.

10. From the Creating the Cluster screen the first node is going to be established. Click Next.
11. At the completion screen, you can view the log of the entire procedure. When you are ready, click Finish.

To confirm the first node of your cluster is up and running, open up Cluster Administrator and expand the name of your cluster. Then expand Groups and Cluster Groups and you will hopefully see that your cluster is online, as you can see in Figure 10.8.

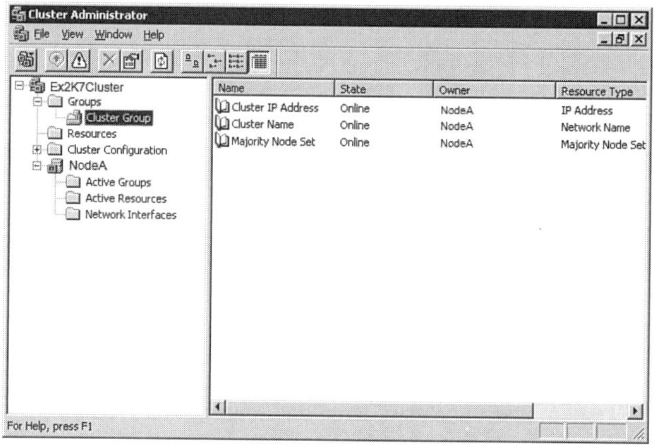

FIGURE 10.8
Confirming that the primary node of your cluster is online.

Having a cluster with one node is not an effective high-availability solution. So, we need to add the second node. To do this, perform the following:

1. Open Cluster Administrator from your cluster tools.
2. Right-click the primary node server name, select New, and then Node. This will start the Add Nodes Wizard. Click Next.
3. Type the name of your second node and click Add. Remember, we are adding only two nodes for our CCR cluster.
4. The wizard will analyze and confirm that everything is in place to form the cluster. When complete, click Next.
5. You are asked for the cluster service account again, which you should have in place already. Add that information, and click Next.
6. The Proposed Cluster Configuration page will display and you can confirm the setting choices you made. If everything is correct, click Next.
7. After the cluster is complete, click Finish.

To confirm that your two-node cluster is up and running, open the Cluster Administrator and you should see the cluster. You should be able to see two servers (your Node1 or NodeA and your Node2 or NodeB). You should see in the State column that they are both Up, as shown in Figure 10.9.

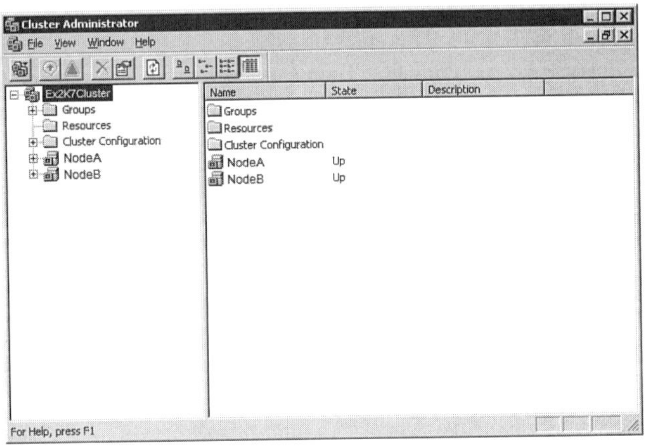

FIGURE 10.9
Confirming your cluster is online.

NOTE Another method to confirm that the cluster is up and running is to go to a command prompt and type **`cluster group`** or **`cluster node`**, and you will see a response regarding your cluster or nodes and the status.

After your cluster is set, you need to establish the file share you configured to be your MNS quorum witness. This works if you installed the hotfix and if the share is correct. To do this you need to go to a command line and type

```
Cluster res "Majority Node Set" /priv MNSFileShare=\\servername\sharename
```

At this point, you are ready to perform the installation of Exchange 2007 for the Mailbox server roles for the active and passive side.

The installation begins like a typical installation:

1. Insert the DVD or mount the ISO for the Installation screen to display. Select the link from Step 4 to begin the Installation Wizard.
2. You will be taken to the Introduction screen. Select Next.

3. You are taken to the License Agreement screen. Choose I Accept the Terms in the License Agreement, and select Next.
4. You are taken to the Error Reporting screen. Make your choice before selecting Next.
5. This brings you to the Installation Type screen, where you can choose either a typical or custom Exchange Server installation. In this case, select Custom Exchange Server Installation.
6. Under Server Role Selection, select Active Clustered Mailbox Role, as you can see in Figure 10.10. The Management Tools are selected by default. Select your options and choose Next.

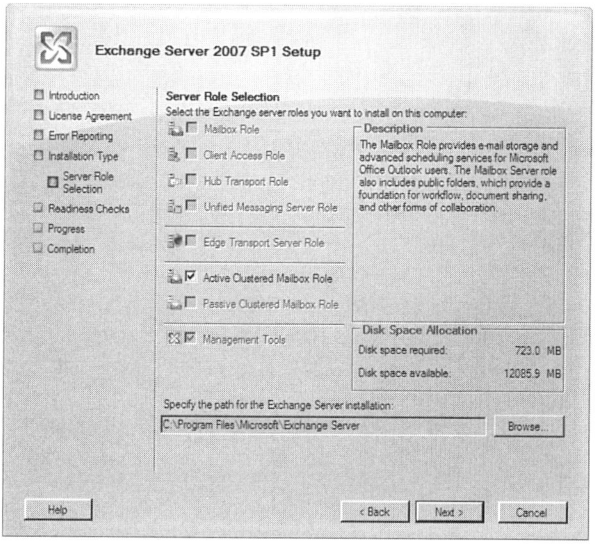

FIGURE 10.10
Choosing the Active Clustered Mailbox Role.

7. Under Cluster Settings, shown in Figure 10.11, you want to choose the Cluster Continuous Replication option. You also need to provide the Clustered Mailbox Server Name (CMS). This is the name your Outlook clients use to connect to the server. You can alter the path to the Clustered Mailbox Server database files if you like by choosing the Browse button. When you are ready, click Next.

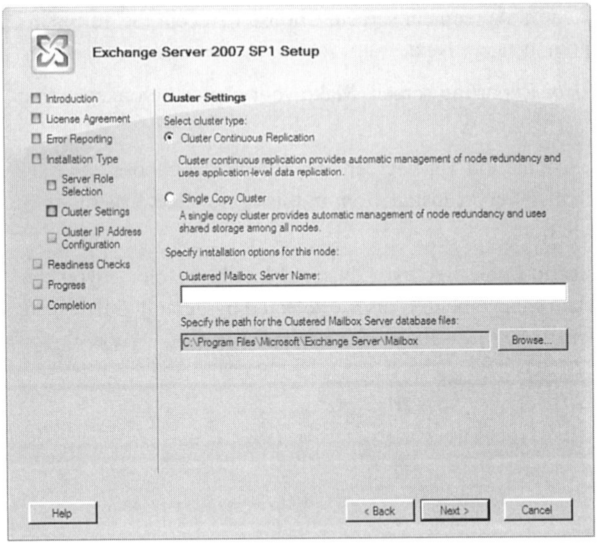

FIGURE 10.11
Configuring CCR within Cluster Settings .

8. On the Cluster IP Address Configuration screen, you have the ability to define more than one subnet, as you can see in Figure 10.12. You can determine the use of IPv4, IPv6, or both. (Note that it is possible to use a DHCP-assigned address, but it is not recommended.) When complete, click Next.

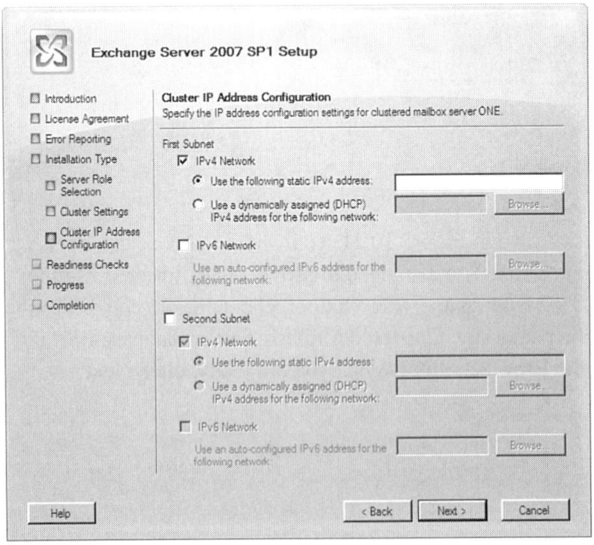

FIGURE 10.12
The Cluster IP Configuration screen.

9. The Readiness Checks screen checks to make sure your system is ready for the installation of the server options you've chosen. After you are clear to move forward, choose Install.
10. The Progress screen walks you through the process of the actual installation. When complete, it takes you to the Completion screen and shows you what has been installed successfully. Click Finish.

After you install the active side, the next step is to install the Passive Clustered Mailbox role. Follow the same steps but choose the passive mailbox.

Configuring Cluster Services with Server 2008

Some people might wonder whether it is better to use Server 2008 over Server 2003. This is logically true. There are enhancements with the clustering services, now called Failover Clustering, that can assist you in creating a more stable and secure cluster for CCR. Some of the new features are multiple subnets, support for geo-clusters, failover across two subnets, and support for IPv4 and IPv6.

In addition, there is a new Failover Cluster Management console based upon the MMC 3.0 changes, shown in Figure 10.13.

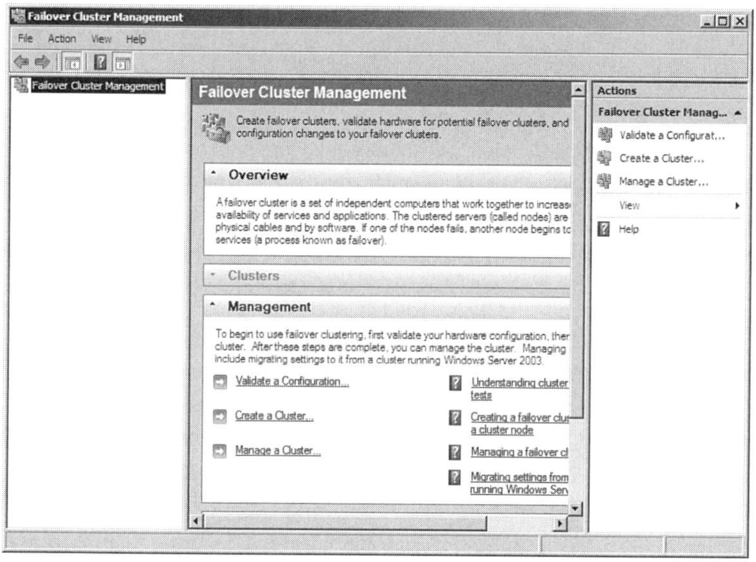

FIGURE 10.13
The Failover Cluster Management console.

There is a new quorum model that allows four different hybrids from which to choose:

- Node Majority—For use with clusters with an odd number of nodes (for use with clusters of three or more), which is really only helpful in an SCC situation (even though you can use it for CCR, it isn't practical because you can use the file share witness and not waste an entire system acting as a node).

- Node and Disk Majority—For clusters with an even number of nodes. Each node gets a vote, as does the witness disk, which might reside on shared storage.
- Node and File Share Majority—For clusters with special configurations, which is the equivalent of the Majority Node Set that we have with Server 2003, and the one we use for CCR.
- No Majority: Disk Only—This is what they might call traditional shared quorum clustering. It can sustain a failure of all the nodes except one. It cannot sustain a failure of the quorum disk. (Note that although this option is available, the instructions clearly say, "This configuration is not recommended because the disk is a single point of failure.")

To perform the preparation process for the CCR, setup on Server 2008 requires some of the same steps for Server 2003.

To configure cluster services, perform the following:

1. You should create a separate account for the cluster services and make that account a member of the Exchange Server Administrators group or Exchange Organization Administrators group. The account should also be put in the local Administrators group for each node.
2. On a Hub Transport server in the same site as the clustered nodes, create a folder and give it any name you like (within reason, such as MNSCluster) and share that folder on the network. Set the share permissions to Full Control for the cluster administrator's account that you created.
3. Configure your network adapters. You should have a public and private connection. It's recommended, for the sake of organization, that you properly label these in your Network Connections so that you know which one you are looking at quickly. You want to have static addresses for both the public and private networks. The private network needs to use a different IP addressing scheme, and Microsoft recommends the addresses 10.10.10.x for both (you can go with 10.10.10.10 and 10.10.10.11 for the active and passive private connections). Check your binding order on the network adapters, too (on the Adapters and Bindings tab of the Advanced Settings for your connection) and put the Public connection to the top of the binding order. Note that IPv6 is installed by default with Server 2008, and you are welcome to work that, too. IPv6 is the way of the future.
4. On a Server 2008 system, you have to add the Failover Clustering feature from the Add Features Wizard through Server Manager. You want to ensure you have IIS and PowerShell installed. The active and passive servers still require all the same requirements for Exchange that they do for a typical installation.

After you have the prerequisites in place, you need to proceed with the creation of the failover. To do this, perform the following:

1. On the active server click Start, Administrative Tools, and then select Failover Cluster Management.

2. This will launch the Failover Cluster Management console. Under Management you will see a link to Create a Cluster. Select that link.
3. The Create Cluster Wizard will launch. On the Before You Begin screen, you are given information about the wizard and to ensure you are prepared to move forward. When you have read the information, click Next.
4. On the Select Servers screen, shown in Figure 10.14, you are asked to locate the servers you want for the cluster. In this case, you should have two servers selected. Then click Next.

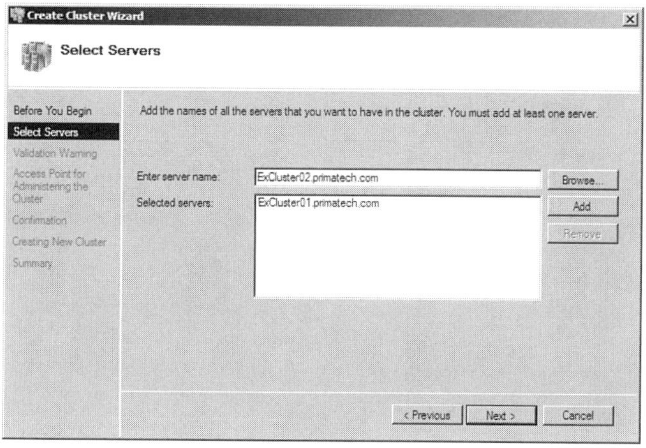

FIGURE 10.14
Selecting your servers for the two-node cluster.

5. You are taken to the Access Point for Administering the Cluster screen. You are asked to provide a cluster name (which is not the name of the cluster that will be accessed by Outlook clients; that name is configured when you perform the install of the active and passive mailbox nodes). You are also asked to provide an IP address for administrative connectivity. After these are set, click Next.
6. From the Confirmation screen, you can confirm the settings you have chosen, and click Next.
7. You are able to watch the process as the new cluster is created. Then you are taken to the Summary pane, where you can select View Report for a detailed report of the process, and click Finish.

Now that you have the failover cluster in place, certain aspects still need to be configured. For example, you need to select which interface is public and which is private (that is, for the heartbeat that lets each side of the node know that the other is alive and well).

To begin, open the Failover Cluster Management tool, expand Networks, and then open the properties page of the public network interface, as you can see in Figure 10.15. You might want to make changes to the name to make it easily identifiable as the public side. Then make sure you select the radio button, Allow the Cluster to Use This Network, and the checkbox, Allow Clients to Connect Through This Network.

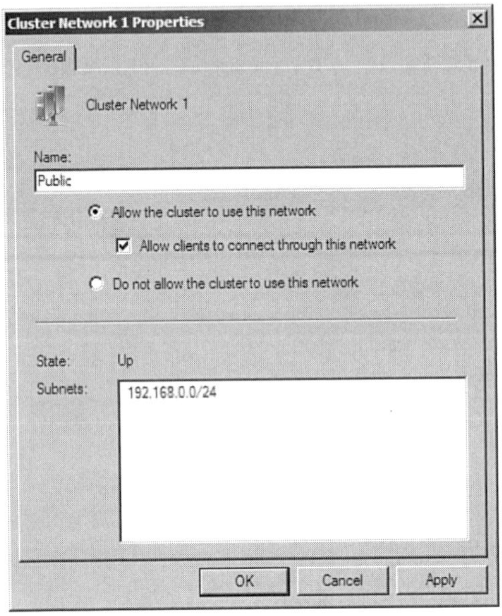

FIGURE 10.15
Configure various network settings for your cluster.

Next, open the private network interface and do the same, although deselect the checkbox to allow clients to connect through this network.

Configuring the File Share Majority quorum is easier in Server 2008 because there is a wizard now. You still need to create the file share as we noted earlier, typically on a Hub Transport server. Make sure the cluster account receives the proper Full Control permissions over the share. With the share created, you can open the wizard to configure the quorum to use that model and to use the UNC for the share. Perform the following:

1. Open the Failover Cluster Manager on one of the two nodes.
2. From the Actions pane, select More Actions, and you will see the Configure Cluster Quorum settings. Click this to open the wizard.
3. To begin with, you are shown the Before You Begin screen, where you can read a bit about configuration of the quorum. When you are ready, click Next.
4. You are taken to the Select Quorum Configuration screen shown in Figure 10.16, which has the four options we discussed earlier. The third one, Node and File Share Majority (for clusters with special configuration), is the one we want for the CCR cluster. Select that radio button and click Next.

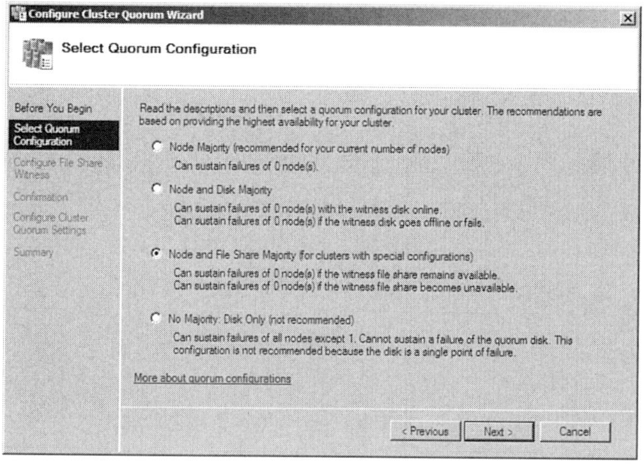

FIGURE 10.16
Selecting the quorum type you require.

5. Under the Configure File Share Witness screen, you are asked to provide the UNC path (or Shared Folder Path) to the folder you shared out. Type that in, or Browse for the location, and click Next.
6. The Confirmation screen simply asks you to verify the cluster quorum. Click Next.
7. After the configuration completes, click Finish.

The next part of the process is to validate the cluster functions properly. To do this, perform the following:

1. Open the Failover Cluster Manager on one of the two nodes.
2. From the Management section, click the Validate a Configuration link to open the wizard.
3. The Before You Begin screen provides information on the validation process; you can read through this and click Next.
4. You are asked to select a set of servers to validate. Choose the two servers in your cluster and click Next.
5. You are taken to the Testing Options screen, shown in Figure 10.17. You are given the option to run all tests or run selected tests. It's your decision, but perhaps the first time you should run all tests (which is recommended) and click Next.

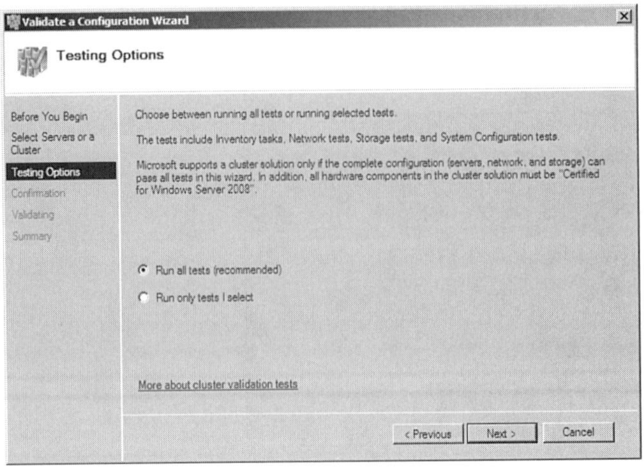

FIGURE 10.17
The Testing Options screen.

6. You are taken to the Confirmation screen, and you can see the list of tests that will be performed on your systems. When ready, click Next.
7. The Validating screen displays. You see your cluster as it is put through one test after another, and you can see the results, shown in Figure 10.18.

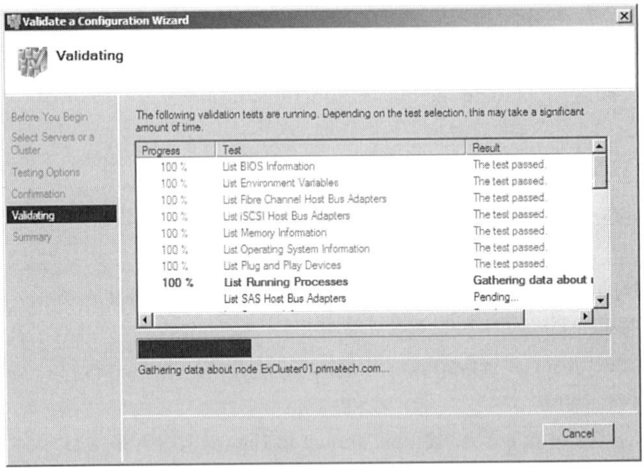

FIGURE 10.18
Selecting your servers for the two-node cluster.

8. After completion, you are taken to the summary page, where you can scroll through and see a report of the process (shown in Figure 10.19). You can also click View Report to see a detailed report of the testing. When you are done, click Finish.

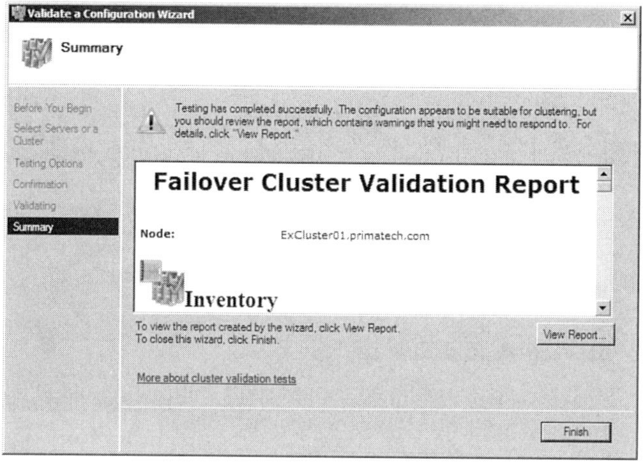

FIGURE 10.19
The Failover Cluster Validation Report.

At this point, you are ready to perform the installation of Exchange 2007 for the Mailbox server roles for the active and passive side.

The installation begins like a typical installation:

1. Insert the DVD or mount the ISO for the Installation screen to display. Select the link from Step 4 to begin the Installation Wizard.
2. You are taken to the Introduction screen. Select Next.
3. You are taken to the License Agreement screen. Choose I Accept the Terms in the License Agreement, and select Next.
4. You are taken to the Error Reporting screen. Make your choice before selecting Next.
5. This brings you to the Installation Type screen, where you can choose either a typical or custom Exchange Server installation. In this case, select Custom Exchange Server Installation.
6. Under Server Role Selection, select Active Clustered Mailbox Role. The Management Tools are selected by default. Select your options and choose Next.
7. Under Cluster Settings, choose the Cluster Continuous Replication option. You also need to provide the CMS. Your Outlook clients use this name to connect to the server. You can alter the path to the Clustered Mailbox Server database files if you like by choosing the Browse button. When you are ready, click Next.
8. On the Cluster IP Address Configuration screen, you have the ability to define more than one subnet. You can determine the use of IPv4, IPv6, or both. (Note that it is possible to use a DHCP assigned address, but it is not recommended.) When complete, click Next.

9. The Readiness Checks screen checks to make sure your system is ready for the installation of the server options you've chosen. After you are clear to move forward, choose Install.
10. The Progress screen walks you through the process of the actual installation. When complete, it takes you to the Completion screen and shows you what has been installed successfully. Click Finish.

After you have the active side installed, you next step is to install the Passive Clustered Mailbox role. Follow the same steps but choose the passive mailbox.

Making Changes to the Transport Dumpster

In the RTM of Exchange 2007, you could configure the transport dumpster through the EMS using the `Set-TransportConfig` cmdlet. However, in SP1 there is a GUI method now through the EMC.

The default configuration for the dumpster is to have the Maximum Size Per Storage Group (MB) option set at 18 and the Maximum Retention Time (Days) option set at 7. If you feel the need to alter this, you can. To do this, you go through the Organization Settings work center, click the Hub Transport node, and under the Global Settings tab you can view the properties of the Transport Settings. On the General tab (shown in Figure 10.20), you can make changes.

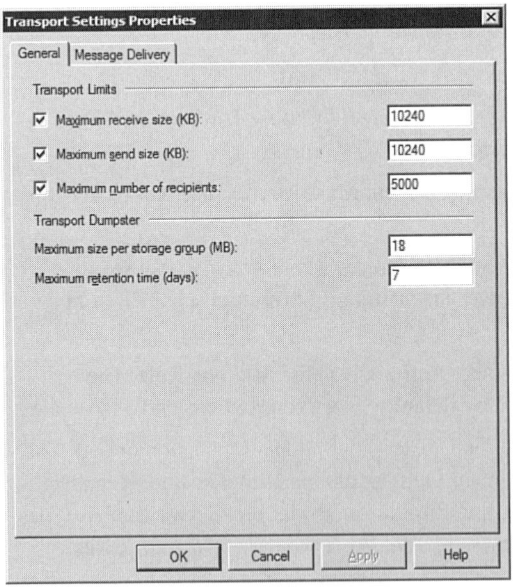

FIGURE 10.20
Altering transport dumpster settings for all Hub Transport servers within the organization.

NOTE Microsoft recommends you set the maximum size to 1.5 times the size of the maximum messages allowed through your system. So, a size limit of 10MB would be a transport dumpster size of 15MB. Microsoft recommends seven days of retention time. So, overall, the defaults are probably fine depending on your maximum message size allowed.

Confirm the CCR Cluster Is Performing Properly

With the RTM version of Exchange, we had to use the EMS to determine whether our CCR cluster was healthy, but now there are ways to check within the EMC. For example, much like with LCR, you can view the properties of the server, and there is now a Clustered Mailbox tab. This shows you if the cluster is online and which node is active.

If we view the properties of the storage group, we can see a new Cluster Continuous Replication tab and see whether our Copy status is healthy.

A new wizard in SP1 called the Manage Clustered Mailbox Server Wizard allows you to move the mailbox to another node, and stop or start the clustered mailbox server. This wizard can be located in the Actions pane if you select the CMS from the Server Configuration work center.

Implement Standby Continuous Replication (SCR)

Scenario/Problem: SCR is the newest of the four high-availability solutions, and you might be confused about what it offers, how and when to use it within your environment, and how to implement it. Let's clear up the mystery of SCR.

Solution: SCR provides a solution that we did not have with the RTM of Exchange and the initial clustered solutions of CCR and SCC—a combination of site resilience and high availability.

By site resilience, what we mean is under a 2003 cluster, both nodes had to be in the same subnet. There was still a way of placing each node in different locations or physical sites. However, they needed to be on the same network, and you might be using a virtual LAN to accomplish the illusion for the cluster.

However, with Server 2008 and Exchange 2007 SP1, we have new clustering abilities and site resilience added to the mix. We can now place our nodes in two different sites.

The simplest use of SCR is along the same lines of LCR, but across two different systems (not just two different disks). You can see how this can be taken to the next level, and you can place these systems in two different sites. However, SCR can do much more. It can create secondary copies of CCR and SCC sources. The source might be a cluster, but the target of the SCR configuration doesn't have to be a clustered target. It can be a single mailbox server or a passive node waiting to spring into action.

Due to the complexity of SCR, we do not cover each possible scenario. Rather, we suggest that you research your specific needs and solutions online. However, we review the basic requirements and configuration options to get SCR up and running.

Some of the requirements for an SCR solution include the following:

- As with other implementations, there can only be one database per storage group.
- Both the source (or active copy) and target (or passive copy) have to be in the same AD domain.
- The source and target have to use the same OS. The target must have the Mailbox role installed (if a cluster, it must be a passive role).
- Either the Enterprise or Standard Editions can be used for SCR.
- The database and storage group paths have to be the same for both the source and target.
- SCR does not use cluster services—it uses the replication service to perform the continuous replication process.
- There is a 50-log lag between the source and target by default. There is also a 24-hour replay time that you can configure.

In our simple scenario, imagine we have two servers—Ex01 (our source) and Ex02 (our target)—and each has the typical installation with Hub Transport, CAS, and Mailbox roles. Both are running Server 2008, and they are both in the same AD domain.

To implement SCR in a simple scenario where you wish to have the database and log files under a storage group called SCR1 on one system replicated over to another system, perform the following:

Open the Exchange Management Shell and type the following command:

```
Enable-StorageGroupCopy -Identity SCR1 -StandbyMachine Ex02
➥ -ReplayLagTime 0.0:4:0 -TruncationLagTime 0.0:5:0
```

What exactly did we type here?

Well, the `-StandbyMachine` is the location of the target system for the passive copy. The `-ReplayLagTime` is a predetermined amount of lag before replaying of the copied log files occurs. This is to prevent a corrupt database and logs from continuing. The format is days.hours:minutes:seconds, so we gave this a 4-minute delay (although the default time is 24 hours, with the maximum being 7 days). There is a predetermined 50-log limit by default, so that regardless of our settings, there is always a 50-log delay to prevent corruption of the passive database. Finally, we have the `-TruncationLagTime` where we specify the amount of time the replayed log files can sit before they are deleted from the target.

There are several ways of knowing that your SCR procedure worked. The first is to check the event viewer and look for Event ID 2114, which tells you that replication has begun.

You can also open an EMS shell and type **`Get-StorageGroupCopyStatus -StandbyMachine (target server name)`** and you will be shown if the status is healthy, if logs have replayed, and so on.

You can also perform the same test we did with LCR, which is to look at the source transaction log location and the target transaction log folder and see that copies are being made (taking into consideration that there is a delay built in).

NOTE Remember, there is no visual confirmation from the EMC that you have succeeded in your task of enabling SCR. If you look at the target server, you do not see anything different in the EMC regarding that server. Perhaps SP2 includes a more graphical implementation of SCR, but for now we need to use the EMS to perform a visual check of the target server to see whether something is replicating.

You may wonder: What if your source goes bad and you need to bring the SCR copy online? There are a few different options for activating SCR copies. In fact, Microsoft has an excellent article at http://technet.microsoft.com/en-us/library/bb691321.aspx.

Utilize Single Copy Clusters

Scenario/Problem: A few years back during the SAN/NAS craze, imagine that your company purchased a huge appliance that is still in use. It works great and has plenty of RAID capability, and your company would like to keep it in production for your Exchange environment. The company has two servers it plans to use the appliance as shared storage for and some form of high availability is desired. SCC seems to be the way to go, so what should be kept in mind?

Solution: Recall that SCC only provides you failover for your systems. The fault tolerance of your servers is going to have to be looked after by the appliance features itself, which no doubt are quite adequate.

Much of what you know already from the CCR information presented previously applies here. You need to configure a cluster and then perform the installation of the active and passive nodes. The only difference is that you choose SCC instead of CCR when performing the installation of the mailbox servers.

One of the biggest differences with SCC on a Server 2008 system is that you choose a different option for configuring your quorums. During the quorum configuration portion of the Configure Cluster Quorum Wizard, you want to choose Node and Disk Majority (recommended for your current number of nodes). Then on the Configure Storage Witness screen, you want to indicate the storage volume you want to use as the disk witness.

Design CAS High Availability

Scenario/Problem: How do you provide higher availability for your Client Access server roles?

Solution: Installing additional Client Access servers provides multiple points for access, but not necessarily high availability. Remember, your CAS servers are responsible for OWA, ActiveSync, and several other solutions that require availability through well placed and uniquely configured CAS servers.

However, keep in mind that the majority of the services provided through a CAS server are handled through your IIS settings. Network Load Balancing (NLB) clusters provide high availability for IIS.

In the event you want higher availability for a CAS server, you can always use NLB. On the one hand, NLB distributes client requests across multiple servers, so that offsets some of the load. On the other hand, if one server goes down, the others continue. NLB is also provided for both the Standard and Enterprise versions of Server so you don't need any special software to implement it.

Logically, there are some differences in how to configure NLB, depending on whether you are using Server 2003 or Server 2008. To enable NLB on your CAS server (running 2003), perform the following:

1. Create a record for the NLB cluster in your DNS Manager. To do this, click Start, Administrative Tools, and then DNS. Expand the Forward Lookup Zones container, right-click the zone for your AD, and click New Host (A). Type the name and IP address (within the same subnet as your two CAS servers) you want to use for the NLB cluster.
2. Your next step is to configure your network adapters. Each CAS server should have two adapters for the NLB cluster. One is Public and the other Private (or NLB). First, you might want to name the connections, so that you can easily locate the right one when you return to the servers. Then change the binding order so the Public connection comes first (which is done by going into Advanced Settings from the Network Connections dialog and under the Adapters and Bindings tab, making sure the Public connection is first).
3. To enable NLB on the first server, go to your NLB adapter and go into the properties. On the General tab, you can turn on Network Load Balancing and go into the properties.

4. Under Cluster Parameters, enter the IP address and subnet mask as well as the full internet name. These are the same settings we configured in DNS. Make sure the cluster operation mode is Unicast.
5. On the Host Parameters tab, input the IP and Subnet mask of the network adapter itself.
6. On the Port Rules tab (delete the default), configure the port range for those connections that you have coming in (HTTP, SSL, POP, IMAP) depending on the work of our CAS servers.
7. After you have the settings complete, you need to add the cluster IP address to the TCP/IP property page of the network adapter itself. To do this, go into the Advanced TCP/IP Settings off the adapter and add the IP address.
8. Adding the second CAS server to the mix is done using the Network Load Balancing Manager, which is opened from Administrative Tools.
9. To add the second server, select Cluster from the menu and then Add Host. Type the name of the second CAS server, and then click Connect. Select the cluster name and click Finish.
10. You are taken to the Host Parameters tab. Type the IP address and subnet mask of the adapter that is part of the NLB cluster. Then you see in the manager that the two servers are NLB-connected.

If you want to perform the same actions in Server 2008, consider the following:

1. In Server 2008, NLB is a feature you need to turn on in the Features. Open your Server Manager, and add the feature.
2. With Server 2008, you can go through your Network and Sharing Center and turn NLB on for the adapter you want to enable NLB clustering on; however, to configure it, you are told to go to the Network Load Balancing Manager, which is found under Administrative Tools.
3. After you open the Network Load Balancing Manager (after you have turned on NLB for your adapter), notice that you have the initial part set up, but it is Unconfigured in the Status. To fix this, select your connection (which might be 0.0.0.0) and go to the Cluster Properties. Here, you see familiar screens if you have done this before in Server 2003—Cluster IP Addresses, Cluster Parameters (shown in Figure 10.21), and Port Rules.

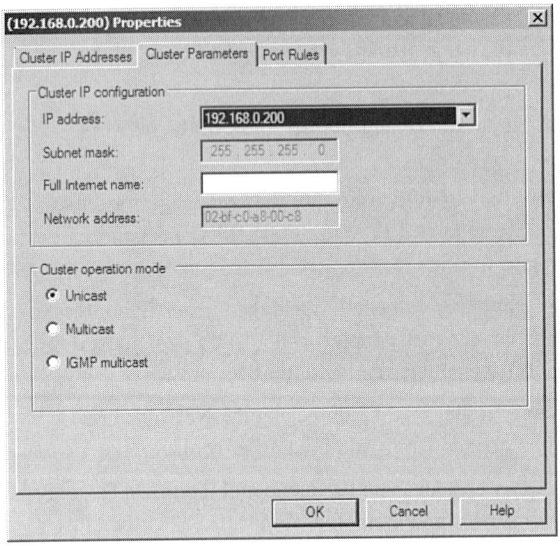

FIGURE 10.21
Configuring cluster parameters.

NOTE In the next section, we discuss the capability of the Hub Transport server role to automatically load balance when you have more than one in an Active Directory site. However, if you need to load balance (which is necessary under certain situations), configuration is the same as what we have here for the CAS server.

Design Hub Transport High Availability

Scenario/Problem: How do you provide higher availability for your Hub Transport server role?

Solution: By default, Hub Transport servers are resilient. The Hub Transport role is registered in Active Directory; therefore, as you add more servers with the role, they are noted in the event of a failure. Load balancing within the site is automatically configured with however many Hub Transport servers you use.

The only time this isn't the case is when the HT role is installed on the same server as the Mailbox role. This is logical because the Mailbox server will automatically use the local HT server.

Sometimes you might have a need to load balance your Hub Transport services. You wouldn't do this for most scenarios; however, you might have an application that requires the relaying of messages. In the RTM version of Exchange, you might have considered a round-robin DNS or MX records, but with SP1, you have the capability to use a hardware or Windows-based NLB solution.

NOTE If you do need to use Windows NLB for your Hub Transport servers, the steps are pretty much the same as what we have for the CAS server to enable NLB between your servers. However, remember that NLB is not supported for load balancing your internal Hub Transport connections (which are handled automatically). You would seek only to use this solution on inbound SMTP connections from applications (perhaps a Microsoft Office SharePoint Server or a System Center Operations Manager solution) that submit messages to an Exchange organization through an SMTP relay (because the applications cannot log directly into a MAPI mailbox). These are unique scenarios, and we encourage you to research thoroughly your solution before load balancing your Hub Transport servers.

Design Edge Transport and Unified Messaging High Availability

Scenario/Problem: How do you provide higher availability for your Edge Transport server role?

Solution: Unlike the Hub Transport server, which automatically load balances between them (due in part to Active Directory), the Edge Transport servers do not have this capability.

You can deploy multiple Edge Transport servers and then use DNS MX (Mail Exchanger) records to ensure the Edge Transport servers have the load balancing aspect, and at the same time, if one fails, there is another to keep messaging flowing in and out of your organization.

In the case of Unified Messaging servers, the concept is similar. Deploy multiple servers where two or more are in the same dial plan. For load balancing, you can configure your VoIP gateways to route calls in a round-robin method, so that if a call is not accepted by a server (in the event it has gone down or is out for maintenance), the call is sent to another UM server.

CHAPTER 11

Configure a Unified Messaging Server

IN THIS CHAPTER

- Envision Unified Messaging Within Your Environment
- Examine Your Hardware Needs for Unified Messaging
- Configure a Unified Messaging Server
- Enable UM Users
- Put the Pieces Together

Envision Unified Messaging Within Your Environment

Scenario/Problem: Unified Messaging (UM) brings with it new terms and concepts that most Exchange administrators have never heard of before. What exactly does UM offer us in Exchange 2007? What are the features our users will enjoy and how complicated will it be for administrators to grasp the implementation aspects?

Solution: First, Unified Messaging in Exchange 2007 unifies voicemail and incoming faxes with your email services. It sounds easy, but consider that voicemail and faxes are typically analog services whereas email services are digital, and Exchange administrators traditionally are more aware of the digital side.

Pulling the voicemail and fax services into the digital world isn't a new concept, but it might be new for Exchange admins. That might make you slightly nervous. Remember, though, if you already have a solution in place for voicemail and you have a telephony person or team assisting with that, they can assist you with this, too. You don't have to become proficient at a new career. It might help, however, for you to be thoroughly familiar with the Exchange side and for you to become familiar with certain voice system terms.

Unified Messaging Features

On the surface, some have defined UM in Exchange as being a way to retrieve your voicemail, incoming faxes, and email all through your Inbox. That is true. It is also only a piece of the story. UM is more than just a glorified voicemail service connected to your inbox. Here is a look into some of the primary features that are provided with Unified Messaging:

- Outlook Voice Access (OVA)—Enables users to access their mailbox using a voice user interface (VUI), which can include a phone, cell phone, Office Communicator 2007 (or some other solution such as Skype, as long as your PBX/VOIP system allows you access to call in). Using either voice-enabled menus or touchtone, you can listen to your email (the UM Server will read the messages to you using text-to-speech capabilities), listen to your voicemail, and make a call to your personal contacts or to persons listed in the company directory. The only item you cannot voice is your PIN, which is not the same as your login to the network.
- Multiple Languages Speech-to-Text—Although OVA supports only English for voice commands coming in, there are features in UM that allow menus and speech-to-text where email can be read from the user's mailbox in a variety of languages including English (U.S.), English (U.K.), English (Australia), French (France), French (Canada), German, Japanese, Italian, Spanish (Spain), Spanish (Mexico), Brazilian Portuguese, Korean, Mandarin (PRC), Mandarin (ROC), and Dutch. So, if you receive messages from different parts of the world, in different

languages, the system will detect the language and read it to you in the correct language.

- Calendar Management Through Phone—Through OVA, you can manage calendar appointments by accepting/declining meetings, sending notices to persons letting them know you will be late, or making calendar changes such as canceling appointments altogether.
- Voice and Fax Messaging—Incoming voicemail or faxes are accepted by the UM Exchange Server and can be accessed through Outlook, OWA, Outlook Mobile, clients with an ActiveSync license, and OVA. Faxes come in as .tif files and are put in user's mailboxes.
- Outlook and Outlook Web Access—UM extends the functionality of these Microsoft email applications in that you can retrieve your voicemail through your Inbox, as you can see from Figure 11.1. From there, you have various playback options where you can play, pause, or stop playback of a voicemail. You can also play the voicemail on a phone.

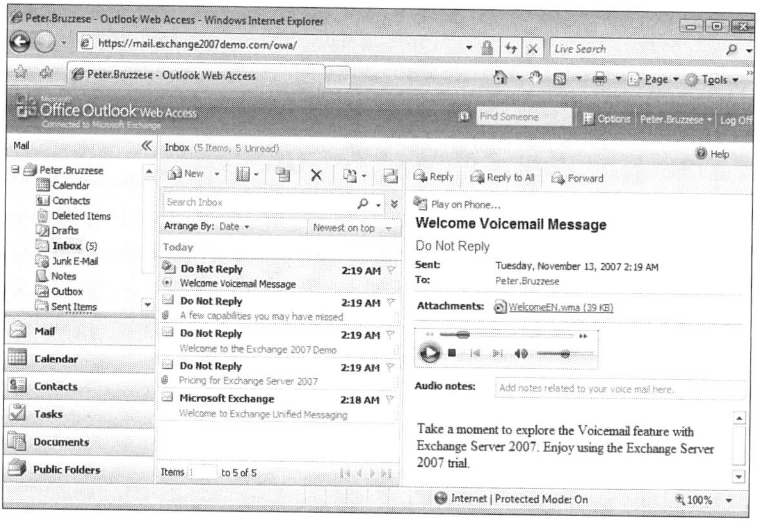

FIGURE 11.1
Outlook Web Access and Voicemail Playback options.

- Play on Phone—When you check email and see you have a voicemail, instead of being forced to listen to it over your computer's speakers (in the event you don't have a headset waiting for you to plug in), you can route the voice messages to your phone. Just supply the number and it will go to your cell phone or your desk phone.

- Auto Attendant—This is your personal voicemail operator. You can configure this to enable for directory lookups of people within your organization, or route calls with menus such as "for technical support, please press 1." A caller can speak to the Auto Attendant or use touchtone menus if the attendant is having a hard time understanding responses. You can even create custom greetings, holiday greetings, and more.

NOTE For a full list and explanation of Unified Messaging features, visit http://www.microsoft.com/exchange/evaluation/features/unifiedmessaging.mspx. For a list of feature improvements/additions with SP1, visit http://technet.microsoft.com/en-us/library/bb691398.aspx.

So far, the features might seem worth the pain of learning new technology as an administrator. What do you really have to learn? Well, you have to grasp some of the basics of telephony from a physical standpoint—lines coming in, PBXs, Public Switched Telephone Networks (PSTNs), hunt groups, and so on. Then you need to learn the configuration aspects of UM on the Exchange server. From a positive perspective, you already know and feel comfortable with the Exchange interface, so that takes much of the stress out of the equation.

Examine Your Hardware Needs for Unified Messaging

Scenario/Problem: You have a legacy PBX in your environment. Can you use it for Unified Messaging? Do you need to get a separate server for your UM role? These are some of the concerns you might have, and it is important to get your facts in order before you make any decisions.

Solution: Consider the layout and equipment in Figure 11.2. The diagram shows that your company has multiple ways for users to access their mail from external sources. The method for external access to the UM server is through a PBX (through a VoIP Gateway) or an IP-PBX.

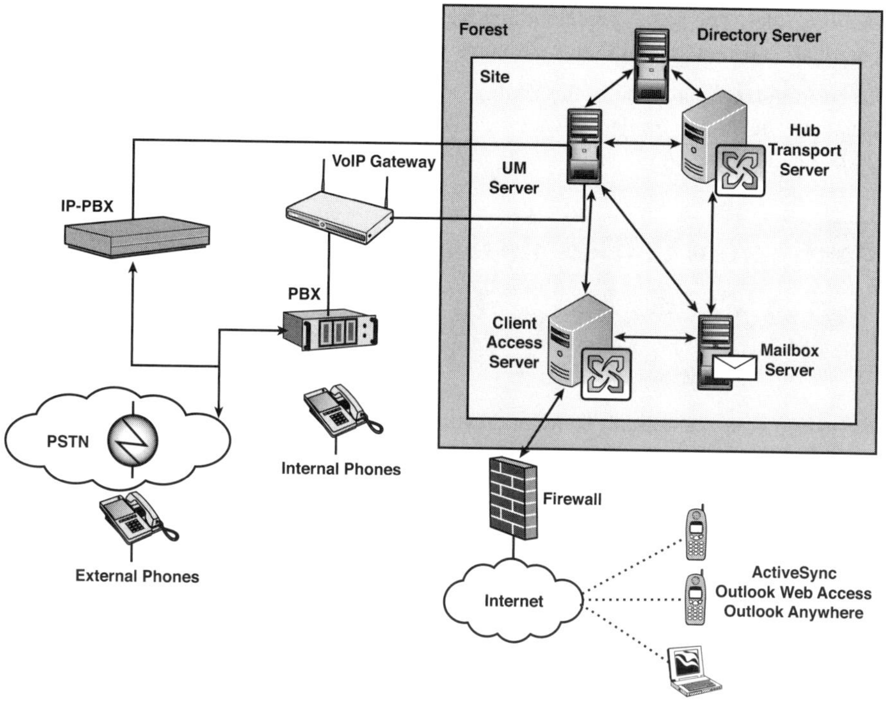

FIGURE 11.2
Designing Unified Messaging.

What exactly is a PBX? It stands for Private Branch Exchange. Its primary function is to allow a small number of incoming lines to be usable by however many people work within the company. So, imagine a company has five paid-for lines coming in from the phone company. However, the company might have 20 people working in the company. They share the collective bandwidth of those lines thanks to the PBX.

Although legacy PBXs are great devices, you need something more to connect to your Unified Messaging servers. You need to have a device that connects your circuit switched phone network with your IP-based packet switching network. That device is a VoIP Gateway.

However, if you don't already have a legacy PBX, you might do well to purchase a single piece of equipment called an IP-PBX.

To find out whether your legacy PBX device, IP-PBX, or VoIP Gateway is supported by Microsoft, consult the Telephony Advisor at http://www.microsoft.com/technet/prodtechnol/exchange/telephony-advisor.mspx.

As far as the hardware involved for the UM server itself and the number of servers you need for deployment, you can install the UM role as a standalone role or with every other role, with the exceptions of the Edge Transport role or the Active and Passive mailbox roles. The actual processor and memory requirements are not that intense (one core with 2GB is the minimum; four cores with 1GB per core is recommended).

To perform the installation of the Unified Messaging server role, you perform a Custom installation (similar to what we considered in Chapter 3, "Install Exchange 2007") and choose Unified Messaging Role from the Server Role Selection screen.

Configure a Unified Messaging Server

Scenario/Problem: After the IP PBX is functional and the UM server role is installed, what is involved in configuration of the UM server?

Solution: There is actually a method or pattern to the configuration process, and we are going to walk you through each set of steps. Obviously, certain choices are your decision based upon your particular environment. However, after the legacy PBX (with the IP Gateway) or the IP-PBX is functioning and the server role is installed, the next steps must be performed in the following order:

1. Create a dial plan.
2. Create a UM IP Gateway.
3. Configure the UM mailbox policy.
4. Configure the Auto Attendant.
5. Enable UM and assign a UM policy to users.

Create a Dial Plan

First, what is a dial plan? These are objects that are created in Active Directory. They are logical representations of an in-place telephony dial plan. If you are just testing these features, you can create whatever you like. However, if you are implementing UM in a real-world environment, you need to discuss the dial plans with your telephony administrator. Your UM server must have at least one UM dial plan to function (although in more complex environments you might have multiple dial plans in place). The whole purpose of the dial plan is to ensure that extensions are unique, which can sometimes be a problem if you have multiple PBXs.

Users within the same dial plan can call each other by using only the extension number, and each person has a unique extension within the same plan. So, for example, you might be 5-9898, and your friend in the cubicle next to you is 5-9899. Looking at it from that perspective, we can see that a user can only be part of one dial plan.

To create a dial plan, perform the following:

1. Open the Exchange Management Console (EMC).
2. From the Navigation Tree, expand the Organization Configuration work center and click Unified Messaging.

3. From the Actions pane, select New UM Dial Plan to open the wizard, shown in Figure 11.3.

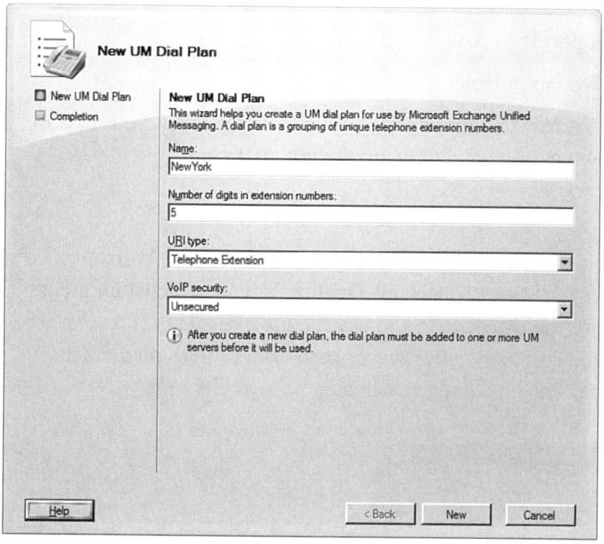

FIGURE 11.3
Creating a new dial plan.

4. Provide a name for the dial plan, which might be a location, depending on how many dial plans you need to establish.
5. Enter a number in digits for the extension number.
6. Select a URI Type (Telephone Extension [default], E.164, or SIP URI) depending on your IP Gateway or IP PBX.
7. Select VoIP Security (SIP Secured, Unsecured [default], or Secured).
8. Click New.
9. When complete, click Finish.

Upon creation of the new dial plan, a UM mailbox policy is created and associated with that dial plan.

When you are asked for a URI type, this is a Uniform Resource Identifier (URI). By selecting a URI type with your dial plan, you have to ensure that your IP Gateway, IP PBX, or PBX supports the selection you make. The purpose of the URI is to enable your VoIP devices to communicate with the Unified Messaging server and services using agreed upon protocols.

When choosing VoIP security, the method you select can protect the network traffic being sent back and on to your Unified Messaging servers.

You might think creating a dial plan is simple. However, when you select the plan and go into its properties, you are presented with seven tabs to work with.

General

Here you can see basic information about the dial plan. Associated UM servers and IP Gateways are included. You can also select checkbox options including the following:

- Send a Nondelivery Report if Message Delivery Fails
- Enable Users to Receive Faxes (selected by default)

You can also select the down arrow to choose VoIP security, in the event you need to change your selection from when you originally created the dial plan.

Subscriber Access

On the Subscriber Access tab, shown in Figure 11.4, you are shown the Welcome Greetings section, where you can leave the default greeting or create a custom greeting. Select Modify and choose the .wav file to modify the greeting. This is a nice option for situations where the company president or perhaps a professional voice actor can replace the welcome for the company when someone calls in.

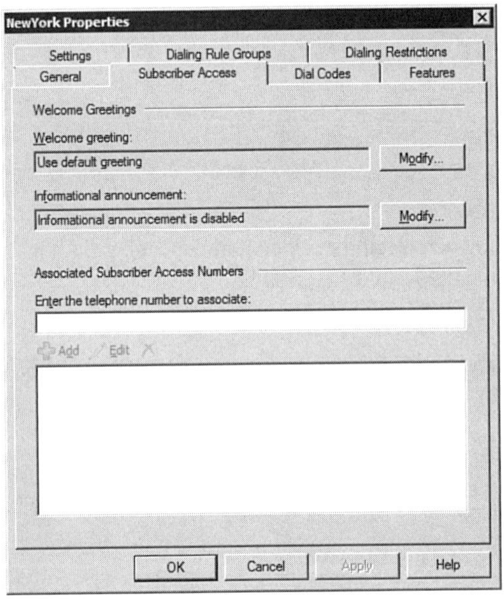

FIGURE 11.4
The Subscriber Access tab within a dial plan.

You can configure the informational announcement, which is disabled by default. This might be something that changes frequently (perhaps different promotional or informational information after the greetings that might change each month). You can select a checkbox to allow the informational announcement to be interrupted.

Under Associated Subscriber Access Numbers, you can provide a number to be associated for the OVA. You have to configure at least one number, be it an extension or external number (or SIP URI if you use an IP-PBX), so that you have OVA.

Dial Codes

There is a section for both incoming and outgoing configuration. Options such as dialing a 9 to access an outside line, common in many company phone systems, are configurable here. You can also configure an international access code, national number prefix, and country/region code for outgoing configuration and in-country/region or international number formats for incoming configurations.

Features

The Features tab, shown in Figure 11.5, enables you to configure important features of the dial plan. For example, there are checkboxes, turned on by default, for Allow Callers to Transfer to Users and Allow Callers to Send Voice Messages.

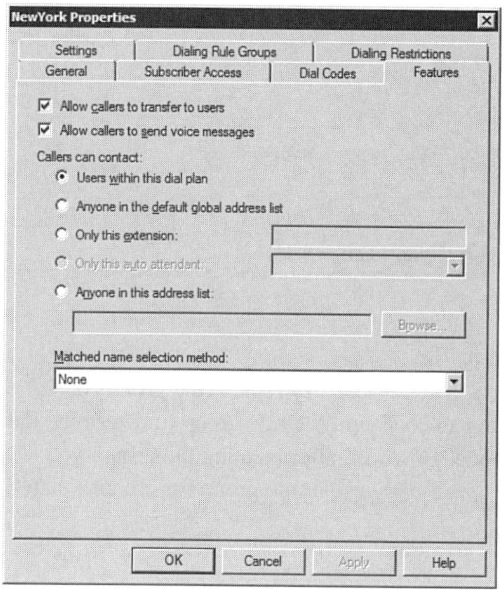

FIGURE 11.5
The Features tab within a dial plan.

You can establish who callers can contact. For example, the default radio selection is Users Within This Dial Plan, but you can choose Anyone In the Default Global Address List; Only This Extension; Only This Auto Attendant; or Anyone In This Address List where you can browse to the address list you want to allow callers to access.

The Matched Name Selection Method field is used to differentiate people with the same names. If someone calls for Joe Smith and you have more than one, the caller can be offered the opportunity to select the person based upon their Title, Department, Location, or Alias.

Settings

The Settings tab is filled with options for you to configure, including the ones listed in Table 11.1.

TABLE 11.1 **Configuration Options on the Settings Tab**

Setting	Default	Options (if available)
Dial by name primary method	Last First	Last First, First Last, SMTP Address
Dial by name secondary method	SMTP Address	Last First, First Last, SMTP Address, None
Audio codec	WMA	G.711, WMA, GSM
Operator extension	(Blank)	
Logon failures before disconnect	3	
Timeouts and Retries		
Maximum call duration (min)	30	
Maximum recording duration (min)	20	
Recording idle time-out(sec)	5	
Input idle time-out (sec)	5	
Input retries	3	
Input failures before disconnect	3	
Language Settings		
Default language	English (United States)	

Dialing Rule Groups

The Dialing Rule Groups tab enables you to add in-country/region rule groups or international rule groups. Essentially you can configure the rule group to determine the type of calls users can make within a group. However, after creating the group, you have to configure the mailbox policy to specifically use a rule group for policies that you will then apply to different users.

Dialing Restrictions

This tab enables you to configure dialing rules for those users who call in to a subscriber access number from a UM dial plan.

The Allow Calls to Users Within the Same Dial Plan checkbox is selected by default. The Allow Calls to Extensions option is deselected by default. If you enable this option, users who call in to the subscriber access number can place calls to other users who might not be UM-enabled. If disabled, they cannot place calls to users who are not UM enabled.

From there you can create allowed in-country/regional groups and allowed international rule groups by selecting the Add button and configuring the allowed groups.

Create a UM IP Gateway

Although the dial plan might represent the logical grouping of users within Active Directory, the UM IP Gateway represents the actual, physical connection between the

Unified Messaging server and the physical gateway (IP-PBX or IP Gateway). UM IP Gateway creates a logical connection that links the IP Gateway device with a UM hunt group.

To create a UM IP Gateway, perform the following:

1. Open the EMC.
2. From the Navigation Tree, expand the Organization Configuration work center, and click Unified Messaging.
3. From the Actions pane, select New UM IP Gateway to open the wizard, shown in Figure 11.6.

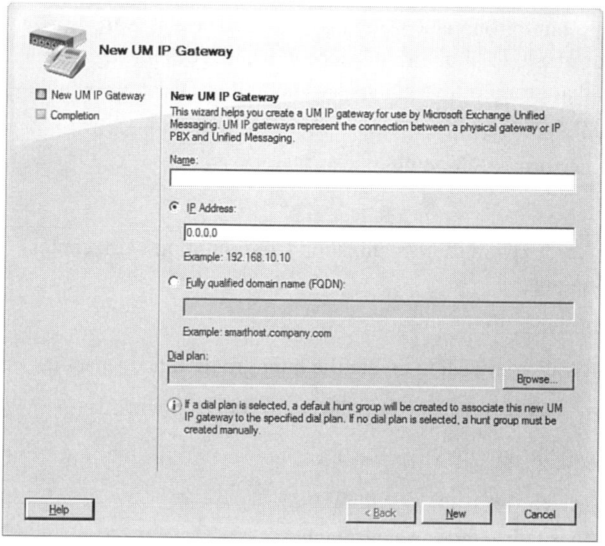

FIGURE 11.6
The UM IP Gateway Wizard.

4. Provide a name for the UM IP Gateway.
5. Select the radio option to provide either of the following:
   - IP Address
   - Fully Qualified Domain Name (FQDN)
6. Select Browse, and choose a Dial Plan. (After a dial plan is selected, a default hunt group is created to associate this new UM IP Gateway to the specified dial plan.)
7. After the wizard is complete, select Finish.

After the UM IP Gateway is created, you can right-click the Gateway and go to the properties. The properties are the same as what we saw during the wizard creation; however, the Allow Outgoing Calls Through This UM IP Gateway is selected by default.

Beneath the UM IP Gateway, a default hunt group has been created. A hunt group represents a connection between a UM IP Gateway inbound call number and a UM dial plan. It associates that dial plan with a pilot identifier. The pilot identifier is an ID that is configured on the PBX or IP PBX. It can also be an extension number or SIP URI, depending on your IP PBX. So you might configure extension 5200 as the pilot number on the PBX. When a call comes in for that extension, it looks to see where it can deliver the call—perhaps 5201, 5202, and so on.

From a physical perspective, a hunt group is a grouping of lines. There is a group of extensions that a caller has available to him, and when he calls, he goes through the hunt group to gain access to that group of extensions. A line will usually be available if you have enough lines in your hunt group.

To create a new hunt group, perform the following:

1. Open the EMC.
2. From the Navigation Tree, expand the Organization Configuration work center and click Unified Messaging.
3. Select the UM IP Gateways tab.
4. Locate the UM IP Gateway you wish to create the hunt group in and select it.
5. From the Actions pane, select New UM Hunt Group to open the wizard.
6. Provide the name of the hunt group.
7. Select the Browse button to locate the Dial plan.
8. Type in the pilot identifier that relates to your device.
9. Click New.
10. When complete, click Finish.

NOTE It is important that you define the pilot number correctly; otherwise calls will not be answered and call routing fails.

Configure the UM Mailbox Policy

With the creation of the UM dial plan, you also have a UM mailbox policy created and associated with that plan. You can create new policies, or you can configure the one you already have created.

To create a new policy, perform the following:

1. Open the EMC.
2. From the Navigation Tree, expand the Organization Configuration work center and click Unified Messaging.
3. Select UM Mailbox Policies to see the policies that currently exist.
4. From the Actions pane, select New UM Mailbox Policy to open the wizard.
5. Provide a name for the policy.
6. Then click Browse and locate the dial plan to associate the policy with.
7. Click New.
8. When complete, click Finish.

After you have the policy created, you want to access the properties of the policy to make adjustments. To do this, select the policy and from the Actions pane select Properties.

There are four tabs to work with (General, Message Text, PIN Policies, and Dialing Restrictions). The following four sections give a brief description of each tab:

General

Here you can alter the name of the policy and see the associated dial plan. You can also configure the maximum greeting duration (minutes) with the default set to 5 (and valid ranges being 1 to 10). This will determine the number of minutes that users have to record their greeting.

You also have a checkbox selected by default to allow missed call notifications. A missed call notification is an email sent to the user if the user didn't answer an incoming call. If a user misses a call, she receives the voicemail a person leaves (if the person leaves one), and she receives an email that lets her know she missed a call. Sometimes this is thought to be unnecessary, so you can create a policy that turns it off for those users who don't want it.

Message Text

This enables the administrator to configure text to coincide with various events. In Figure 11.7, notice that you can include the fax identity at the top. When a sender's fax machine sends a message, he will receive this text in return to identify the receiving system.

Some of the other messages you can configure include the following:

- Text Sent When a UM Mailbox Is Enabled
- Text Sent When a PIN Is Reset
- Text Included With a Voice Message
- Text Included With a Fax Message

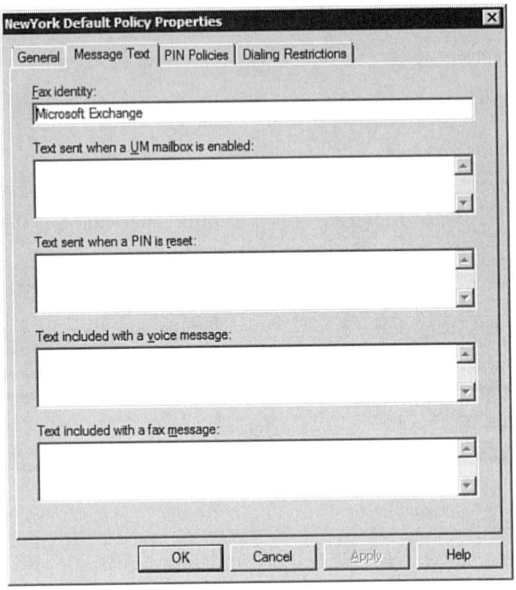

FIGURE 11.7
The Message Text tab for the UM mailbox policy.

PIN Policies

PIN policies are for users who access their Inbox through the telephone. You can configure settings like the ones listed in Table 11.2.

TABLE 11.2 **PIN Policy Configuration Settings**

Setting	Default
Minimum PIN length	6
(Checkbox) PIN lifetime (days)	60
Number of previous PINs to disallow	5
Failed Logons	
Number of incorrect PIN entries before PIN is automatically reset	5
Number of incorrect PIN entries before UM mailbox is locked out	15

Dialing Restrictions

These settings have two checkboxes at the top that are enabled by default: Allow Calls to Users Within the Same Dial Plan and Allow Calls to Extensions.

Beyond that, you have the ability to add allowed in-country/region rule groups from the dial plan and allowed international rule groups from the dial plan. So, when we created the dial plan and configured the dialing rule groups from there, those are the rule groups we see when creating our policies and choosing the restrictions for the policies.

Configure the Auto Attendant

The Auto Attendant is helpful as a guide for users that call. Often you might find that when you call automated systems, the Auto Attendant is not helpful. The reason is that you ultimately want to speak to a human and feel the Auto Attendant is acting as a barrier to your ultimate goal. However, some situations are perfect for an automated guide.

UM is one of those situations because, if guided properly, you can accomplish the tasks of speaking to the person you want, leaving a voicemail, or of checking your voicemail, calendar, and so on.

To start, we have to create a new Auto Attendant. To do that, perform the following:

1. Open the EMC.
2. From the Navigation Tree, expand the Organization Configuration work center and click Unified Messaging.
3. Select the UM Auto Attendants to see the current attendants (the default is to have none).
4. From the Actions pane, select New UM Auto Attendant to open the wizard, shown in Figure 11.8.

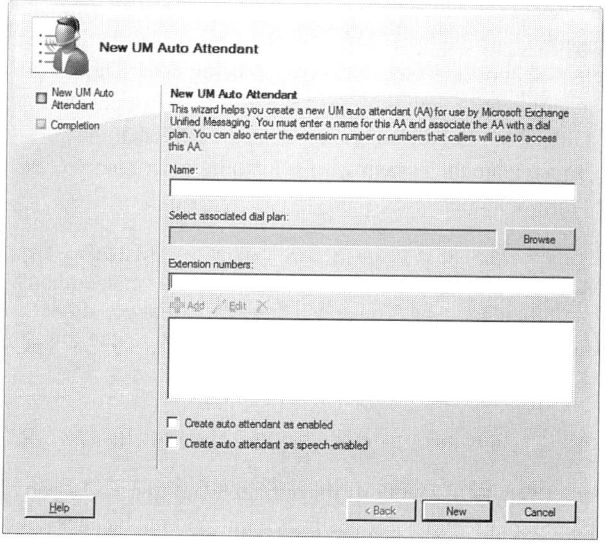

FIGURE 11.8
Create a new Auto Attendant.

5. You are asked for a name for the Auto Attendant (AA).
6. You are asked to associate the AA with a specific dial plan.
7. You want to add the extension numbers that callers can use to reach the AA (up to 16 extensions). The number of digits for the AA doesn't have to match the dial plan you have selected because direct calls to the AA are allowed.
8. You can select the checkbox Create Auto Attendant As Enabled to have the AA active immediately upon completion of the wizard.
9. You can select the checkbox Create Auto Attendant As Speech-enabled, which is not the default setting. Without this option, enabled users can only respond to the system or prompts with touchtone phone input. However, with it, enabled users can use voice input, too.

After you have the AA created, you can right-click it and select Properties or select it from the Actions pane. You are presented with six tabs that you can configure even further for the AA.

General

The General tab presents some basic information about the AA, such as the status, associated dial plan, and last time modified.

You can configure the extension numbers to associate with the AA here if you didn't do so during its creation or you can add, edit, or remove extensions.

The option to speech-enable the AA is on this tab, and you can turn that on or off.

There is also an option to use the DTMF fallback AA. DTMF stands for dual tone multi-frequency and can be used only if the Speech-enable checkbox is selected. A DTMF AA is used when the AA cannot understand the speech being used. The DTMF doesn't work from speech navigation but requires keypad input. It is recommended that you use either a DTMF fallback or include an operator extension so that the person calling has the ability to navigate the system with something other than voice (in case she has difficulty with voice automated systems).

> **NOTE** To create a DTMF AA, you simply create an AA with all the same configuration options that you have for your front-running AA. The only difference is that you do not speech-enable it. Then you select the Browse button off the General tab to use this DTMF AA.

Greetings

Here we see that we can create a variety of greetings for our attendant to use. As you can see in Figure 11.9, you configure greetings for business hours and nonbusiness hours. You can add an information announcement.

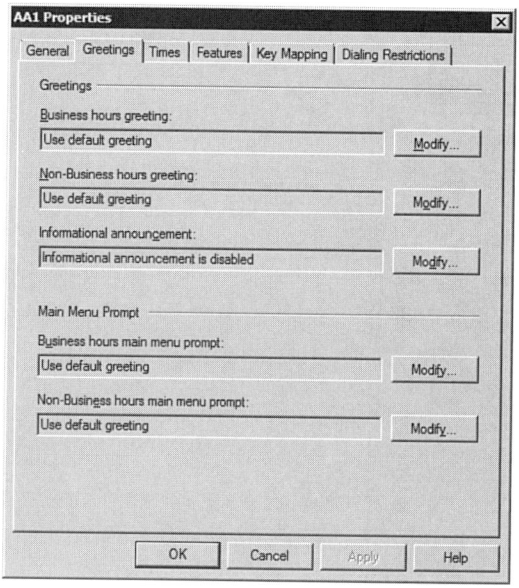

FIGURE 11.9
The Greetings tab from the Auto Attendant properties.

You can also configure the main menu prompt information for both business and nonbusiness hours. The main menu prompt is actually your list of options for users to choose to get started. For example, the prompt might say, "For Sales press or say 1."

Times

You might have noticed in the Greetings tab that there are business and nonbusiness hours. The Times tab enables you to establish the company business/nonbusiness hours. You can configure your time zone.

You can also configure the holidays that your company recognizes so that the system knows which days are not workdays (although ordinarily they would be). During the process of adding holiday dates, you can also include specific greetings for each holiday so that you can provide instructions on the number of days your company might be closed or simply provide a holiday greeting.

Features

The Features tab, shown in Figure 11.10, includes features we've addressed for users, but this is from the perspective of the AA and persons calling in from the outside.

You can choose the language the caller hears when contacting the AA for this dial plan. By default, if you installed the English version of Exchange, the English language setting is chosen. However, you can go to the Microsoft website and download additional Unified Messaging language packs for Exchange Server 2007. Although every language is not available, there are many to choose from.

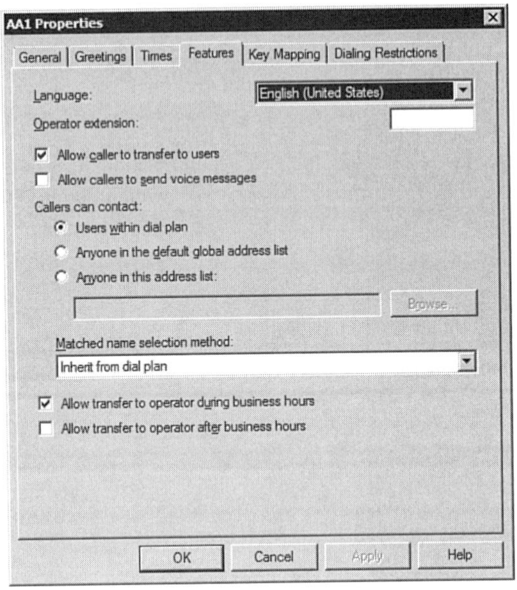

FIGURE 11.10
The Features tab from the Auto Attendant properties.

You can input an operator extension, which is used to connect a caller to an actual operator or perhaps a UM-enabled mailbox to leave a voicemail.

You can select the following checkboxes:

- Allow Caller to Transfer to Users—Enables users in the dial plan to transfer calls to other users in the same dial plan. After you select this, you can configure the section callers can contact.
- Allow Callers to Send Voice Messages—Enables callers to send voice messages to users.

In the Callers Can Contact section, you can configure the caller to be able to connect with users within the dial plan, anyone in the default global address list, or anyone in this address list, where you have to browse for the address list of your choice. The matched name selection method can be inherited from the dial plan, or you can configure the method to include the Title, Department, Location, Alias, or None.

You can also configure the caller to allow transfer to operator during business hours or allow transfer to operator after business hours.

Key Mapping

You can select the Enable Business Hours Key Mapping and the Enable Non-business Hours Key Mapping checkboxes. Here you can provide the connections for when users type or say a response. For example, if they press or say 1, they are sent to the extensions you provide. You might have one extension set for business hours and one set for nonbusiness hours.

If you click the Add button, you can see the Key Mapping Entry options (shown in Figure 11.11). From here you can determine what key must be pressed or expression said (and you can configure multiple phrases to ensure the system understands the response). Next, you configure the action that will occur. Perhaps you want an audio file to play (in the event it is nonbusiness hours), and sometimes you want the person transferred to another extension or another AA that is configured for that selection to handle additional choices.

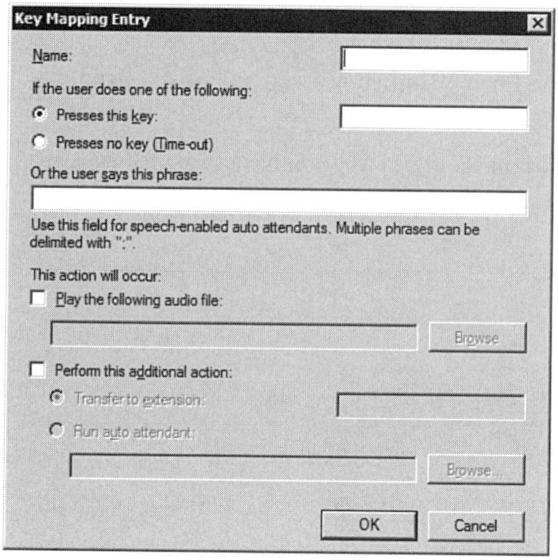

FIGURE 11.11
The Key Mapping Entry options from the Auto Attendant properties.

NOTE You might connect with a primary AA that presents you with a group of options from which to choose. You make your selection, but now you are dealing with a different department and different options for you to choose. The way to accomplish this is to have your first AA pass you off to another AA that might be defined for Sales, Research, and so on. That AA might pass you off to still another AA until you narrow down for what or who you are looking.

Dialing Restrictions

This tab enables you to select the checkboxes Allow Calls to Users Within the Same Dial Plan or Allow Calls to Extensions. Then you can configure for the AA the in-country/region rule groups or international rule groups, which were already created for the dial group. You are just selecting the ones that apply to the AA.

Enable UM Users

Scenario/Problem: After you have the Unified Messaging server set up and receiving calls, how do you enable users to be able to use UM features?

Solution: To enable a user's mailbox with Unified Messaging, perform the following:

1. Open the EMC.
2. From the Navigation Tree, expand the Recipient Configuration work center.
3. Select the user mailbox.
4. From the Actions pane, select the Enable Unified Messaging link to open the wizard.
5. On the Introduction screen, shown in Figure 11.12, you have to start by selecting a policy. Click Browse and locate the policy you want to apply to the mailbox.

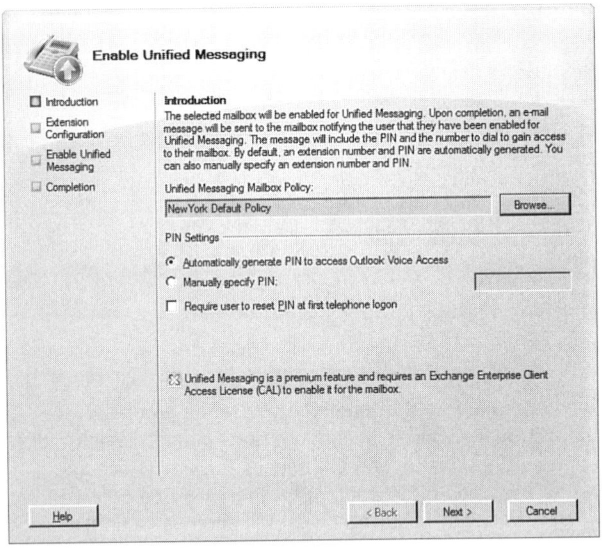

FIGURE 11.12
UM-enabling a user mailbox.

6. Under PIN Settings, you can choose the following:
   - Automatically Generate PIN to Access Outlook Voice Access (the default)
   - Manually Specify PIN (and then indicate the PIN)
   - Require the User to Reset PIN at First Telephone Logon

7. When you are done, click Next.
8. From the Extension Configuration options, you can provide the following information:
    - Automatically Generated Mailbox Extension—This is grayed out unless you have the Business field on the Address and Phone tab of the user's properties in the EMC populated with a number or the Telephone Number field on the General tab of the user account in the AD Users and Computers. This option is for a Telephone Extension plan, but not available if you have an SIP URI or E.164 dial plan.
    - Manually Entered Mailbox Extension—With E.164 or SIP, you can provide the extension for the users manually. It must match the number of digits you specify for the dial plan itself.
    - SIP Resource Identifier—Here you can choose Automatically-Generated SIP Resource Identifier or Manually Entered SIP or E.164 Address.
9. When the settings are configured, click Next.
10. Review your Configuration Summary, and click Enable if everything checks out fine.
11. When complete, click Finish.

NOTE There is a note within the wizard that reminds us that UM is a premium feature and requires an Exchange Enterprise Client Access License (CAL) to enable it for the mailbox.

PS NOTE The cmdlet in the EMS to enable UM for a user's mailbox is `Enable-UMMailbox`, but there are lots of different parameters involved. The easiest solution to perform bulk UM enabling is to use the EMC Wizard to enable one user with the proper configuration settings and then when the command completes, click Ctrl+C to copy the exact PowerShell command. Then you can use that (with some tweaks) to enable UM on multiple users.

After a user is enabled, you can enter the user's Properties and locate the Mailbox Features tab. From here you can select the Unified Messaging option and select the Properties button. This takes you to some of the properties that you can change, as you can see in Figure 11.13.

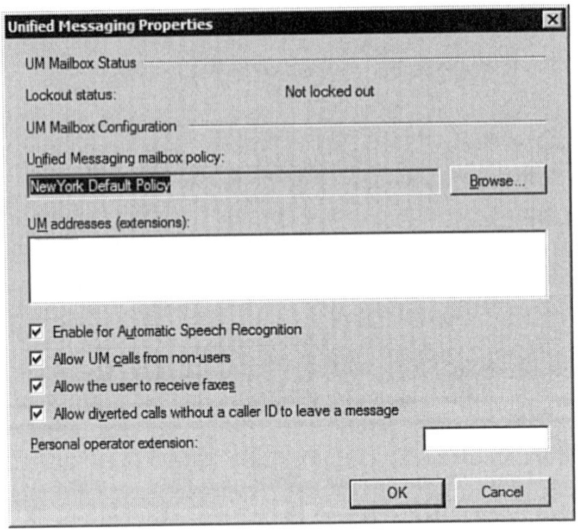

FIGURE 11.13
UM Properties on the mailbox.

You can change the mailbox policy and UM address (extensions). You can also select or deselect the following checkboxes

- Enable for Automatic Speech Recognition
- Allow UM Calls from Non-users
- Allow the User to Receive Faxes
- Allow Diverted Calls Without a Caller ID to Leave a Message

You can also provide a personal operator extension.

Put the Pieces Together

Scenario/Problem: Perhaps you grasp all the preceding steps and all the terminology is swimming through your brain, but you simply cannot see it all working together. You have all these puzzle pieces—how do they fit together?

Solution: That is an interesting question because the truth is that you are expected to establish and configure the logical structure of all of this without really understanding the underlying physical structure first. That is a hard thing to mentally put together. Let's see if we can break this down, now that you know all the steps and pieces.

From the physical perspective, we have a PSTN. Imagine this as the equivalent to the Internet (which is an IP-based packet-switched network), but it is a circuit-switched telephone network. Put simply: two different types of networks.

There are lines you pay for from the phone company that are coming into your network. Now, you might have a fancy IP-oriented network in place, but let's assume you have lines coming in, typically called trunk lines. The trunk lines connect to a PBX (or IP-PBX). The PBX takes the trunk lines and splits them into extensions that connect to individual phones that typically sit on a user's desk. The idea is to have fewer trunk lines than extensions (hoping all users in the company don't pick up their phones at the same time to make a call). This is where the hunt group concept comes from. A hunt group is a method that distributes calls from a person through an available line. The system hunts for an available line.

So you have this PBX with lines coming in, and you have extensions coming out that go to fax machines and phones and other devices. To get the PBX to communicate with your IP-based network, you need an IP Gateway. Or, perhaps you have an IP PBX, which enables you to connect your network with a PSTN and provide VoIP capabilities.

Physically, you have the connectivity and the devices. However, there must be protocols underneath all this that enable it all to work. This is where you start hearing terms like SIP (Session Initiation Protocol).

After you have your telephony folks come in and you have your PSTN all set, your PBX (with IP Gateway) or IP PBX all set up (which includes hunt groups configured and so on), you are now ready to install and configure the UM server.

Most of your UM configuration is the creation of logical objects that relate to and control the interaction with all of the physical objects we were just discussing.

So, imagine a dial plan as a logical grouping in Active Directory for your AAs under that plan, your mailbox policies under that plan, and your users. These are connected to UM gateways, which are logical representations of hunt groups that connect to real hunt groups off your PBXs.

Essentially, after you have the physical and logical pieces in place, there will be calls made. The numbers and extensions are all part of the configuration and take some planning on your part; this isn't all automatic. Calls coming into the system or going from one user to another within the system will relate to voicemail, fax, OVA, Play on Phone, and the AA calls. All these will need to be configured and tested to ensure you have it all working properly.

> **NOTE** One of the best parts to this entire discussion, unless you decide to become a UM-only Exchange Admin, is that you only have to know your system for your particular environment. The protocols in use, the extensions, and so on will be an investigation and discussion with your telephony team. However, in the end, after you document and configure the UM services, you won't have to deal with all this on a daily basis.

CHAPTER 12

Monitor and Troubleshoot Your Exchange Environment

IN THIS CHAPTER

- Monitor Your Exchange Environment
- Use the Exchange 2007 Toolbox to Troubleshoot
- Use the EMS `Test` Cmdlets for Troubleshooting

Monitor Your Exchange Environment

Scenario/Problem: From the moment you create and enable your first mailbox and mail begins flying through your organization and in and out of your mailbox servers, your Exchange environment begins the process of atrophy. Disk space, once plentiful, evaporates. Network bandwidth, once a 10-lane highway, is now a traffic jam. The key to staying on top of this is monitoring (and logically reporting). Where does one begin?

Solution: There are two sides to monitoring—the manual side and the automatic side. Obviously, as a busy administrator you want to automate the process as much as possible. To accomplish that, you have to first determine what you really need to watch and then manually configure the software to monitor and report on itself.

NOTE Microsoft uses a methodology called the Microsoft Operations Framework to control the process it calls lifecycle management. This includes a great deal of time and planning along with mediation on the cycle and how you can maintain your infrastructure. Within the plan, Microsoft includes schedules you can use to help monitor Exchange. Go to the TechNet site at http://technet.microsoft.com/en-us/library/bb266969(EXCHG.80).aspx and note that there are daily, weekly, monthly, and as needed tasks to care for. You can print operations checklists too, or tweak them to make them your own.

Some of the tools you can use to assist you include the following:

- Performance Monitor
- Event Viewer
- Performance Troubleshooter
- Microsoft Operations Manager (MOM 2005)
- Systems Center Operations Manager (SCOM)

Let's consider the use of each one.

Performance Monitor

The Reliability and Performance Monitor (which is the new tool introduced to us in Windows Vista, used for performance monitoring in Server 2008) is still a fine tool for checking out our Exchange situation. However, there is a Performance Monitor option from within the Toolbox that is already set up with all the needed objects and counters.

To use the EMC's preconfigured Performance Monitor, perform the following:

1. Open the Exchange Management Console (EMC).
2. From the Navigation Tree, select Toolbox.

3. Scroll down to the Performance tools, select Performance Monitor, and then, from the Actions pane, select Open Tool.
4. Here you can see (in Figure 12.1) the preconfigured options, some of which are server-oriented, such as Processor (% Processor Time) and Memory (Pages/sec). Others relate to the MSExchange Store Interface, the Information Store, the IS Mailbox, the Transport Queues, and the Transport SMTP Send and Receive.

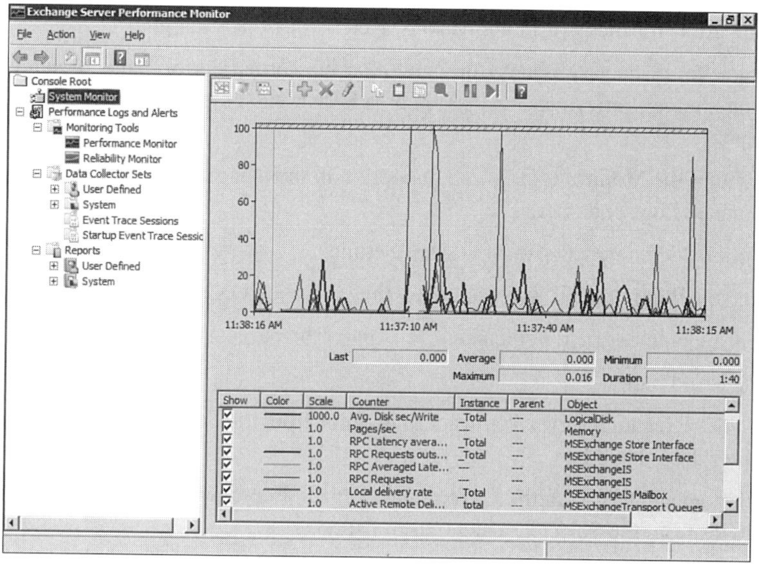

FIGURE 12.1
The Exchange Server Performance Monitor.

5. If the screen appears too busy, you can deselect the checkboxes for the counters you do not need.
6. If you want to add new counters, you can click the plus button and choose the objects and counters you need.

Later in this chapter, we discuss what Microsoft is pushing for your Exchange monitoring tool—MOM 2005. One of the necessary features to any monitoring tool is the capability to alert an administrator when there is a problem. That problem can be something as simple as your server reaching low disk space, and you want to know about it as soon as possible.

However, even if you do not have MOM 2005 and don't intend to purchase it and use its features in your environment, you can still use Performance Monitor to alert you to Exchange-oriented issues.

NOTE Keep in mind that the Performance Monitor tool for Server 2003 is different from Server 2008. With Server 2008, we now have Data Collector Sets, which you can use to define certain actions and alerts to occur. We present both methods of configuring the alerts.

Server 2003 Perfmon Alerts

You can create alerts for many different reasons. Here is just one example.

To place an alert for disk space issues (through either the normal Performance Monitor or the Exchange Server Performance Monitor) on a Server 2003 system, perform the following steps:

1. From within the Monitor tool, locate the option in the navigation pane called Performance Logs and Alerts.
2. Right-click Alerts and choose New Alert Settings.
3. Type in something logical, such as **`Low Disk`**, and click OK.
4. There is a Comment field you can use to explain the purpose of your alert.
5. Click the Add button.
6. Choose the Exchange server you want to monitor from the Select Counters from Computer drop-down box.
7. Choose Logical Disk from the Performance Object drop-down, and choose Free Megabytes from the Select Counters From list box.
8. Confirm your choices and click Add. Then click Close.
9. Select Under from the Alert and type in a number in MB that represents the amount of disk space you wish to be worried beyond. Perhaps it is 25%, 20%, 15% and so on—figure out the amount that percentage is in relation to the disk drive and use the MB.
10. Alter the Sample Data Every settings to once per day.
11. Select the Actions tab and select the way you want to be alerted.
12. From the Schedule tab, you can choose the time the alert can run (or set it to be run manually).
13. Click OK.

Server 2008 Perfmon Alerts

You can create alerts for many different reasons. Here is just one example.

To place an alert for disk space issues (through either the normal Performance Monitor or the Exchange Server Performance Monitor) on a Server 2008 system, perform the following:

1. From within the Monitor tool, locate the option in the Navigation pane called Performance Logs and Alerts.
2. Expand out the Performance Logs and Alerts.
3. Expand Data Collector Sets.
4. Select and then right-click User Defined.
5. Choose New and then Data Collector Set to open the wizard.
6. From the opening screen, shown in Figure 12.2, you can input a name (perhaps **`Low Disk Space`**), and then choose Create Manually (Advanced). Click Next.

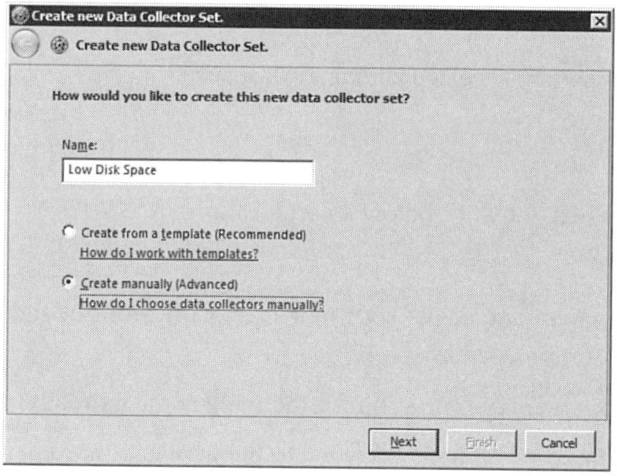

FIGURE 12.2

Creating a Data Collector Set to monitor performance counters on disk space.

7. When asked, "What type of data do you want to include?" select the Performance Counter Alert radio option. Then click Next.
8. When asked, "Which performance counters would you like to monitor?" click Add.
9. Choose the Exchange server from the Select Counters From Computer drop-down.
10. From the Available Counters list, select LogicalDisk.
11. Then select % Free Space or Free Megabytes as the counter. Choose Add, and it will be added to the Added Counters section, as shown in Figure 12.3.

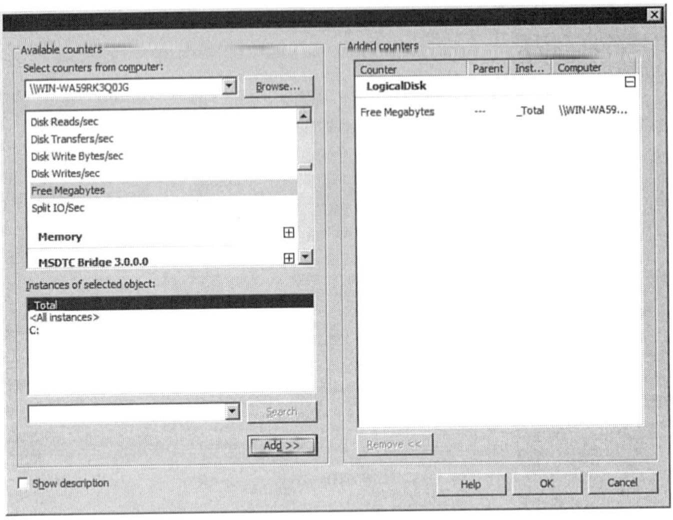

FIGURE 12.3
Creating a Data Collector Set to monitor performance counters on disk space.

12. When ready, click OK.
13. Then you can choose to alert when above or below a certain limit.
14. Click Next and Finish.
15. To configure the alert you want to occur, select your new Data Collector Set and then click Properties from the Actions pane.
16. On the Alerts tab, you should see the configuration for the collector set already.
17. Select the Alert Action tab and choose to write an entry to the application event log. (Note we discuss the Event Viewer in the next section.) You can also start another Data Collector Set if the alert criteria is met.
18. Select the Alert Task tab to choose a Windows Management Interface (WMI) task and arguments to run if the criteria are met.
19. When you are finished, click Apply, and then click OK.

Event Viewer

In both Server 2003 and Server 2008 (which includes the more advanced and complicated form of Event Viewer), there are Application logs. Because Exchange is considered an application, your informational or failure events are located here. This makes Event Viewer an essential part of your monitoring of Exchange.

There is software that automatically checks through event logs for predetermined flags with Exchange. However, you can manually open the Event Viewer to look for problems, too.

As you can see in Figure 12.4, you have Error, Warning, and Informational types of levels that are reported. The source might come from a variety of different places and the event IDs can range from the lower numbers into the thousands, so it is almost impossible to try to keep track of all this. Another solution that is programmed to keep track of all of those events would be a better solution, as we will see with MOM and/or SCOM. However, there are times when there are obvious codes or events that you are looking for, and you can use the filtering features of Event Viewer to track these down.

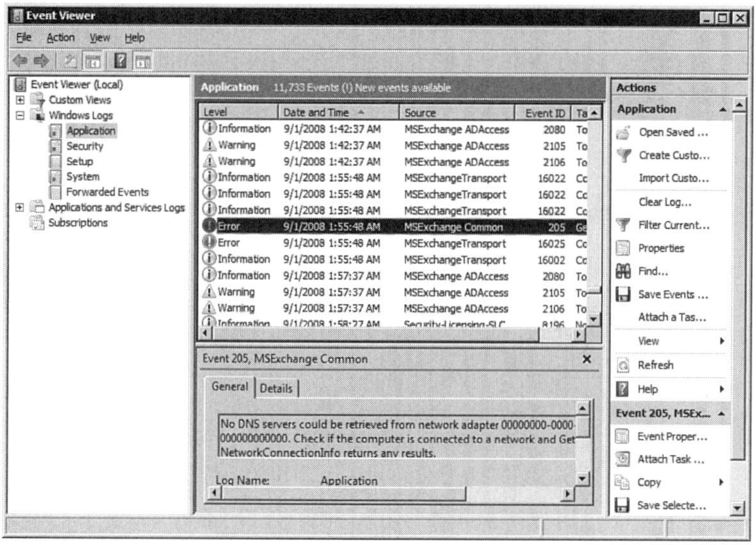

FIGURE 12.4
Using the Event Viewer to monitor Exchange events.

Attach a Task to an Event

Another feature of the Event Viewer in Server 2008 is the capability to attach a task to an event. Let's say you see an error is repeating on your server. You want to know the next time it happens immediately. So, you locate the error in the Event Viewer and perform the following:

1. Select the event to which you wish to attach a task.
2. From the Actions pane, select Attach Task To This Event to begin the Create Basic Task Wizard.
3. The first screen should have the name of the task already, but you can modify this. You can also include a description, and then click Next.
4. Because you are creating this task to occur based off of an actual event, the Log, Source, and Event ID are already filled in for you (and grayed out) on the When a Specific Event Is Logged screen. Click Next.

5. On the Action screen, you can choose to perform the following:
   - Start a Program.
   - Send an E-mail.
   - Display a Message.

6. Depending on the option you select in Step 5, you are able to configure which program you want, the email you wish to send, or the message you want displayed on the screen. Select your action and click Next.
7. Input the details of your action and then click Next.
8. On the Summary screen (shown in Figure 12.5), you are shown the name, the trigger (what will kick off the action), and the action. You can choose the option Open the Properties Dialog For This Task When I Click Finish in the event you want to make further adjustments to the task.

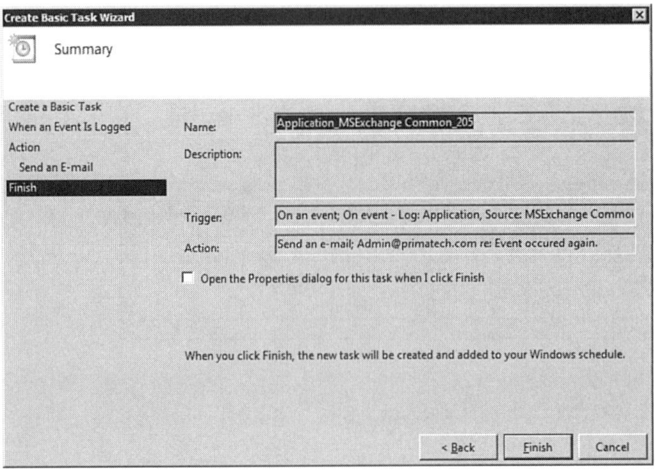

FIGURE 12.5
Create an alert task based on an existing event.

9. Click Finish.

Performance Troubleshooter

In the Toolbox, directly beneath the Performance Monitor is a tool called the Performance Troubleshooter. This can be a monitoring tool or a troubleshooting tool, depending on what it is you are concerned about with your Exchange server. It can even assist with solutions to your problems or performance issues.

To use the Performance Troubleshooter, perform the following steps:

1. Open the EMC.
2. From the Navigation Tree, select Toolbox.
3. Scroll down to the Performance tools, select Performance Troubleshooter, and then from the Actions pane, select Open Tool.
4. You are first taken to the Update the Exchange Troubleshooting Assistant. If no updates are needed, select the Go to the Welcome Screen link.
5. You are asked to label the analysis that will be performed. Then select either the option Troubleshoot New Performance Issue or the Analyze Previously Collected Data option. If this is your first time looking at Performance Troubleshooter, you want to choose Troubleshoot New Performance Issue. If you have an analysis you want to view, choose Analyze Previously Collected Data. Then click Next.
6. You are asked, "What symptoms are you seeing?" and you can choose one of the following:
   - Multiple users are complaining of delays while using Outlook or are seeing the Outlook cancellable RPC dialog frequently.
   - The number of RPC operations per second is higher than expected.
   - The number of outstanding RPC requests is high.
7. Make a choice depending on the problems you notice, and click Next.
8. You are asked for a Server Name. The Global Catalog Server Name is usually filled in by default. You can Show Advanced Login Options and alter the credentials to be used. Then click Next.
9. In the Configure Data Collection section, there are many options. You are shown the root-data directory and you can start the collection immediately or set a scheduled time. If you show advanced data collection options, you can turn on or off settings such as the following:
   - Collect PerfMon Data
   - Collect ExMon Data
   - Collect Function Call Log (FCL) Data
   - Collect Event Log Data
10. Review the options, make the changes you prefer, and click Next.
11. The analysis is performed and the Connectivity Test Results page is displayed, as shown in Figure 12.6.

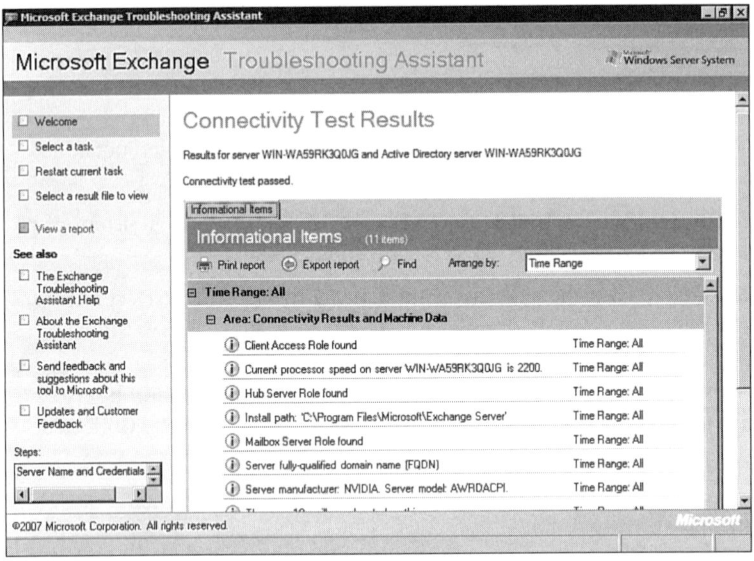

FIGURE 12.6
Connectivity test results.

NOTE ExMon is the Exchange Server User Monitor, a tool that was developed to collect performance data regarding Outlook (MAPI) clients and their performance. Unfortunately, it is not easily obtained for Exchange 2007. It seems you have to open a support incident with Microsoft or be an MS Gold Partner to obtain the tool.

Now you can perform the analysis of the gathered data, either immediately or by restarting the process at a convenient time. To do so, perform the following:

1. From the Connectivity Test Results page, click Next.
2. The files are read and analyzed. In the end, you are presented with a Performance Summary tab, a Performance Details tab, and an Informational Items tab.
3. The tool offers to investigate user activity. Click Next.
4. You are presented with a variety of options from which to choose. For example, if high RPC is found on the server, there could be a third-party Outlook add-in to blame, so you are asked to provide additional information regarding the users of the server. Then click Next.
5. Your system will check the following items:
    - Disk drives
    - Location of the data files

- Health of the physical disk
- Queue performance
- LDAP health
- Network performance
- Miscellaneous checks
- ExMon RPC analysis
- FCL analysis

6. You are finally presented with a final set of results with the Overview of all items, Performance Issues, Execution Issues, Recommendations, and General Information, as you can see in Figure 12.7.

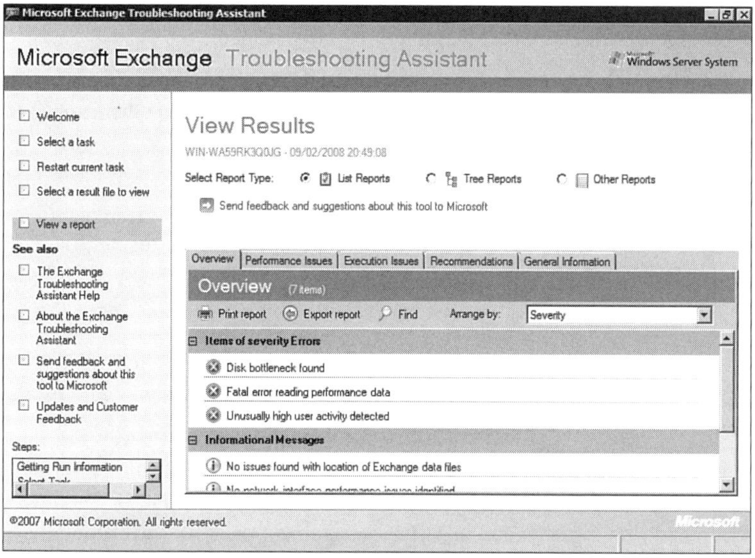

FIGURE 12.7
The analysis results.

7. You can change the report type from List Reports to Tree Reports or Other Reports. You can see the various issues and print the report, export the report, use the Find option to locate something specific, or arrange by severity or issue.

This tool can be used for troubleshooting, but it is better to use it for monitoring and reporting first. Fix the problems before they grow too large.

Microsoft Operations Manager (MOM 2005)

It is beyond the scope of this book to venture into the world of Microsoft Operations Manager 2005. It's an event and performance management system that watches event logs and does proactive alerting and reporting. It looks at a baseline and can perform trend analysis.

NOTE MOM 2005, although widely used in the workplace, has been replaced by Systems Center Operations Manager (SCOM) 2007. You can continue to use MOM if that is what is used in your environment, and Microsoft provides Management Packs for its continued use. However, if you do not have MOM in place, you should consider implementing SCOM, which also has management packs for Exchange 2007 SP1.

In terms of Exchange 2007, it can identify peak workload hours, detect abnormal behavior, and provide detailed reports regarding your environment.

To get MOM up and running, you need to install the SQL Server first and then the MOM database. Finally, to extend the functionality of MOM to give you the Exchange features, you need to install the Exchange Management Pack.

PS **NOTE** The Exchange Management Pack takes advantage of the `Test` cmdlets (which we discuss in detail toward the end of this chapter), returns the results to MOM, and presents them in an easy-to-read report.

You need to install Internal Agents on the internal Exchange servers, such as the Hub Transport, Client Access, Unified Messaging, and Mailbox servers. Or, you can install External Agents to work with the Edge Transport servers.

You can download the management pack from Microsoft; it's a free download. It comes in as an MSI file and you have to open it and extract the files first. If you have MOM already up and running, you can install a management pack by performing the following:

1. Open the MOM 2005 Administrator Console. Click Start, All Programs, Microsoft Operations Manager 2005, and then click Administrator Console.
2. From the Navigation pane, you can see the Management Packs section. If you expand this and select Computer Groups, you see a variety of different MOM options, but none relate to Exchange 2007.
3. Click Management Packs.
4. Right-click Management Packs, and select Import/Export Management Pack to open the wizard. Click Next.

5. You can choose to import or export management packs. Select the radio button to import, and then click Next.
6. You can choose where the pack is located (which is where you extracted the files), and you can choose the type of report you want to perform. In this case, select Import Management Packs only. Click Next.
7. You are asked to select the management pack, and then you have to select import options. Choose either Update Existing Management Pack. Custom Rules, Enabled/Disabled Settings, and Company Knowledge Will Be Retained or Replace Existing Management Pack.
8. You can choose to back up the existing management pack and browse for a location. Then click Next.
9. You are shown the Import Status as it imports the information. When you return to the console and look at the Computer Groups again, you can see in Figure 12.8 that you now have a lot of Exchange 2007 options.

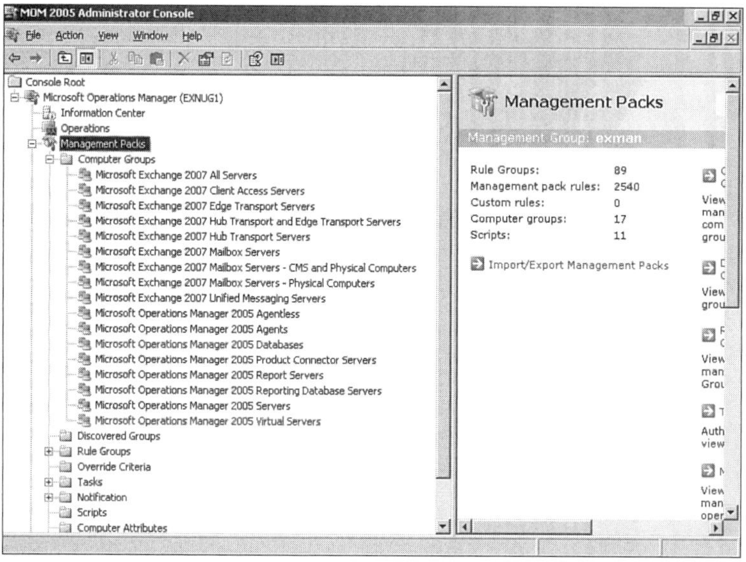

FIGURE 12.8
The MOM Administrator Console with the Exchange Management Pack installed.

Next, you install agents. You can do that from the wizards provided in the Administrator Console for internal agents (for the Hub, CAS, MB, and UM roles). However, for your Edge transport servers, you have to install the agents manually.

Use the Exchange 2007 Toolbox to Troubleshoot

Scenario/Problem: There are all sorts of different tools in the Toolbox. How do you know which one to use when trying to work out a problem?

Solution: Each tool has its own purpose and we consider them now, starting with the top.

NOTE Keep in mind that many other tools exist beyond what we have in our Toolbox. Troubleshooting is not an easy task at times, and we need to reach for a different set of tools, such as Eseutil.exe, which is used for offline defragmentation and analysis of the database's integrity. Other tools can be located on Microsoft's website and can be used to perform everything from benchmarking (Load Generator, Exchange Stress and Performance 2007, and Exchange Server Jetstress) to gathering information (Exchange Profile Analyzer and Information Store Viewer) and more. The point is that you should investigate more tools if you plan to be a solid Exchange Administrator.

The Best Practices Analyzer

Considered a management tool, the Exchange Best Practices Analyzer (ExBPA) performs monitoring and troubleshooting by ensuring best practices are being followed between your Exchange servers and the AD environment.

NOTE We discussed this tool earlier in Chapter 3, "Install Exchange 2007," because it had a readiness check before installing your first Exchange server.

With the ExBPA, you can perform a baseline of your system to report differences it sees from that baseline and future scans. You can also perform a health check, a health/performance check, a permission check, a connectivity check, and the readiness check.

To run the tool, perform the following:

1. Open the EMC.
2. From the Navigation Tree, select Toolbox.
3. At the top, under Configuration Management Tools, select Best Practices Analyzer, and click Open Tool from the Actions pane.
4. The tool checks for updates, and then you can click the link Go to the Welcome Screen.
5. You can begin a new scan or look at a preexisting scan you performed at an earlier time. In this case, click Select Options for a New Scan.

6. You are asked to provide the name of the AD server (usually this is filled in for you), and you can show advanced login options if you need to change your credentials to access the AD server. Then click Connect to the Active Directory server.
7. As you can see from Figure 12.9, you need to provide a name for the scan, select a scope (an entire organization or individual servers), and then choose the type of scan to perform. Keep in mind that if you choose a baseline, it could take up to two hours. Then choose the speed of the network and click Start Scanning, or you can schedule a scan to occur at a better time.

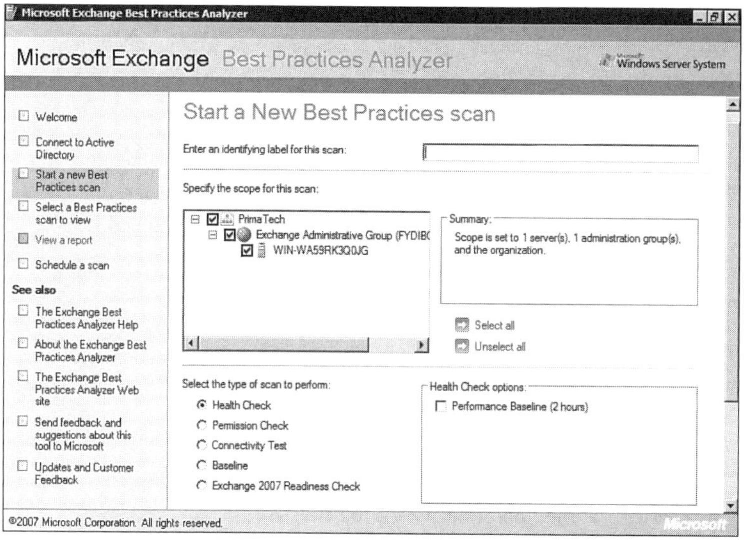

FIGURE 12.9

The Exchange Best Practices Analyzer tool.

8. After the scan has completed, you can choose the link View a Report of This Best Practices Scan.
9. You are shown a report that provides critical or informational issues that are affecting the health and performance of your Exchange organization. Suggestions are also made to correct the problems that are found.
10. When you see a problem, select it and you are shown options to learn more about the problem and how to resolve it.
11. When complete, close the analyzer.

Disaster Recovery Tools

Within the Toolbox, we have two disaster recovery tools.

Database Recovery Management

When a disaster strikes with your database (or disks), the Database Recovery Management tool can help you to bring your system back online.

To run the Database Recovery Management tool, perform the following:

1. Open the EMC.
2. From the Navigation Tree, select Toolbox.
3. Under Disaster Recovery Tools, select Database Recovery Management and click Open Tool from the Actions pane.
4. Select Go to Welcome Screen.
5. You are asked for server and user information. Provide a label. Make sure you have both an Exchange server and domain controller name in the required fields. If there is a need to alter your logon options, you can select Advanced Logon Options and then click Next.
6. You are asked to select one of the following tasks:
    - Manage Databases
        i. Analyze log drive space
        ii. Repair database
        iii. Show database related event logs
        iv. Verify database and transaction log files
    - Manage Recovery Storage Group (if you have one created; otherwise you have to create one first)
        v. Merge or copy mailbox contents
        vi. Mount or dismount databases in the recovery storage group
        vii. Remove the recovery storage group
        viii. Set up 'Database can be overwritten by restore' flag
        ix. Swap databases for 'dial-tone' scenario
    - View Results
        x. Go to Results Page

Obviously, there are many different ways to go with this tool. In fact, we already discussed recovery storage groups and dial-tone recovery quite extensively in Chapter 9, "Design and Deploy Disaster Recovery Settings."

Database Troubleshooter

This tool is not quite as powerful as the Recovery Management tool. You use this tool in situations where the database won't mount or there are inconsistencies in the log file—perhaps you have run out of disk space or the log files have run out of numbers for the log file naming (which is unlikely, but it can happen).

> **NOTE** The procedure for running the Database Troubleshooter tool is straightforward; you simply provide the number of minutes of database events that you want to detect (0 indicates all). The default is set to 120.

Mail Flow Tools

When you have a problem with your Exchange server that isn't a database issue or a physical problem with a server, oftentimes it is a mail flow issue. Mail isn't flowing properly, mail is getting stuck somewhere, mail isn't leaving your organization to go to the outside—these issues can cause frustration on the part of your users.

Several tools within the Toolbox can assist in this regard. Let's examine them one at a time.

Mail Flow Troubleshooter

When using the Mail Flow Troubleshooter, you can indicate the symptom that you are trying to track down. The symptoms include the following:

- Users receive unexpected nondelivery reports when sending messages.
- Expected messages from senders are delayed or are not received by some recipients.
- Messages destined to recipients are delayed or are not received by some recipients.
- Messages are backing up in one or more queues on a server.
- Messages sent by user(s) are pending submission on their mailbox server(s) (for Exchange Server 2007 only).
- Problems with Edge Server synchronization with Active Directory (for Exchange Server 2007 only).

Message Tracking

This is not a new tool in Exchange, but it is one that has evolved over time and we appreciate its purpose. Message tracking is enabled by default on the Hub and Edge Transport servers and the Mailbox servers.

You can use the Exchange Management Shell (EMS) to search message-tracking logs; however, the EMC offers a search tool with a simple interface to work with. If you wish to use the EMC to search the message tracking log, perform the following:

1. Open the EMC.
2. From the Navigation Tree, select Toolbox.
3. Under Mail Flow Tools, select Message Tracking, and from the Actions pane, click Open Tool.
4. On the Message Tracking Parameters page shown in Figure 12.10, you can select checkboxes to include criteria in the message-tracking search. You can configure the following:

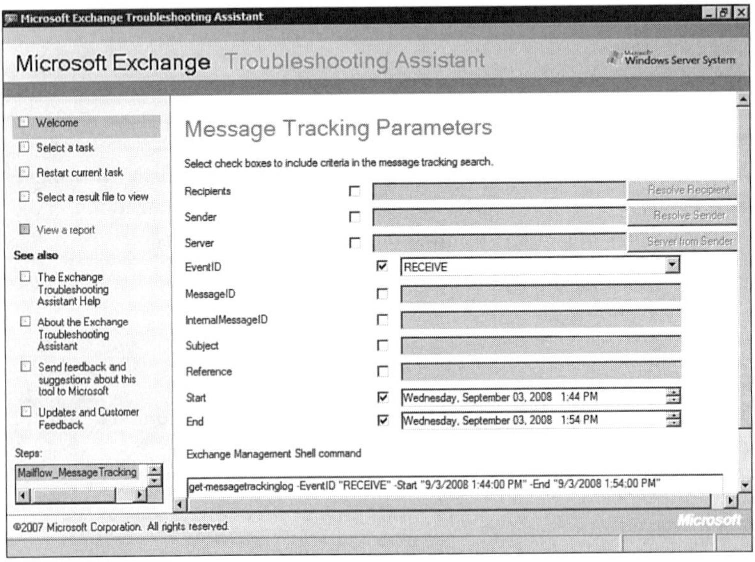

FIGURE 12.10
The Message Tracking tool.

- Recipients
- Ender
- Server
- EventID (by default is set to RECEIVE)
- MessageID
- InternalMessageID
- Subject
- Reference
- Start
- End

5. Make your configuration choices and then click Next.

PS NOTE You can see the Exchange Management Shell command listed at the bottom of the Message Tracking Parameters with the options you have provided.

It's impossible to say what you will look for at any given time, so these options change depending on your needs. Notice the extreme flexibility in this tool. Here you have the EventID, where, if you select the down arrow, you can see several options such as RECEIVE (which is used to look for messages received by the server), DELIVER (used to search for messages delivered to a mailbox), or SUBMIT (used by Mailbox servers that submit items to the Hub Transport servers).

Queue Viewer

The Queue Viewer is a tool that shows SMTP messages that have not completed their journey. These might be inbound or outbound messages, and they can be delayed for any number of reasons.

From within the Queue Viewer, you can choose the server you wish to connect to (the default is the local server). You are shown three different views of the queues: all queues on the server, all messages in all queues on the server, and all messages filtered for a specific queue.

You might be able to determine whether messages are sitting in the queue because DNS is failing, Hub Transport servers are not available, or perhaps the destination server is unavailable. Another feature is the capability to remove with NDR and remove without sending NDR, which is great for spam that is coming into your server.

NOTE If the Queue Viewer doesn't start because the Transport Service isn't starting, you might have an IPv6 issue. Before you try to start the service, go to your network properties, and even if IPv6 is enabled, provide a static IP address for the connection. Then start the Transport Service and you will have no trouble starting Queue Viewer.

Routing Log Viewer

The Routing Log Viewer is a new tool in Exchange 2007 SP1. It is designed to work on the Hub Transport and Edge Transport servers. This tool can help analyze the routing topology and determine whether the way mail moves is the best method for the site topology.

When you open the tool, it is a blank box. To open log files, perform the following:

1. From within the Routing Log Viewer, select File, and then select Open Log File.
2. You can type the name of the transport server, browse server files, or browse local files, depending on where you are running the tool. If you are on the Hub or Edge Transport server already, just click Browse Local Files. Then select a document you wish to analyze and click Open.

3. Here you can see the following tabs:
    - Active Directory Sites and Routing Groups—Shows your sites and routing groups. You can see if a site whether a hub site (and if it is, the next hop site will be indicated, too). You can see the total cost to deliver mail to the site. The Backoff path is shown, too (in the event there is a problem delivering a message).
    - Servers—Lists all the servers within your Exchange organization. You can see the proximity from the local server to those other servers, so you are able to see a map between the servers. You can see server roles for each server, and the total cost to send messages from the local server to other servers.
    - Send Connectors—Shows a list of all SMTP connectors for your Exchange organization (including foreign connectors and routing group connectors).
    - Address Spaces—Shows address spaces within the organization. Each space has a cost-associated connector that is ordered.
4. If you note any configuration changes that must be made, such as if you determine that messages are not routing according to the lowest cost path, consider reviewing your topology and making some changes.
5. When you are finished analyzing, you can close the tool.

One of the more interesting features of the Routing Log Viewer tool is that you can load different routing table logs and see the differences between them. If there are changes between them, they are highlighted and you can see the modification quickly.

Use the EMS `Test` Cmdlets for Troubleshooting

> **Scenario/Problem:** There are `Test` cmdlets in the Exchange Management Shell that you can use to quickly perform troubleshooting of your server and messaging environment. What are these cmdlets and how do they work?

Solution: There is a grouping of cmdlets that all begin with the verb `Test`, including the following:

- `Test-ActiveSyncConnectivity`—Lets you perform a complete synchronization with the Client Access Server and a specific mailbox.
- `Test-EdgeSynchronization`—Checks to ensure the Edge Transport servers are synchronized correctly with the Hub Transport servers.
- `Test-ExchangeSearch`—Ensures search is enabled and indexing.
- `Test-ImapConnectivity`—Verifies that the IMAP4 service is up and running.

- `Test-IPAllowListProvider`—Tests the configuration on servers running the Hub or Edge Transport role (because these are the only two servers where the antispam settings can be configured).
- `Test-IPBlockListProvider`—Tests the configuration on servers running the Hub or Edge Transport role (because these are the only two servers where the antispam settings can be configured).
- `Test-Mailflow`—Determines whether the System Mailbox can send or receive mail.
- `Test-MAPIConnectivity`—Determines whether there is MAPI functionality on the server. You can indicate a specific server or, if you do not indicate a server, it will use the System Mailbox.
- `Test-OutlookWebServices`—This actually verifies that the Autodiscover service settings are running for the CAS server.
- `Test-OwaConnectivity`—Verifies that Outlook Web Access is running.
- `Test-PopConnectivity`—Verifies that the POP3 service is running.
- `Test-ReplicationHealth`—Checks all forms of replication-like cluster services, storage group replication, and so forth.
- `Test-SenderID`—Determines whether an IP address is legitimate.
- `Test-ServiceHealth`—Checks to see whether all the required Exchange services that are set to start automatically have started.
- `Test-SystemHealth`—Has been described as a mini-ExBPA because it checks the system and analyzes it according to best practices.
- `Test-UMConnectivity`—Tests that the UM server role is functional.
- `Test-WebServicesConnectivity`—Verifies Outlook anywhere on a CAS server.

PS NOTE These cmdlets have parameters that make up a syntax for each one. Some can be run without the syntax, whereas others require all the parameters. Being that it is beyond the scope of this book to provide all the PowerShell syntax to every cmdlet, we recommend that you go to http://technet.microsoft.com and do a simple search for any of the PowerShell cmdlets you are interested in using, now that you know what their functions are.

A

B

C

D

E

F

G

H

M

N

O

P

Q

R

T

U

V

W-X-Y-Z

UNLEASHED

Unleashed takes you beyond the basics, providing an exhaustive, technically sophisticated reference for professionals who need to exploit a technology to its fullest potential. It's the best resource for practical advice from the experts, and the most in-depth coverage of the latest technologies.

Microsoft SQL Server 2008
ISBN-13: 978-0-672-33056-8

Microsoft SQL Server 2008 Analysis Services
ISBN-13: 978-0-672-33001-8

Microsoft SQL Server 2008 Reporting Services
ISBN-13: 978-0-672-33026-1

Microsoft SQL Server 2008 Integration Services
ISBN-13: 978-0-672-33032-2

Microsoft Dynamics CRM 4.0
ISBN-13: 978-0-672-32970-8

Microsoft ISA Server 2006
ISBN-13: 978-0-672-32919-7

Microsoft Office Project Server 2007
ISBN-13: 978-0-672-32921-0

Microsoft SharePoint 2007
ISBN-13: 978-0-672-32947-0

Microsoft SharePoint 2007 Development
ISBN-13: 978-0-672-32903-6

Microsoft Small Business Server 2008
ISBN-13: 978-0-672-32957-9

Microsoft SQL Server 2005
ISBN-13: 978-0-672-32824-4

VBScript, WMI and ADSI
ISBN-13: 978-0-321-50171-4

Unleashed books are available at most retail and online bookstores. For more information or to order direct visit our online bookstore at **informit.com/store**

Online editions of all Unleashed titles are available by subscription from Safari Books Online at **safari.informit.com**